ISBN: 9781290503884

Published by:
HardPress Publishing
8345 NW 66TH ST #2561
MIAMI FL 33166-2626

Email: info@hardpress.net
Web: http://www.hardpress.net

THOMAS BOWMAN STEPHENSON

The Life of the Reverend
THOMAS BOWMAN STEPHENSON
B.A., LL.D., D.D.

FOUNDER OF
'THE CHILDREN'S HOME'
AND OF THE
WESLEY DEACONESS INSTITUTE

BY
WILLIAM BRADFIELD
Warden of the Wesley Deaconess Institute

London
CHARLES H. KELLY
25-35 CITY ROAD, AND 26 PATERNOSTER ROW, E.C.

PREFACE

I HAVE endeavoured in this book to give to the many friends of Dr. Stephenson, and to those who may wish to inform themselves about him and the work which he accomplished, such a record of the facts of his career as can now be obtained, and I hope I have done so with a good degree of accuracy. I have been able to use his own words to state the underlying principles of his work. These have been given with considerable fullness, as I believe they are still well worth the careful study of Christian workers. So far as I am able I have tried to sketch a true picture of the man. I have aimed at drawing a portrait, not at making a dissection. But I have not consciously used any false colouring in so doing. I am deeply conscious that I have not been able to satisfy the demands of the love of his 'boys and girls,' his helpers in the work, and his deaconesses. I do not possess the rare gifts necessary for such a portrayal as their hearts would acknowledge to be adequate. I sympathize with them, and can only plead, with the writer of the Second Book of Maccabees, that 'this is such as I could attain unto.'

I have felt obliged to be very ruthless with regard to the large number of existing stories of the Children's Home and the redemption it has accomplished in multitudes of lives. Unless such stories directly illuminated his life and character, I have not recorded them. Had I done otherwise, this book must have grown to more than twice its size. But I think there is room for a book which should contain them. Mr. Curnock's admirable *History of the Children's Home,* if it were brought up to date, might well serve the purpose. Stories of redemption are worth saving.

In telling of Dr. Stephenson's doings as a leader of the Wesleyan Methodist Church, I have remembered that the book may be read by many who have little knowledge of our affairs, and I have inserted brief explanations for their benefit, though I have been conscious that these might well appear stale and unprofitable to readers who know the organization and life of our Church as well as I do myself.

I have not attempted to write the history of England with regard to social reform, and especially with regard to children, during the last half-century. But I have felt that it needed to be written, and that when it is written, Dr. Stephenson will be seen not only to have rendered service of the highest value, but also to have contributed important and, indeed, vital ideas which have enriched the conceptions and enlarged the vision of the social workers of our day.

The problem of emigration to Canada has interested me greatly, as I have met with it in this task. I have carefully refrained from giving any opinions of my own with regard to it, but have taken pains to bring out Dr. Stephenson's opinions as clearly as I could. Whether given as direct quotation or not, there is, I think, no line in this book on that subject which does not come from him and express his mind on the subject.

Except in so far as he gives it himself, I have not tried to state the doctrine with regard to woman's place and work in the Church which underlies his deaconess organization. I think this may soon need doing, but it will be better done when the work itself has grown more familiar, and a larger experience has been accumulated with regard to it.

I have to acknowledge the large assistance given to me by Mrs. Stephenson in the preparation of this book; also the kindly interest and wise counsel of the Rev. Nehemiah Curnock, who more than once has laid aside his own great task of giving the world a complete and trustworthy edition of Wesley's Journal, to afford me the benefit of his memories and experience. I am indebted to the Rev. Arthur E. Sharpley for kindly writing the chapter on Dr. Stephenson as a musician, to the Rev. S. Carroll Myers, of the Children's Home, for the loan of old magazines and portraits and much other valuable assistance, and to many other friends for help whose value they will recognize as they read this book. And the name of Sister Margaret Gibson claims my most grateful acknowledgement. It is not too much to say that, but for her efficient and sympathetic secretarial work, the book could never have been written at all.

WILLIAM BRADFIELD.

WESLEY DEACONESS COLLEGE,
ILKLEY,
September, 1913.

CONTENTS

[illegible]

CHAPTER I

[illegible]

CHAPTER II

[illegible]

CHAPTER III

[illegible]

CONTENTS

PAGE

CHAPTER XII

CHAPTER XIII

CHAPTER XIV

CHAPTER XV

CHAPTER XVI

CHAPTER XVII

LIST OF ILLUSTRATIONS

Thomas Bowman Stephenson

CHAPTER I

Introductory

A LIFE of Dr. Stephenson will be wanted by the people who love him. The old boys and girls of the Children's Home, to whom the memory of 'the Doctor' is a very sacred one, will wish for an account of the man to whom they owe so much; and the past and present workers in that great Institution, who were trained under his care, will not be behind the children of the Home in this desire. The Wesley Deaconesses also, to whom 'the Warden' meant as much as 'the Doctor' to the Children's Home people, will seek to keep his memory green. And the Wesleyan Methodist Church, and the Christian Church at large, will feel that it has a right to some record of the doings of one who was great both as an evangelistic leader and as an ecclesiastical statesman.

Dr. Stephenson's life was interwoven with much of the history of his time, his country, and his Church. The Lancashire cotton famine, the establishment of a national system of education, the problem of emigration and the development of Canada, the establishment of closer relations between English and American Methodism, the admission of laymen to a share in the supreme governing authority of our Church, and the position of women in its work, are all matters which were woven into the very texture of his life; and with regard to many of them, his activities were full of influence in shaping the course of events and the thoughts of men.

And in that deeper Church history which tells of the movements of the Spirit of God, and the inspirations and visions that are received and transmitted from land to land and from generation to generation, his name will form an important link between the evangelical Church of Germany in the years following the Napoleonic wars, and the evangelical Churches of England (including specially, of course, the Methodist Church) in the three later decades of the nineteenth century and the beginning of the twentieth. For the 'Inner Mission' of the Lutheran Church was not only the inspiration of the two special developments of Christian activity with which his name is connected, namely, the Children's Home and the Wesley Deaconess Institute, but also of some other things which he attempted, and of a spirit which, largely through him, has become the common property of our Churches to-day. He was not merely a link in a chain; the spiritual ideas of the Inner Mission were reborn in his mind, and came forth from it not as mere pale imitations, but as thoughts and deeds of his own. Nobody objected to his schemes as 'made in Germany,' for by the time he brought them forward, they had become thoroughly English; and they have proved themselves as completely natural among us as ever they did in the country of their origin. His institutions have rooted themselves firmly in the life of our Church, and show that spiritual vitality, which not only maintains itself, but is a source and fountain of new and better things still to come.

The more intimate personal life of Dr. Stephenson is not easy to tell. Sometimes there is a gleam of self-revelation so frank that sheer reverence forbids its exposure on the printed page, and more than once the most complete confession of his own soul's life is made in some public utterance; but he had not many intimate friends, and he did not write to them the things that were nearest to his own heart. In the case of one, perhaps the closest friend of his life, Mr. Cuthbert Bainbridge, of Newcastle-on-Tyne, it is believed that a very intimate correspondence did exist, but if so it cannot now be found. All that exists in the way of record is fragmentary, and no complete 'history of the soul' can be attempted here.

CHAPTER II

Parentage — Centenary Fund — Childhood — Education — Conversion—Wesley College—Miss Lupton—First attempt at Preaching.

WHEN, at the Conference of 1822, the Stations were being made up, it was found that there were not men enough to fill all the vacant posts. The Secretary of the Conference, the Rev. Robert Newton, was, however, equal to the occasion. 'I know a young man,' said he, 'named John Stephenson, who is a very good preacher, and would like to come into the ministry.' 'Put him down,' they said; and John Stephenson was sent to Lincoln to be the assistant of the Rev. Thomas Galland. Next Conference, his name appeared upon the *Minutes* as a missionary appointed to the West Indies.

He came from the neighbourhood of Barnard Castle, and had met a young lady at Darlington who greatly attracted him. During the next few years, while he was in the West Indies, he corresponded with Mary Bowman, and asked her to be his wife. She consented, on condition that he would come home and take her out to the West Indies with him. He did not obtain permission to do this until the year 1828, when he returned to England, and the marriage was arranged to take place soon after Conference. But at that Conference there was nobody ready to go to a vacant appointment in the Shetland Islands; and Dr. Adam Clarke, who had taken the Islands under his special care, spoke with some warmth and bitterness about the unwillingness of the young men of the ministry to volunteer for such hard and difficult work. It was more than John Stephenson could stand. 'If nobody else will go, I will,' he said, and the Conference took him at his word, and put him down forthwith for the Walls and Sandness Circuit. Poor Miss Bowman's wedding trousseau, prepared for the West Indies, had to be changed in great haste for one more suitable to the Shetland storms. However, like a brave woman, she went with her husband, and they spent three years there, and then came away with a very warm affection for the Islands, which they both retained to the end of their lives.

Mrs. Stephenson proved to be a very capable and unselfish woman, who not only bore the burden of providing for her family on the very small income which ministers in those days received, but found time to be a class-leader, a visitor of the sick, and a helper in every good work ; and her six children grew up in an atmosphere of prayer and devotion, as well as one of constant, active Christian service.

Thomas Bowman, the youngest of the six, was born at Red Barns, in the Newcastle-on-Tyne Circuit, on December 22, 1839, and was baptized in Brunswick Chapel by the Rev. Robert Newton, who had introduced his father to the ranks of the ministry in the unceremonious and expeditious fashion we have already recorded.

The year 1839 was the Centenary Year, which celebrated the hundredth anniversary of the foundation of the 'Society of the People called Methodists.' All who have read John Wesley's Rules for this

Society know their first words: 'In the latter end of the year 1739, eight or ten persons came to me in London who appeared to be deeply convinced of sin, and earnestly groaning for redemption. They desired (as did two or three more the next day) that I would spend some time with them in prayer, and advise them how to flee from the wrath to come, which they saw continually hanging over their heads.

'This was the rise of the United Society, first in London, and then in other places.'

At the end of one hundred years, this Society had grown into one of the largest of the Protestant Churches of the world. The Centenary was celebrated by the raising of a great fund, which was mainly divided between Foreign Missions and the establishment of two Colleges at Richmond and Didsbury for the training of the ministry. It was the first instance since John Wesley's days of a great general collection throughout Methodism for Connexional purposes, and has since been followed by the Jubilee Fund, the Thanksgiving Fund, and the Twentieth Century Fund, all of which are land-marks in this biography.

John Stephenson had five children when the Centenary movement began, and Thomas Bowman made his appearance upon the scene before the end of the year. In recognition of this happy event, his father gave an extra guinea to the Fund. It was a great pleasure to Dr. Stephenson to recall his early personal connexion with the first of these great Connexional collections. When the Jubilee of the Wesleyan Missionary Society was celebrated in 1863, in giving his own contribution to the Jubilee Fund, he associated it with the name of his then recently widowed mother, and with the memory of his father, and of the uncle whose name he bore, and also with that of the great missionary advocate who had baptized him. And when later he took a very prominent part in the gathering of the Thanksgiving Fund, he used to recount with much satisfaction his share in both the great collections which had preceded it.

During his infancy his mother was in very poor health, and he lived with one of his aunts for more than three years. He speaks of her as 'kindness, gentleness and wisdom personified, a true saint, a member of the Church of England, with a perfect respect for Methodism.'

John Stephenson was appointed Secretary of the Contingent Fund in 1847. This was not at that time a 'Departmental' appointment, in the present Methodist sense of the word; that is to say, he was not 'set apart' to it, but held it in connexion with his ordinary circuit work. The year 1849 was the time of the great secession, in which the Wesleyan Methodist Church lost a hundred thousand members, and received the most staggering blow that has ever been given to it. John Stephenson held the office of Secretary to the Contingent Fund right through this dark and difficult time, and his painstaking and valiant work did much towards maintaining and reconstructing the organization that had been so severely shaken. He continued to hold the office until the year 1854, when the Rev. Thomas Dickin took his place. Three years later, in 1857, the name of the Department was changed to the 'Home Mission and Contingent Fund,' and the Rev. Charles Prest was 'set apart' as its Secretary. John Stephenson had left his mark upon the office, and had done much towards increasing the resources of the Fund, and giving Home Missions the position they have since taken in the Methodist Church. It has been felt by some who remember these troublous times that the valuable service he then did for the Connexion has scarcely had the appreciation that it deserves.

When his father was stationed at Bedford, Thomas Bowman was sent to the endowed school there, known as the 'Bedford Charity.' It had already become a power in the education of boys, though at that time it was not much more than a Preparatory School. He was one of the youngest of its scholars.

On his father's removal to Louth, he went to its ancient Edward VI. Grammar School, where Tennyson had not long before been a scholar. Dr. Stephenson's chief memory of it seems to be of the brutal method in which punishment was administered. He also tells us that no desks were provided, except for scholars in the senior class. Each boy brought a box with him, containing his books, and these boxes, arranged in a semicircle, were all the furniture which was then thought necessary.

Three years later his father was appointed to Dudley, and Bowman attended the Grammar School, the Head Master of which was an accomplished scholar and an excellent teacher.

It was while at Dudley that a spiritual crisis came to the lad, which resulted in his conversion and consecration to the work of Christ. He tells about it himself:

'One of my father's colleagues—Michael Johnson—regularly held a meeting for children on the Saturday afternoon. Football, cricket, hockey, and other games had not yet become fine arts, and had not claimed both the half-holidays of the week. At that time, in the hands of a capable and sympathetic minister, the children's meeting on the Saturday afternoon was a great power. To me it was the opportunity of decision. I do not remember any particular circumstances leading up to it. I am pretty sure it was not in connexion with a Mission. Week after week, the man of God taught us the best things, and pressed upon us the joy and the duty of belonging fully to God. When the meeting was over, and my young heart palpitating with its new joy, I ran home, and there I found my father and mother, who stood with clasped hands, and with tears of joy running down their faces, as they thanked God for the surrender which their youngest child had made to the Saviour-King.

'Several years passed, during which my "experience" was like April weather, shadow and shine alternating; but I never ceased to feel God's ownership of me. And presently I found myself at Wesley College, Sheffield. I had reached the danger-point where manhood and boyhood meet. I clung, however, to the hope of the gospel, and was confirmed in good things by the powerful preaching of Dr. Waddy. His strong, manly, and appropriate preaching made me realize the width of the gospel message, and the nobility of a life wholly given up to God and His Church. But I think I should have followed my star in choosing the law as my profession, if a strong "revival of religion" had not "broken out." Ah! how much these old phrases, now seldom heard, mean! Half a century ago, a revival was not something to be engineered by advertisement, but often with no visible cause, the pulse of the Church began to beat quicker, and the revival " broke out." So at Wesley College a notable revival took place ; not the greatest known there—that was years before the time of which I write—but a great revival nevertheless. Two of the youths, who afterwards became most influential, were William H. Tindall (so well-known by his relation to the Southport Convention), and James Wood, who was fervent in spirit and generous in beneficences, till death claimed him too early. Many others of the boys chose Christ as their portion, and a good many of them are prominent and earnest workers in the Church of their fathers to this day. It was the influence of those days of grace which finally decided me to become a preacher of the gospel, in which sphere I have found the highest and sweetest pleasure for fifty-three years.'

The next appointment his father received was to the Bramley Circuit, in 1854. We find from the *Minutes of Conference* that, after having been Superintendent for eighteen years, and for one part of the time Chairman of the Bedford District, and also for the last seven years Secretary of the Contingent Fund, John Stephenson was appointed to Bramley as the second minister, and a successor was appointed to the secretaryship of the Contingent Fund. He only remained at Bramley one year, and then resumed his superintendency at Whitby. It is natural to conclude that he must have had some breakdown in health, which made him for the time unable to carry the burdens he had previously been bearing.

The appointment, whatever significance it may have had to himself, was one of the greatest importance for his son, for it was at Bramley that

Bowman Stephenson, a boy of fourteen, first made the acquaintance of Ellen Lupton, whom he afterwards married. She was the youngest daughter of Mr. John Lupton, cloth manufacturer, a prominent Bramley Methodist, whose family still remain in the town and in connexion with the Methodist Church.

It was from the Bramley Circuit that he was sent to Wesley College, Sheffield, and he must have been there for more than a year before that revival broke out to which he refers in the story of his conversion. Of Wesley College he speaks as follows :

'Although a good deal was needed to lift the school into its proper position, there were many fine elements in its life, of which not a few of my comrades of long ago have spoken with hearty gratitude. I there began to prepare for matriculation at the University of London. At that time, the older universities were closed against all those who would not accept the teaching of the Church of England ; and London University, in spite of many difficulties, was the main protection of Nonconformists against this cruel narrowness.

'The religious tone at Wesley College was high. A few there were whose influence was altogether bad ; most of the boys, however, thankfully accepted the religious life of the place. Many of them have done well, some of them notably well ; amongst these may be mentioned Sir William Stephenson, Judge Waddy, Dr. Agar Beet, and Thomas G. Osborn.

'The ministry of Dr. Waddy in the school pulpit was one of the most helpful forces. Dr. Waddy was a great preacher, and he accomplished the very difficult feat of preaching in a manner intelligible and interesting to the boys and at the same time admirably helpful and stimulating to adults.

'While at the college, I myself made a few attempts at preaching, for by this time the conviction had taken hold of my heart that I must give my life to the work of Christ. On one occasion, as I was starting for one of my appointments, Dr. Waddy gave me a cheerful bit of advice. "I hope," he said, "you have something good to finish with. When I was a young man I always had by me a finish that could be screwed on any sermon I was preaching." And, with this advice and a twinkle in his eye, he wished me well. On another occasion, preaching in a village near Sheffield, I had exhausted the provision which I had made for the occasion, and seeing that the clock, placed in a most conspicuous position, was telling everybody that it was only twenty minutes to twelve, I made an attempt to add to what I had already said, such scraps as rose in my mind, and so dragged the sermon out until the orthodox twelve o'clock. An old Yorkshireman, typical of his race, came afterwards into the vestry, and shaking hands, he said to me, "Young man, you did very nicely until twenty minutes to twelve, but you ought to have stopped then, for you had naught more to say." The old man's advice was exceedingly appropriate, and it has more than once stood me in good stead.

'Meanwhile, the years were running on. My father was now stationed at Whitby, and in the holiday which I was spending in that delightful seaside resort, I was asked to 'take an appointment in the little village of Sandsend. My name did not appear on the plan, but according to the custom of the time, a star indicated the appointment I was to take. Engaged in business in the town was a young man who, like myself, had ambitions for the pulpit. He encouraged me, and we went out occasionally together. But to this day Dr. Waller remembers that the first text from which he heard me preach was, "And when they saw the star they rejoiced with exceeding great joy." '

At one of these Wesley College appointments, an afternoon service at Carver Street Chapel, among the handful of worshippers who gathered to hear the young preacher was the poet James Montgomery, whose hymns, especially 'Hail to the Lord's Anointed,' have been such favourites with the Methodist people.

Robertson of Brighton once said there were two rocks on which every young man either anchors or splits—God and woman. This seventeenth year of his life saw Bowman Stephenson coming to anchorage in both cases. One of those private diaries, that are too sacred for quotation, shows that the aspiration after the divine life and the aspiration of a youth in love were both of them working their will in his heart ; and while the flame of religious devotion purified the earthly flame, the other most certainly had its powerful though less recognized effect upon the passion for holiness of life.

We will, however, dare to take from the diary in question a description of Miss Lupton from her lover's hand.

'How well I recollect the first time I ever saw her ! It was just at the gate of Bramley Chapel Yard. She was dressed in mourning for the death of her sister, and she was just going to her class. Oh ! what a look was on her face—that beautiful face I have so often admired! There was not a trace of pride, there was no predominant passion written there, but on every lineament there was written devotion. She seemed as one who had given up the world—a saint on whose pure brow was written "Holiness to the Lord."'

More than thirty years afterwards, when she died, her husband wrote about her as follows:

'My first vivid remembrance of her shows her to me, on a quiet summer's afternoon, going to her class-meeting. Her bonny face, with the sunny hair forming a more beautiful halo than any painter ever gave to the Madonna, had on it the light of a perfect peace. Thank God for the young women who have grown up in the pure and sheltering circle of a godly home, and have the true basis of character and life in a simple faith, and a lowly, obedient love. Such used to be the maidens who afterwards became the centres of many a lovely home life; and if the circle of their thoughts was somewhat narrower than the "culture" of to-day would approve, they were highly educated in the best sense of the word "education," and their lives and characters had a genuine wholesomeness not often to be found amongst those whose taste demands the spiced wines of fashion, or who are always panting after notoriety.

'Her home was one of high respectability and complete comfort, in which the tradition of early Methodism still prevailed. Her ideas as to the books women ought to read, the amusements they should indulge in, and the dress they should wear, retained to the end the tinge early given to them, and were none the worse for that. Her mother died when she was an infant, and she owed much to the care of her eldest sister, who has long since passed home to heaven. For her father she had a great affection and a most reverent memory. During her last illness she said to me, " I am so thankful for a good father. He was a holy man." Then turning to her daughter, she said, " Dora, you will follow in your grandfather's steps, won't you ? " At another time as she was murmuring to herself, " Jesus, precious Jesus," she suddenly opened her eyes and said to me, " That's what my father used to say." Who can estimate the power, both for restraint and impulse, of such a fine and sacred memory ? '

CHAPTER III

Call to the Ministry—Candidature—Peter Mackenzie—Open-air preaching—College days—Gough and Punshon.

ON leaving Wesley College, it was arranged that Bowman Stephenson should spend some time in private study in preparation for the London Examinations. To make this possible he went to Gateshead to supply the place of a minister who was ill. It was while he was doing this work that he felt himself definitely called to the Christian ministry. He writes about it as follows:

'I very much wished for twelve months' private study in preparation for the university examination, and it was whilst so engaged that my conscience and heart demanded that I should enter the holy ministry. I had been preaching for several weeks, with apparent appreciation by the congregations, and with a growing sense of the holiness of the work, which is a supreme equipment of the preacher. We Methodists are accustomed to look for signs and wonders in the name of Jesus, indeed we doubt whether any man can be sure of his own vocation for the ministry unless, in the minor office of local preacher, he had commended himself to the people and had received the heavenly stamp upon his work. One week I had been greatly troubled because I could not trace any direct spiritual good to anybody

THOMAS BOWMAN STEPHENSON, B.A.
(At the time when he took his London degree.)

[face p. 30.

as the result of my preaching ; and on my knees I had pleaded with God that if He wished me to give myself to the work of soul-saving He would be pleased to give me some sign of His goodwill and favour. I was to preach in a Tyneside village on the following Sunday night. I went, and from the first moment the service seemed to be baptized with a heavenly glow. The majority of the congregation were intelligent working men. They entered fully into sympathy with the preacher ; many wept ; some uttered prayerful ejaculations. That same night twelve of those fine Tynesiders chose Christ as their Saviour and Leader. I felt that this was a sign and a call which I must not neglect. It decided my career. Fifty years afterwards, being in that neighbourhood, one of those men, now grey-headed and bent with years, took my hand and thanked me for the word spoken that night so long ago.'

The gathering of the Candidates for the Ministry in the year 1858 was of a very remarkable character. There were one hundred and sixty of them, by far the largest number that had offered in any year since the Reform Agitation, and their character and ability was much higher than the standard of preceding years. Throughout the Connexion their offer was taken as a sign that the Wesleyan Methodist Church had fully recovered from the heavy blow that had been received nine years previously. There was a great wave of evangelical earnestness and power among these men and their contemporaries, though, alas, it was to a large degree checked and repressed by the timid, cautious, conservative bearing of many of the older men, who had passed through the storms of 1849, and had learnt in those storms to fear and distrust everything outside the beaten track. This over-weight of caution continued to burden the ministry for many succeeding years, and was in many ways one of the worst legacies left to Methodism from the great struggle.

The going up to London of the candidates made a very deep mark upon more than one of their number. Dr. Stephenson has himself left a record of it.

'We had to travel up to London in the old-fashioned third class, and the journey took about twelve hours. At a wayside station two or three candidates boarded the train, and we soon knew that one of them was a gifted man alike with genius and high devotion. The carriages being divided only half-way up, afforded an excellent opportunity for saying some profitable words. I remember how our voices rang through all the rattle of the train, and how Peter Mackenzie, for it was he to whom I refer, seized the opportunity to speak a word for God to those strangers thus gathered together. Yes, he was a genius! To his preaching thousands owe their salvation; some have thought that he might have been more wisely guided, and more profitably used for the winning of souls; but, however that may be, none could be for ever so brief a time in his company without realizing that the stamp of God was upon him. In that same examination were some who have achieved greatness, many who have fulfilled their course triumphantly, and a few, after half a century has passed, who are still working, or waiting until the call to the higher worship of the skies shall come to them.

'This year was fruitful in presenting to the Church

a large number of able men. No less than five of them in due time became Presidents of the Conference, and some of them would obviously have attained that honour if circumstances had been favourable.'

Another of the candidates, the Rev. Nehemiah Curnock, in his *History of the Children's Home*, gives a very vivid picture of the same gathering:

'We were lodged, for the examination days, in the Westminster Wesleyan Training College, it being summer holidays for the students. Sunday came—a hot summer's day. After dinner, one of our number, a minister's son, whose father led the way in the earliest days of Methodist Home Missions, proposed an open-air service, for which there was no lack of volunteers. A band of about twelve was quickly formed. As we sallied forth into the unknown streets, some of us, probably, were just a little nervous, for we knew not into what den of peril our captain, who had, to our thinking, a dare-devil air about him, might lead us. By what route we went, or where precisely we landed, I cannot now tell; but of the place itself I have a very distinct recollection. It was a by-street, at the right-hand corner of which stood a tobacconist's shop—open. The owner, coatless, in a spotlessly white shirt, with arms folded, was standing in the doorway, sunning himself. As we trooped round the corner, I remember glancing at the fellow and saying to myself, "That man thinks himself lord of all he surveys."

'Half-way down the street, our leader halted at a door, and by some wizardry of look or tone which I did not then very well understand, he charmed the woman who answered his knock into lending him a chair. This he straightway mounted, and began to sing. Since then, many on both sides of the Atlantic and at the Antipodes have heard that voice singing for Jesus and His little ones. But in my ears it has never sounded more sweetly than when, in that queer London street, I first listened to it. Street-preaching was not so common then as now, and our mere presence—a group of unfledged parsons in black coats and white ties—proved sufficient to draw a crowd of children and loose-enders.

'As by magic, the singing doubled the congregation. At open doors and windows, as well as in the roadway, they stood—all the sorts the street could provide, from the wrinkled grandmother to the babe in arms. Presently the pair of white shirt-sleeves hove in sight, and soon their owner began noisily to dispute our right to invade his domain. At first the crowd sympathized with the fellow, and things began to look dangerous. Our first attempt at missioning in London seemed doomed to end in ignominious failure.

'Suddenly, however, a strange champion put the enemy to flight. He was only a city arab—a shrewd little urchin, who, attracted first by the singing, had somehow been fascinated by the preacher. There stood the lad—ragged and grimy—devouring every word, like one who was pining for good. I could see that the tobacconist's interruptions annoyed him, and that he wanted to hear the service out. Just when the blatant uproar was at its worst, the lad sprang in with shrill cockney voice, "Never heed him, sir, he sells ceegyars." Something in the twang, or in the comical look on the lad's face, tickled the public fancy. The crowd burst into a roar of laughter, the white shirt turned tail and skulked off, and we were left to finish our service in peace.

'Little did any one of us dream that that London street boy was the first of a long succession of children whom the singing preacher within a few years was to captivate. Who the lad was, or what became of him, I do not know. But I dream of a coming day, when as we walk the streets of the City of God, we shall see him, and shall learn that the song and the sermon, that Sunday afternoon, were not in vain.

'The singing street preacher was THOMAS BOWMAN STEPHENSON.'

Mr. Curnock also tells of a prayer-meeting that was held in the morning for the candidates at Westminster, in the room now known as the Waller Memorial Hall. He remembers going into a terrific uproar. 'There was a young man kneeling with his sleeves turned up, showing the crimson lining of his coat, his face dotted with the blue marks of the coal-pit, and he was praying with a passionate earnestness which was calling forth a perfect storm of response.'

He remembers also that Peter Mackenzie, when the examination was over, gave a final address to the candidates, by their special request, on 'Christian Perfection'; and that in this address he dealt with the temptations of a young minister in a most faithful and competent fashion, so as to surprise everybody at his ability to realize a position that must have been so foreign to anything he himself had experienced.

A month after this examination, Thomas Bowman Stephenson was accepted by the Conference as a candidate for the ministry, and sent for training to Richmond College.

On the college staff were the Rev. Alfred Barrett, a saintly man, and a wise administrator, and the

Rev. Benjamin Hellier, afterwards of Headingley, who won the loyalty and reverence of many generations of students. Both these men had daughters who were little girls at the time, Mrs. Hugh Price Hughes and Miss Hellier. Each of them still possesses lively memories of a particularly merry-hearted student, whose explosive gaiety was the very life of the College. The Rev. Thomas Jackson still held the post of Theological Tutor, though far advanced in years; and as Assistant Tutor, William Fiddian Moulton was the sympathetic helper of every student. Between Mr. Moulton and Bowman Stephenson an intimacy sprang up which ripened into life-long friendship—a friendship which grew stronger as it adapted itself to all the vicissitudes of the two great careers, so unlike in their outward seeming, which lay before them.

An interesting record, giving a picture of one aspect of his career as a student, exists in the shape of a story that he wrote for one of the Twopenny Soirées at Bolton a few years afterwards. We transscribe part of it for the sake of the light it throws on himself as well as the sketch it gives of some of his companions.

'My college was a Gothic building with a very extended frontage. In the centre rose a tower, containing the entrance hall, with its marble statue of the founder, and above that the library with its twenty thousand volumes. The curtains of the building between this central tower and the wings were occupied by lecture rooms and dining hall, on the first floor, with sitting rooms, and on the second with bedrooms. The wings were filled, in every story, with the men's chambers, and in the west wing, on the second floor, myself and my cousin, freshmen of the same year, had our rooms, the doors of which were exactly opposite to each other, one on each side of the passage which ran up the centre. My cousin was a very Adonis in comparison with myself. We used to be popularly known as "Beauty and the Beast"; although I flatter myself that my ugliness was comparative rather than absolute. But if he had the advantage externally, I used to cherish a secret suspicion that I had the pull on him in brains; and so my envy never became bitter. Besides, as things went with us in those days, we were necessary to each other—for the proximity of our rooms, and an informal partnership in crockery, and other paraphernalia, rendered each dependent on the other. So that when either gave a supper, the other was necessarily one of the guests; and when the edibles had been discussed in one room, it was customary to leave the fragments and retire to the other.

'Very pleasant are my memories of those social hours, when care was as yet not difficult to charm, and not a man amongst us ever thought of his digestion. But a wreath of cypress is twined with the holly; for how can I forget that thou, Strickland, with thy tall figure, and dark eyes, and envied silken whiskers, art known no more on earth—having finished thy short term of life almost before thou hadst entered on its realities? But then the treacherous consumption had not betrayed itself, and thy laugh was free, and thy step elastic.

'But the others still remain on earth, though the four quarters of the world now hold us, separated for ever. Meadow went to China as a missionary, and last, but not least, Tom Trelawney is a Broad Church curate at Nottingby. Now, it was a general opinion amongst us, that Trelawney was a great genius. He used to manufacture verses with a ring about them which proved the presence of some real metal, even though he was sometimes overcome by the rhyming difficulties which young climbers of Parnassus find specially trying. He was, moreover, slightly heterodox in his opinions—just sufficiently to give an interesting flavour to his sentiments, for he was an exponent of "Muscular Christianity," a Hercules then in its cradle. And moreover, he had a beautiful face. Yes, beautiful is the word. It wasn't pretty, like Tom's, nor handsome like Strickland's—it was beautiful, and that because of its great mobility. The expression of his face would change with a suddenness which seemed almost magical, and resembled nothing so much as the aspect of a landscape when the sun has broken forth from behind a cloud which a high wind had driven across its face. Then he had the gift of oratory in no mean degree : he could lower or raise his voice, and throw in a dramatic shudder whenever the circumstances required it, and, indeed, was just the man, who, if he had talked Arabic, would have made his fortune as a story-teller in the East.

'One night I had given a supper to these worthies and two or three other men. We sat round the fire, in easy-chairs of very original patterns, having our legs disposed with all the liberty prevalent in bachelordom, and giving utterance to our views on all things supernal and inferior. Then having, to our own satisfaction at least, settled the affairs of the world, we betook ourselves to story-telling ; and after several minor squibs had been exploded, Trelawney reared himself from his horizontal position in a Derby chair, extinguished the lamps, so that the room remained lighted only by the feeble glimmers of the fire, now burning low; and commenced his story of the Vampire. The story was of the regulation pattern, and we may perhaps be excused if we spare our readers the recital of it. The climax was as follows:

'"For one moment more, Madelaine stood with eyes upraised to heaven; then with the step of resolution, went down into the shadows. Sometimes her feet trod on the moss, which yielded to her step, like a dead hand: sometimes struck against a bone awanting to his fellows of the skeleton. But on she went, till on the coffin she saw the mark made by the witch. Her limbs trembled under her, and to her straining ears the vault seemed filled with the low whisperings and laughter of fiends; but she held the first nail to its place, and struck, once, twice, thrice. Then in the coffin there seemed to be a shaking, as though some prisoner were struggling to free himself from fetters. Again she drove a nail, and the struggle became wilder—what seemed the efforts of despair, and the very coffin moved on its stone slab. A third time she struck, once, twice, thrice, and then she heard a sort of smothered cry, and out of every crevice of the coffin came dark blood, fluent as in life, but cold as in death; and Madelaine fell fainting

. . . .

'Just at this moment, on the door which hung closed and locked, behind our circle round the fire, there came three knocks, slow and seeming timid. Trelawney's sentence was cut off without its finish;

and each man felt his hair creep; but in a moment or two, recovering self-possession, I opened the door, and there in the passage stood a tall, dark figure, with no certain outline, only with a black, shining head-piece, and vomiting forth flame into the room. I fell back discomfited, but was somewhat reassured to hear, issuing from above the flame, the voice of a friendly policeman, who said, "Beg your pardon, gents, but here's one of these doors is open, and I've been wandering all about these here blessed passages a-looking for somebody to shut 'em. Yer'll have thieves in before morning if yer porter leaves the doors unlocked *this* 'ere way."'

The neighbourhood of Richmond to London made it possible for the students to attend meetings of various kinds, and occasionally to hear one of the great preachers. Punshon was then at the zenith of his powers, and his oratory and his spiritual influence had a very powerful effect upon Stephenson.

Another brilliant man of the day was John B. Gough, the celebrated Temperance advocate. Both his eloquence and the great realities of the theme with which he dealt took a great hold of the soul of Bowman Stephenson. He writes:

'I never heard a man who could move the people as he did. He was intensely dramatic. Everything that you heard you also saw. He was so famous that large numbers gathered wherever he went, and once he lectured in Exeter Hall on six successive nights, and each time to a crowd. Two passages recur to me after all these years. In one of them he was illustrating the danger of moderate drinking. He pictured the captain of a ship who had been down to lunch and had had two or three glasses of wine. He was not drunk, but he was just a little excited. He came on deck and cast a look upon the sails. They were fully expanded, and the ship was bearing all that she safely could. But with the stimulus of the drink which he had taken, he gave an order for further sails to be set. For a moment they bore the strain, then—crash—they came down, and the ship was rolling helpless in the sea. The captain was not drunk, but the mischief was owing to the order which would never have been given but for the brain excitement produced by the wine-glass.

'On another occasion, Gough was appealing to the audience to preserve their children from this peril. He portrayed in a few skilful words the possible fate of a little child who had grown up under the influence of the drinking customs of the family. Turning in a moment to the first row on the platform, he snatched up a little girl who was there, put her feet on the rail, passed his arm round her waist, and said, " Look at her. Who would not give up his glass to save a child like this ? "

'It was after one of John B. Gough's lectures that I signed the pledge, which I have kept for fifty-three years.'

Bowman Stephenson's College course only lasted two years, and he unfortunately lost through illness a considerable part of even this short period. He was, therefore, unable to continue his Arts course at the University of London until he received an appointment from the Conference of 1860, as junior minister in the Norwich Circuit. On going there, he resumed his interrupted University course, and before long took his degree as Bachelor of Arts.

CHAPTER IV

Early Ministry—Norwich—Bradlaugh—Grosvenor Street, Manchester—Jubilee of Missionary Society—Cotton Famine—Marriage—Bolton, Fletcher Street—Union for Christian Work—Letter from John Fernley—Exhibitions—Temperance Work—Reminiscences—Farewell Speech.

HIS superintendent at Norwich was the Rev. Joseph Moorhouse, a man of judgement, kindliness, and earnest effort for the quickening of the Church. Norwich had suffered very severely in the great Agitation that had swept over Methodism in 1849 and the following years. Two out of the three chapels had been claimed by the Reformers, and the congregation left at St. Peter's, the one chapel which remained, was painfully small. An added difficulty was that the agitation had completely severed the Wesleyan Methodists from any fellowship with the other Nonconformist ministers and people of the town. Mr. Moorhouse wisely determined to let bygones be bygones. Slowly but steadily the relation of the Nonconformist Churches to each other became more cordial, and progress was made towards the restoration of the Wesleyan Church to a more satisfactory and favourable position. The leading Baptist minister, the Rev. George Gould, welcomed Mr. Stephenson to his personal friendship, and they used to meet for brotherly intercourse nearly every week.

Here, at the beginning of his ministerial course, Mr. Stephenson showed that power of assimilating the novel ideas that were in the air, and of acting upon them with energy and success, which was one of his leading characteristics all through his life. Having heard somewhere that in a certain London theatre services had been held on Sundays for evangelistic purposes, he promptly determined to try the experiment in the theatre at Norwich. To the people around him, the step was one of unheard-of audacity, and the critics were numerous and powerful. The congregations were, however, from the first crowded, and this experiment of getting off the beaten track accomplished its purpose so well as to encourage him to make other daring ventures when the time came. So far as is known, this was the first time when Methodist services were held in a building of this description. In the second winter of his ministry at Norwich, the theatre could no longer be obtained, but the Rev. George Gould joined with him in united services on the Sunday night, after the ordinary Church meetings were concluded, in the fine old St. Andrew's Hall. Here also large congregations were gathered, and much good was done.

A prominent incident of the Norwich days was a debate with Mr. Bradlaugh, who used to be a frequent visitor to the city, which was at that time a stronghold of Secularism. He was then known throughout the country as 'Iconoclast.' The debate seems to have been, as such affairs usually are, entirely inconclusive, and ended by Mr. Bradlaugh denying that, at the time of the French Revolution, a woman had been carried through the streets of

Paris naked, in the character of the Goddess of Reason. He insisted that the evidence for such a statement should be produced upon the spot, a method of debate which it is to be feared he was not above using whenever he found himself in an awkward corner.

Mr. Stephenson's singing in his public services, and especially his rendering of ' Jesu, Lover of my soul,' are still remembered by Norwich Methodists. The earnest and popular young evangelist was naturally in much demand, and his preaching outside the limits of his own circuit caused a real awakening in the towns and villages of East Anglia.

In those days it was held that two years was quite long enough for a Probationer to remain in one circuit ; and in two years we find that Bowman Stephenson was removed from Norwich to the Manchester Grosvenor Street Circuit.

Two years previously an experiment had been made in the appointment to Grosvenor Street of an evangelist to do what we now know as ' Mission ' work. The Rev. Richard Harper was freed from other circuit work in order to labour in one of the poorest parts of Manchester, and was thus the first Home Missionary minister, according to our present classification. Bowman Stephenson was appointed to continue the work which Richard Harper had begun. He did so, but departed from the methods of his predecessor. In particular he fastened upon Saturday night as the time of his opportunity with the poor working men and their wives in that city. He arranged in the schoolroom on that evening a weekly programme of music, recitations, and whatever else of a similar character might be secured.

The success was considerable, but when the end of the second year's appointment was approaching, the circuit stewards asked for an interview, and said that the holding of these meetings on the Saturday night was disapproved by many Methodists at the other chapels, and they hoped he would give them up. He at once replied that he would accept no engagement to a circuit which did not leave him sufficient liberty to carry out his work in the only way which he believed likely to accomplish his object. They thereupon reconsidered the matter, and withdrew their request.

The Jubilee of the Foreign Missionary Society fell in 1863, while he was still in the Grosvenor Street Circuit, and great Jubilee celebrations were held in Manchester, which brought Mr. Stephenson opportunity of intercourse with men like William Arthur, Dr. Osborn, Isaac Holden, T. P. Bunting, Thomas Farmer, and W. N. Heald. His personal acquaintance with these men, formed now, was destined to stand him in good stead when his greater work came to him.

The Lancashire Cotton Famine had already begun, and it was a matter of very great surprise to the Methodist Church that Manchester was able, under those circumstances, to give so largely to the Jubilee Fund, though, possibly, the Cotton Famine and the consequent lack of trade really contributed to this generosity. Many men of importance in the cotton trade would find that there were large sums in the bank lying idle, just because they were not able to carry on their business as usual. They would, therefore, be more free to give than in good times when every penny was badly wanted to meet the demands of increasing trade. It is also noteworthy that the general prosperity of the country carried the nation right over this crisis, and although there was much suffering in Lancashire, the public revenue shows that, as a whole, England was still increasing in wealth.

However that might be, throughout Lancashire and parts of Yorkshire people were starving. The skies were blue and bright—a bad sign in districts where a cloudless sky means no work. Great efforts were made to meet the necessities of the people. National subscriptions were raised, and the Northern States of America themselves sent shiploads of food to the relief of Lancashire.

Most of the working people sympathized strongly with the Northern States, and with Abraham Lincoln, for they realized that this was the side that represented freedom. But many of the well-to-do and upper classes leant towards the South, partly because of the irritation that had been caused by what they thought to be the arrogant attitude of the North. A Society was formed to plead the cause of freedom. The Free Trade Hall was crowded at meeting after meeting. Mr. Stephenson took his full share in this agitation, though it increased the opposition and disfavour with which a certain section of the Methodist people looked upon his innovations.

Grosvenor Street, the head of the circuit, was a chapel of great memories. There had been a time when it was continuously full, when the 'best families' in Manchester Methodism were seat-holders, and it had enjoyed the ministry of many of the greatest preachers of the Connexion; but the tide was already receding, and Grosvenor Street was even then feeling the pressure which has since become so heavy.

One little incident of Mr. Stephenson's work there deserves record, if only to show the particularly severe and unbending conservatism about little things that was in those days seriously hampering the free circulation of the life-blood of Methodism. In Grosvenor Street Chapel there were both a reading-desk and a pulpit, and it was the custom for the morning service to be read from the desk, and for the minister to go into the pulpit for the sermon. The gallery was so high that the Sunday school children, who were placed at the back of it, could not see the minister at all when he was in the reading-desk. So Mr. Stephenson explained to the people how anxious he was that the children should hear and see, and thereupon proceeded to take the Bible up into the higher pulpit to read the lessons. Even this little innovation created a great stir, and aroused some very stupidly prejudiced minds. At the same time it had the effect of bringing home to the minds of the majority the need of making some suitable arrangments for the children's worship.

After Mr. Stephenson had been two years in the circuit he was, at the Bradford Conference of 1864, received into full connexion and ordained, and his ordination was promptly followed by his marriage to Miss Ellen Lupton. After these events he did not return to the special charge of Daniel Street, which he had previously held, but a re-arrangement of circuit work was made, and the new home was begun at Droylesden.

Some correspondence that belongs to this period

shows him earnestly discussing with friends and comrades the secrets of the higher life.

When the triennial change came, he had promised to go to Bolton, to take special charge of Fletcher Street. The good people whom he was leaving were very wishful to give him some token of their affection, while at the same time they wanted to assure his successor of a real welcome. Being canny Lancashire folk, with an eye to economy of time, and perhaps of some other things, they arranged that the 'funeral bakemeats' should 'furnish forth the marriage tables.' The Farewell Meeting was held, and speeches were made appreciative of Mr. Stephenson's work. There were some tears, and the presentation clock, which had been covered with a cloth, was exposed and duly handed over to him. Then, in a moment, the scene changed. His successor appeared upon the platform, and the people gave him a most affectionate welcome. 'It was all hearty, all sincere, but rather comical, for the rain of tears was dried up in a moment, and the sunshine of hope gilded the remainder of the meeting.'

A day or two after they removed to Bolton.

Fletcher Street was a good specimen of a working people's church. It is one of those good, old, square preaching-places which still hold so high a place in the affections of the Methodist people. Indeed, there are many who think that the Methodist worship cannot be so effectively offered, nor the Methodist work of winning men by preaching so successfully done in any other kind of building whatever. The Fletcher Street Church was supported by a very vigorous Sunday School. One noteworthy and interesting feature of the social upheaval caused by the cotton famine was the way in which the Lancashire habit of grown-up people attending Sunday School was confirmed and developed. The Fletcher Street School had, at the time of Mr. Stephenson's appointment, sixteen hundred scholars, four hundred of whom were grown up to manhood and womanhood. They possessed the musical voices and instincts which belong to the county, and the singing, led by a fine organ, was a great inspiration.

Mr. Stephenson began his work by banding the people, or as many of them as were willing to join, into what was called the 'Union for Christian Work,' whose object was to win for Christ by varied means all classes of the community. At first about fifty people joined in this association, but afterwards it grew much larger. Its chief object was to carry on the aggressive work of the Church, and to maintain all those 'extras' which are not provided for by the ordinary and regular machinery of Methodism. All the accessory associations of a Methodist Church were to be united under one management. Mr. Stephenson's idea was that three objects would be served :

1. Money would be collected more easily for a central fund that was carrying on all classes of work, than in smaller sums for a number of scattered objects.

2. Committee work would be lessened if, instead of having a separate management for each department, all could be directed by the same meeting.

3. Whenever circumstances required some new mode of work, it could be at once adopted without

the necessity of forming a new organization. Thus order was to be secured, but with it an elasticity that was as vital as order itself to the effective carrying on of Christian work.

A considerable number of visitors were employed in going from house to house, calling the attention of their neighbours to the claims of religion, and inviting their attendance at public worship. They were told that they were not to regard themselves merely as Tract Distributors, but that it was their business to win the confidence of the people, and bring personal influence to bear upon them. The success of these visitors varied very much, for whilst some displayed a most encouraging aptitude, others soon found the work altogether too trying and difficult. The results of faithful persistence and kindly visiting were, however, manifest and permanent.

A set of 'soirées' were a great success. They were kept up for three winters, and an average attendance of five hundred was secured. The lectures were much appreciated, and these social gatherings had a very considerable effect in bringing into more intimate relations with the Church a large number of people, who could not, perhaps, have been immediately appealed to by higher means.

A Savings' Bank was started, but never grew to any large proportions.

The 'Slater Field Mission' gave great satisfaction. Seventy members of Society, a School of two hundred scholars, and two well-attended Sunday services were to be seen as a result of this branch of the work.

A circuit magazine entitled the 'Monthly Greeting' went well, and proved in many ways the power of the press. Some seventy thousand publications, containing nearly two hundred thousand pages, were circulated in Bolton by the Union during the three years of Mr. Stephenson's ministry.

The Sunday-night Mission, whose object was to hold services for people who had not clothes of sufficient respectability to make them willing to go to the chapel, was also a real success, not only in gathering congregations, but in plucking brands from the burning.

The Cottage and Open-air services shared this prosperity, and the Adult Spelling Class, where the illiterate were taught to read the Bible, led to some good cases of conversion.

In view of later developments, it is very interesting to read in the 'Monthly Greeting' for September 1868, of 'Miss Entwistle, our deaconess.' We learn that 'it was through the agency of the Union that her valuable labours had been secured for the neighbourhood.' The Report goes on: 'Of her indefatigable visiting it is not necessary to say a word; but beside this, three Mothers' Meetings are held every week in connexion with her work.'

It is much to notice that a woman was employed and set apart for the work, and supported whilst doing it, but it is certainly striking and unusual that she should be called a 'deaconess,' as in 1868 the use of that word in connexion with English Protestant Churches must have been rare indeed.

At this time the Blake system of Juvenile Collecting was just being started by Mr. Blake, of Harrow, Sherborne, in Dorset, Bradford (Kirkgate), Sheffield,

Manchester, New North Road in the City Road Circuit, and Bolton seem to have been the first places to take it up. Mr. Stephenson was deeply interested, and lent his active assistance to the promotion of it.

He also appears to have had a project in his mind which had some kinship to the establishment of the Fernley Lecture. The following letter from John Fernley, while it does not tell us what this project was, is given for its own interest.

'My dear Sir,

'Previous to the interview I had with you, I had for many years been contemplating the importance of a well prepared sermon or lecture to be delivered at Conference, on a subject either in illustration or defence of Wesleyan doctrine or polity. Your kind visit induced me to turn my immediate attention to it again, and as I visited London a few days afterwards, I took the opportunity of naming my views to two or three of my old ministerial friends. The modest proposition was so well received that I felt encouraged to proceed with my own scheme generally; and then stated that if we could settle upon a satisfactory plan, together with a definition of the object of the lecture or sermon, before the approaching Conference, I would be willing to endow it with £50 annually; the whole to be under the management of a Committee of persons holding office, such as President, Ex-President and Secretary of Conference, some of the Treasurers of our own Funds, &c. I requested Mr. Perks to send me a draft of the scheme and to consult some of our ministers upon it. When we have settled it, my present intention is to send it to Conference for its approval and acceptance.

'As you did me the favour to call to see me at Clairville, I avail myself of this opportunity of conveying the above information. If you can meet with parties willing to sympathize in your larger and more important project, this does not need to interfere with it; both indeed may work harmoniously together, as the object is the same generally, though the mode of operation varies.

'I am,

'Yours very sincerely,

'JOHN FERNLEY.'

With regard to the general results of Mr. Stephenson's ministry, Fletcher Street Chapel was filled, a very large addition was made to the membership of the Church, many scores of additional scholars joined the school, and in every department the work of the Church prospered. The hearts of the people were united in mutual interests and labours, and their piety deepened through their services of benevolence and self-denial.

In connexion with the Union for Christian Work a great many of the methods of what was later known as the 'Forward Movement' were tried, some of them for the first time, and with very marked success. All through the winter months weekly popular lectures were given in the large schoolroom, which held several hundreds of people, and was crowded again and again. The magic-lantern was freely used, electrical experiments were exhibited and explained, and one great triumph was to get a wire through to the House of Commons, and receive on the platform statements of what was being done there at that particular moment.

Everything, however, was subordinated to the public services, and the great central work of evangelization. Open-air meetings were constantly held, and the people were taught that the end of all Christian endeavour was the salvation of men.

It was the custom of the town to begin the New Year with four or five days' holiday. All the paraphernalia of the old-fashioned country fairs came into the town. The moral character of much that went on was more than doubtful, and the irresponsible frivolity and gross vulgarity of these holidays threatened serious interference with evangelistic work. To do something towards mitigating this state of things, Mr. Stephenson encouraged his people to hold an exhibition in the large schoolroom. Many of the men were skilled mechanics, and the women clever with the needle, and some at least of the younger folk could make drawings and models and machinery. To lend dignity and attraction, oil paintings were borrowed from wealthy houses. A large fountain was established in the middle of the great room. The getting a huge tub through an upper window, making it water-tight, disguising it with flowers and ferns, and supplying it with gold-fish was a whole night's work, and a matter of immense interest to a large number of workers. It is a difficult thing to-day to realize how fresh and novel it all was at the beginning of the year 1867.

During the exhibition, a little paper was published

and printed in the Schoolroom, from which we quote the following :

THE FLETCHER STREET TIMES
AND
EXHIBITION CHRONICLE.

JAN. 2, 1867. No. 1.

The New Year has opened very happily—at least at the Exhibition. We may safely say that this is the first Exhibition of the year. It was opened most successfully by the Mayor of Bolton, supported by members of the Town Council ; and during the whole day a succession of intelligent visitors flowed into it, who expressed themselves as being highly delighted and greatly surprised. It was, in truth, a pleasant sight which greeted the eyes of the stranger about eight o'clock. The room was warmly curtained and brilliantly lighted. The lights were reflected from a thousand objects of beauty. Here Chaucer looked upon his visitors with open face, and yonder Tennyson, his latest successor in fame. Here, an engine, driven by electricity, was running to and fro on its brazen rails ; and there, a lighthouse was pouring its light over a stormy sea, and advising the spectators to ' Remember the Draper lifeboat.' There, the ' veiled Vestal ' peeps timidly through her veil at the multitude of by-passers ; who after a long look at the splendid ornamental painting, pass on to see the Fijian trophy, the patent fire engine, and the gas meters, displaying their ' insides.'

Meanwhile numerous applications are being made at the Refreshment Stall for the patent Exhibition Wine, which ' has not a headache in a hogshead of it ' ; and from the other side of the room there comes the laughter of a large circle who are being amused in a most ' shocking ' style ; the Christmas-tree is nodding with its weight, and beseeching the on-lookers to relieve it.

The Piano is making merry music, and 'Charley' is in a neighbouring vestry ventriloquizing in a marvellous manner.

Handbills announcing the various attractions were circulated extensively amongst the people. One of the objects mentioned was a mechanical model of a piping bull-finch. This moved the soul of the venerable superintendent of a neighbouring circuit, who had not so learnt the duty of a minister; and when in May the District Meeting arrived, in which every minister's name may be challenged, he called attention to this very serious matter. He had secured a handbill, and, appealing to the Chairman, asked what was the opinion of the brethren on this subject. He read extracts, and mentioned several items of which he strongly disapproved. 'Here, Mr. Chairman, is another item—a piping bull-finch. Is it by introducing piping bull-finches into our schools, and perhaps into our chapels, that the work of God is to be carried on?' The Synod, of course, dismissed the matter with a laugh, but there were more than a few who had grave doubts when they went home as to whether they had done their duty. It is not easy nowadays to realize the importance which was then placed upon such trifles.

It must not be thought, however, that too great an importance was attached to this side of things by Mr. Stephenson and his helpers. Evangelism was the very core of their work, and was never forgotten. More than fifty years have passed away since then, and yet there remain in the neighbourhood, old men and women who look back with gratitude and thankfulness to the days of their consecration to the service of their Lord and Saviour; and the generation that followed them also felt deeply the strength of the tide of spiritual power which flowed deep and full in those Galilean days.

During his pastorate in Bolton, the manse was gladdened by the arrival of a daughter, Dr. Stephenson's only child, Theodora, afterwards to be so widely known in connexion with her father's work as 'Sister Dora.'

We have seen how Mr. Stephenson was led as a Richmond student, by the oratory of John B. Gough, to sign the temperance pledge. In those days active Temperance workers had to face a great deal of unpopularity and dislike within the Church, as well as to compete with the tremendous evils of drunkenness. He, however, was not the man to be frightened or silenced by such disapproval, and he speedily came to the front among the Temperance leaders of the day. His name is again and again mentioned next to that of the Rev. Charles Garrett, as a vigorous and impassioned advocate and courageous leader in this great reform. And the tragic circumstances connected with the death of his own brother, at the beginning of what promised to be a distinguished medical career, intensified his feelings, and redoubled the energy with which he threw himself into this great conflict.

One of those who still remember him at Fletcher Street, Mr. G. T. Higson, writes:

'I was only eleven years of age when he came to Bolton, but I retain a vivid remembrance of his first Sunday morning service at Fletcher Street. It was his fine singing that got hold of me. He took his hymn-book, and led off in such a way that I found a sensation of my hair standing on end, "like quills upon the fretful porcupine." The singing never dragged when he was in the pulpit. Mr. Stephenson in his singing has ever been an ideal to me of the inspiration a minister may convey to the service in that direction.

'Mr. Stephenson had remarkable success in capturing the young people for Christ and the Church. A very great number attended the prayer-meetings. My brother, the Rev. R. H. Higson, at fourteen years of age, and I myself at twelve, received our first tickets of membership at his hands in Mr. James Ritson's class, in which were men of fifty years of age, as well as a good company ranging from that age to ours. We immensely enjoyed those meetings, as well as the lively prayer-meetings and love-feasts. We used to turn out occasionally at six o'clock on a Sunday morning to the prayer-meeting; and once or twice we—the young people, in their great enthusiasm for their minister—had a prayer-meeting at the back of his residence, in a field at Daubhill. Many of those youths and maidens have remained faithful to this day, and there are many in Australia and America, as well as at home, who have not forgotten their youthful inspirations under Stephenson's ministry. And as the result of that three years' ministry the Church obtained several ministers, many Sunday-school teachers, a great number of prayer-leaders and class-leaders, and a host of fervent worshippers from that time to this. . . . The monthly Soirées started by Mr. Stephenson were very successful. A charge of twopence was made, and in return we were presented with a bag of biscuits and a cup of coffee, and it was our privilege to enjoy ourselves in an 'At Home' fashion for about an hour, and then we were treated either to a lecture or a varied programme of reading and song. Many eminent men were secured, such as W. O. Simpson, and also men of science and art. I think the standard of age for those attending was fourteen or fifteen ; but some of us youngsters invariably managed to squeeze in, and enjoy it with the rest.

'I well remember a great Temperance meeting at which Mr. Stephenson presided at Fletcher Street, at which every available seat was filled, when he had secured twelve men of the place of different trades to give their experience of their ability to do work without drink. It was a great night—every man of them excellent—and very many were influenced for total abstinence and religion.'

The Rev. James H. Hodson, B.D., writes in the *Wesleyan Methodist Magazine* for November, 1912 :

'Mr. Stephenson came to the Bridge Street Circuit, Bolton, in 1865. I was then a boy of thirteen. As quite a child, I heard the call of God to the ministry ; no other purpose than that of being a Methodist preacher ever entered my mind. My father spoke of this to Mr. Stephenson shortly after his arrival, and he, in turn, talked with me about it. The result was that I went to live in his house, my mother taking me to him, and saying, "Like Hannah, I have brought my boy for the service of the Sanctuary ; do you train him for the high calling." So it came to pass that I lived as one of his family till I entered Didsbury College in

1872. I thus had unique opportunities for observing his character and his work. He regarded me as a son, and was a good companion for a boy. When studies were over he would join in boyish pursuits. He fitted up a workshop, where he gave me lessons in carpentry. Once, together, we achieved the construction of a wheelbarrow of such generous proportions that it was too big to go through the garden gate! Another triumph was a summer-house, cunningly contrived out of an old four-post bedstead! Again, as the "field-day" of Fletcher Street Sunday School came near, so deep was his interest in the children that we manufactured a number of kites for their amusement. Like St. Francis of Assisi, he was a lover of animals, keeping all at once a horse, a dog, a goat, and turkeys. When we lived in London, at one time he would carry home some miserable, lost, mongrel cur, of which it cost his wife some scheming to be rid; at another time it would be a tortoise, or, again, a family of white rats, which ere long threatened to become as numerous as those which followed the famous pied piper of Hamelin! His tender heart was speedily touched by the sight of distress. I have seen a poor, wretched man come to the door, and so work upon his sympathy that, but for the timely intervention of his thrifty wife, he would have given the man the only shirt ready for his own use.

. . . .

'College days at Richmond over, he felt within himself the movings of ambition to be a great popular preacher, nor can any one who knew him intimately doubt that such a career was well within his power. But, partly under the influence of William Arthur, and after some inward conflict, he deliberately chose to aim simply at being a winner of souls. Thus he honoured God ; and God honoured him by giving him not the evanescent renown of a merely popular preacher, but a name that Methodism will never allow to be forgotten. In the opinion of competent judges, he never did himself justice as a preacher. He was in great demand for sermons, lectures, speeches, and was so often from home that his preparation for his appointments in his own circuit was sometimes too hurried. But now and again he would preach a sermon of great power and ability, revealing his real quality. He was a fine open-air preacher, and regularly took his stand in spaces carefully chosen for this work. On his village appointments he would, when possible, preach out of doors rather than to the few saints in the chapel. In his open-air ministry he won some remarkable trophies for Christ amongst men deeply sunk in sin. His Sunday-evening services were always followed by prayer-meetings, in which it was usual to see converts, some of whom still live to bless his memory. He had a beautiful voice, which he consecrated to Christ ; his gospel solos and his song-lectures were very popular and greatly owned of God.

'It was at this time that he assisted Charles Garrett and George Maunder to establish the *Methodist Temperance Magazine*, and also succeeded, in conjunction with others, in arranging the first Temperance meeting ever held in connexion with a District Meeting.

'Amid ceaseless activities, he carefully cultivated

his own spiritual life. Sometimes rising very early, he spent hours in meditation and prayer, the subject of Entire Sanctification at that time, and, indeed, all through his ministry, having special fascination for him, and often forming the theme of his sermons.'

His opinions and character at this stage in his career are well shown by a farewell speech made when, on leaving Fletcher Street, he received a presentation of a valuable harmonium, subscribed for in small sums by five hundred friends. He said:

'I am anxious as long as I can to put off the moment of parting, and if I could forget all about it for this night I should be glad to do so, and simply think of the causes which have led you to give me these expressions of your love; that love which has lived, and, if I may judge from my own heart, has grown through the whole period of my residence with you. Forgetting, then, the parting hour, I will try to say some few things in reference to our relationship for the last three years.

'First of all, during the whole time of my residence here, I have striven as far as possible to belong to no party in this society. In all religious connexions there are men who naturally group themselves together and sympathize with each other in their views of certain public questions and matters that may happen within the church; and, without using the words in an offensive sense, in all Christian churches there are parties. It always seems to me to be the first duty, as well as the highest wisdom of a minister of Christ, not to throw himself into the hands of any such party, not to make himself their representative, much less their tool, but ever to maintain towards all within the Church relations of earnest love and kindness.

'Then I have tried in the Church to carry out the principle of co-operation. I believed I was not able by myself to do the work which needed to be done in this neighbourhood, and, therefore, I asked your assistance. I believe in no clerical order. The word "clergy" is utterly misapplied when used of ministers of the Gospel. The whole people of God are the "clergy," in the true sense of the word; and as I do not believe any man on earth is a priest, so I do not believe any man is a clergyman except in that general sense in which these words are applicable to all Christian men who are united by living faith to their living Head. As a consequence, a logical consequence, of this I feel I am only one workman amongst many; that I am only, if you will allow me the expression, the foreman, and it is my greatest wisdom and my greatest duty to endeavour to enlist in the Master's service every person who can do any work at all. And I believe that unless a Christian minister can carry with him the heart, the conscience, and the co-operation of the people, however hard he may work himself, he will not be powerful for any wide and extensive good. I have striven never to tell anybody to do what I would not do myself. I do not believe there is any degradation in any sort of work done for Christ. I believe the reason why in some places such matters as open-air preaching are never heard of, is because ministers do not set the example. I myself should on many occasions like to have been excused from open-air preaching, and however bold a front I have put on, when getting up to preach both indoors and in the open-air, my heart has been beating at a rate that was exceedingly distressing ; but if I had not done such work I could not have dared to ask any of you to do it. Any man who is a commander should also be the leader of his people. Further, I have always tried in carrying on the work here never to shrink from anything because it was extraordinary. The world has never been moved by any man who is not willing to go out of the beaten paths. It is necessary for us to look abroad and see in what new forms old truth can be presented to the people ; and along what new channels it can flow. If I have been enabled to do any good at all, it is because I have not been frightened of a thing because it was new ; but rather thought that, as it was a novelty, I had good reasons for looking at it. I have tried to preach in the old-fashioned style, and, if you like, have had a touch of the " Ranter " about me. I do not shrink from being classed with those of my brethren who are accounted by superfine people as not so genteel as their neighbours ; for I have always comforted myself with this thought : " If I be a gentleman, folk will find it out ; and if I am not, no attempts that I may make to look like one will deceive people." I have never been afraid of a good roaring prayer-meeting of the old-fashioned sort, nor of the practice of kneeling at the penitent-form. I have never been afraid of a good loud " Glory," or an " Amen " ; I am glad to hear these things, and I am thankful this earnest spirit has widely prevailed amongst you. In this I have only been trying to do what my brethren are doing; and I hope there is nothing egotistic in my saying that I feel I do not deserve one tithe of what you have said about me this night. It has very deeply humbled me before God; and did you know my heart and my relations to my God as I know them, my many weaknesses and defects, which very painfully depress my mind, you would not have been able to say so many kind things. God shows me the evil of my own heart, and my utter dependence on Him; and I do not think there is much danger of your spoiling me by your expressions of love and goodwill. Yet I am grateful for them, and they will be a great comfort to me.

'While I have been here I have tried to be useful to the Sunday School, and one of the most pleasant memories that I shall have of Bolton will be the way in which the scholars have spoken to me, and held out their hands to shake mine when I have met them. I have also been a teetotaller, and have never shirked that position; but in all these matters I have tried to illustrate three qualities. I have tried to show in everything honesty, justice, and charity. For instance, you know I am a Liberal, perhaps a Liberal with a touch of Radicalism about me; yet though I have held those opinions I have never shrunk from declaring them. I should have felt disgraced in my own eyes if I had held political opinions which I had hesitated prudently to express; but while I have done so I have felt that some of my Tory friends who held different opinions had the same right to express theirs. . . . As to teetotalism, I do not believe it has won me a single enemy in the town; if I except a few publicans and beer-house keepers. I believe *they* will not be sorry when they know that I have left by mail train for London. But while I have avowed my teetotalism, and have never had so strong an impression as at this moment as to the evil of drinking, yet I have never allowed the fact of a man not being a teetotaller to interfere with my relations with him. I have been never less his friend and co-worker, and have never been shy or suspicious of him ; and, in return I have been frankly treated by such men, and have received from them the most unhesitating and undeviating support. I am touched with the words in the address, " your friends in connexion with Fletcher Street Chapel " ; I am thankful to you for that word " friends." It will be a very pleasant memory for me to think that I have left five hundred friends behind me. I can only say that if you are sorry to lose me, I am far more sorry to go away from you, and however sharp the wrench may be to your hearts, it is a great deal sharper to mine, and it will be a long time before I shall be able to look upon any congregation and society with that same feeling of intimate friendship that I have long felt for you. . .

' In conclusion, I ask you for your prayers. I am appointed to a sphere of labour very different from that which I expected. I hoped to have gone to Leeds ; but as the necessities of our Connexion have withdrawn from a circuit a minister who has been called to be the Connexional Editor, the Rev. Benjamin Gregory, the Conference thought that such a circuit had a special claim, and when that circuit asked for me to be appointed in his place, the Conference seized me and put me down for

Lambeth. When I received the appointment my heart shrank very much from going, but I am trying to tell myself that all must be right, and to say,

"Mould as Thou wilt Thy passive clay."

The circuit, however, is not a poor one, and I have no right to complain that the Conference has appointed me to it, but the chapel and neighbourhood that will be under my special care are perhaps as bad as can be found out of the bottomless pit. My parish will be in "New Cut," Lambeth, and I shall have to go to chapel every Sunday morning through a street crowded, as Bolton Market Hall is crowded on Saturday night, with people engaged in buying and selling, and I shall have to visit members in cellars and garrets in the dense courts of that part of London. The congregation is very small indeed, and it has declined for several years past. Altogether there is perhaps as little to invite a man as could be found in any place, but there is this one thing which does invite me, that I shall have to go to "seek that which is lost."

'In going yonder to work, however, I shall have many advantages. I do not want to represent myself as a martyr, or one on a forlorn hope. I shall have good times and good friends, but still there is hard work to be done, and I have a somewhat dark path before me. Yet when I shall be working two hundred miles away, in the dense courts of Lambeth, it will be a great comfort and cheer to me to think of the many people in Lancashire who have not forgotten me, and are praying for me.'

CHAPTER V

Invitation to Leeds—Appointment to Lambeth—Attracting the Crowds—The 'New Cut.'

TOWARDS the close of his ministry in Bolton, Bowman Stephenson had received an invitation to the Leeds Oxford Place Circuit, after some correspondence with the Superintendent, the Rev. William Davison. This correspondence is interesting as one of the earliest examples of that demand for a 'free hand' for men engaged in Mission work with which the Methodist Church has been made so familiar since the 'Forward Movement' took a prominent place in its history. As ever, Mr. Stephenson is a pioneer. He had evidently written asking for very large concessions in the way of modifying the ordinary administration of the circuit.

Mr. Davison replies from the point of view of the old-fashioned Methodist Superintendent, who has not the slightest intention of allowing any power to pass out of his own hands, and means to work the circuit, and expects his colleagues to help him to do so, on the well-established Methodist plan. He writes :

'It will not only be agreeable to me that Holbeck should be largely worked by its local pastor, but I should greatly prefer a colleague who would work it on that principle to one who would leave his own locality in order to enjoy social life with the more numerous respectable families on the Oxford Place side. I should, therefore, be perfectly ready to give every reasonable facility in that direction, consistently with the well-working of the whole circuit.

'But I think that there are one or two things which you forget. First: You appear to think that the town part of the circuit consists only of Oxford Place, Hanover Place, and Holbeck. But there is *New Wortley*, a very important place, rather nearer to us than Holbeck is, with a society of 172 needing pastoral care, and a place that will well repay efficient working, in a population resembling Holbeck, and itself in the vicinity of Holbeck. Who, on your plan, is to take charge of New Wortley?

'Secondly, I think you a little forget that other ministers may have their special plans, plans for the working of which regularity in the circuit work may be essential. For instance, we have connected with the Oxford Place Leaders' Meeting 894 members (embracing Hanover Place, which has no separate Leaders' Meeting). I should have preferred working these two societies as separate pastorates, but the classes being so intermixed, and my colleague in his third year, it seemed desirable for this year to work them together as best we could. I set to work in earnest pastoral visitation, and I believe made some impression. *But* this is the busiest circuit I ever was in, not excepting Manchester. Four or five meetings a day I have had, &c. Now, how are our 900 members to be watched over? To get time for pastoral work requires indomitable energy, and though it may seem a small matter, to have to devote an hour to the preparation of a Monday-evening sermon at Oxford Place, it may just be the exclusion of four important visits by the busy Superintendent. Besides, Oxford Place is one of the most important congregations in Methodism, and I have generally found that alternation suits our people best. I thoroughly dislike, indeed, the plan of five ministers in a circuit as lately here, for I like to be often before the same congregation if I am to be their pastor. The Oxford Place people will want to see you in your turn. However, I think the case can be sufficiently met by giving you, as far as possible, predominant work at Holbeck.

'As to going out of the circuit, I quite agree that while we ask strangers into the circuit, the Ministers of the circuit may lawfully, in moderation, go out. At the same time, few pieces of foreign work are equal to preaching for a day at Oxford Place, where you have three or four ordinary congregations rolled into one.

'Our work is considerably increased by the division of the circuit. Oxford Place Circuit only lost about three hundred members, and with them two ministers. Our ticket work is very heavy.

'On the whole, I do not think you should make any stipulation with the Quarterly Meeting. They are not the parties to arrange our work, and I could not sit in the Quarterly Meeting, and hear the Plan-making taken out of my hand. Nor do I think they would wish more than a statement that you would feel a special pleasure in thoroughly working Holbeck. Indeed, I think it might be injurious. For there were one or two at the preliminary meeting for inviting you that more or less opposed (neither of them knew much of you), and if there was something exceptional in your offer, it might lead to a divided vote. We have an admirable people, but one or two crotchety ones.

'I have written this note very rapidly, but hope you can decipher my meaning. I have no fear but that we shall comfortably arrange our circuit work, when we get together in one of our early Preachers' Meetings.

'I think it an easy thing to get on with a colleague of earnest and zealous purpose, with whom the worst work may be the endeavour to lop off some little excrescence, whereas if he have neither hands nor feet, what Superintendent can hopefully be associated with him?'

Mr. Stephenson's letter, in reply, shows a very clear conception of his own purpose, and a very plain demand for a 'free hand' to carry it out.

'You appear to have an objection to coming beforehand to any understanding; though you kindly suggest that the case may be met by giving me "as far as possible, predominant work at Holbeck." Now, if that meant in your mind what it meant in mine, I think it would be all that I could desire. . .

'What I want is to have a limited area; appointments as regular as possible; and personal responsibility for a certain district, with all that that implies; so far as can possibly be made consistent with circuit work. In a word, I want as nearly the position of a Home Missionary Minister as can be without a direct Conference appointment.

'Now I wish to be very honest with you, my dear

sir, before entering the circuit. I tell you frankly that many of my modes of operation are unusual; in some instances they have been questioned by good, but timid, people. It is quite possible that I may shock some prejudices—though I shall studiously avoid doing that unnecessarily; and it is possible that what some may consider excrescences, I may hold to be a very necessary part of a system of work. I have had here a large amount of liberty. In all matters of prerogative I have carefully guarded the Superintendent's position, but the details of our operations in the limits of my own district have been left almost exclusively to myself. The theory of superintendency has been applied in an exceedingly liberal manner. Now, I think this to be very necessary. I work very much out of the usual ruts. There are very few men in Methodism who do; and I take it that all latitude should be given to those, which is at all consistent with our system.

'Now, I hope you will not imagine that I say this because I think *you* are at all disposed to assert your prerogative unduly. I do not think so. If I had, I should have promptly declined the invitation. But I don't want to become your colleague under any sort of misunderstanding, and I have, therefore, expressed myself frankly.

'I take it that the stewards at any rate know my style of work, and are inviting me with their eyes open. I should earnestly wish that. If I come to the circuit, I shall try to do my work with the universal approval of the circuit; but I shall not be stopped by the fear of offending anybody's prejudices, amongst the laity. I want to come to make every man, woman and child in Holbeck feel the influence of Methodism. Then I must get at them in my own way.'

At the close of this correspondence the invitation followed in due course, and appears to have been practically unanimous; so we may presume that the Superintendent had been able to make satisfactory arrangements with his proposed colleague.

Concerning this invitation, Mr. Stephenson tells the following story:

'Some two or three years before I had found it more convenient and comfortable to let my moustache grow, and in the Quarterly Meeting at Leeds, when it was proposed to invite me, an aged and venerable man opposed the suggestion solely on the ground that I wore a moustache. As a matter of fact, I believe that myself and two or three others were the only ministers in Methodism who then let their hair grow on their faces. Some years previously a serious matter of discipline had arisen in this connexion. A minister came to the Conference adorned by this appendage, and Conference was informed that the dislike of the people to it was so great that it would not be possible to appoint him to any circuit. The difficulty was created, not by any prejudice amongst the ministers, but by the strong objection of the people.

'Subsequent to this incident, however, the public feeling with regard to the wearing of the moustache had greatly changed. Things French had become popular at the time of the Crimean War. Boys' caps were made after the French shape; trousers were worn after the peg-top pattern; and even in the Leeds Quarterly Meeting a great majority voted in favour of inviting a minister who had himself followed the growing fashion.

'I was not the first, however, to adopt it. Dr. Rule led the way. He was a man of small features, and for some reason thought that he would gain both in health and in dignity if he allowed the hair to grow on his lip after the patriarchal fashion. He first appeared in this new adornment in the District Synod, at which William M. Bunting was in attendance. The latter was a ready wit, and took the first opportunity of expressing in the Synod the pleasure of them all in having Dr. Rule amongst them, but went on to say, "Our only regret is that we shall see his face no more."'

However, something of quite different import interfered with the invitation to Leeds. When Stations were before Conference, a plea was put in on behalf of the Lambeth Circuit. Their minister, the Rev. Benjamin Gregory, had been taken away by the Conference to fill the office of Connexional Editor, and as circuits always do in such cases, they claimed that special consideration should be given to them, and fixed upon Mr. Stephenson as the man whose appointment would best mitigate the severity of their loss.

At that time, the Lambeth Circuit included all the territory between Blackfriars Bridge and Clapham Common. Lambeth was still the head of the circuit. It had already suffered from that outreaching of the people into the suburbs which has so affected the civic and religious life of London's vast population. His special charge was the chapel in Waterloo Road. It stood immediately opposite the London and South Western Railway Station. A constant flow of people moved along Waterloo Bridge, and thence outwards to various parts of South London, though the traffic was very considerably checked by the fact that a halfpenny toll was charged for passing over the bridge. When, a few years later, mainly through the exertions of Sir William M'Arthur, this toll was abolished, the number of foot passengers crossing the bridge rapidly and largely increased.

In Mr. Stephenson's days, however, the toll and its effect on the traffic made the position of the Waterloo Road Chapel serious and difficult. Hard by it was the 'New Cut,' then notorious as one of the black spots in London. The chapel stood back some thirty feet from the footway. Mr. Stephenson fixed his attention on the vacant space in front of it as admirably adapted for open-air services. He determined to establish a preaching-place there. A platform was built and roofed in. It had doors which could fold back against the wall, and strong lights fixed, giving it, as he tells us himself, 'something of the appearance presented by a cheap-jack's establishment.' A small desk and a harmonium completed the outfit. Chairs, however, were wanted to retain the passers-by. Even though a good many of them should take a chair for a rest, rather than through any anxiety to hear the preacher, still, if they had a chair they would listen to him. So Mr. Stephenson made his first appeal to the Methodist Connexion for two hundred chairs, or two hundred half-crowns with which to buy them. The response was immediate, and when the chairs were provided the new preaching-place proved most effective.

Night after night open-air, gospel, and temperance

meetings were held. His singing was a great attraction, and large audiences assembled. The Rev. J. H. Hodson tells us that he used to act as curate on week evenings, and on Sundays they had a student from Richmond College. One of these, who came for a considerable period, was the Rev. W. J. Williams, since President of the New Zealand Conference. It is interesting to find Mr. Williams in after years, when he was Secretary of the New Zealand Conference, sending collections from New Zealand to support the Children's Home, and writing about it with the warmest sympathy.

At certain seasons, and especially on Derby Day, there were great multitudes passing by. Mr. Stephenson met the case by keeping up services throughout the evening. He commenced one address by saying, 'Pretender has won the Derby, and the suicides have begun,' and always showed himself able to accommodate himself to the character of his audience.

At another time on this same open space, a camp-meeting was held. By a little ingenuity, and the use of some timbers and canvas, they managed to turn it into a commodious and comfortable gathering-ground. The small room at the back served for conversation with those who were impressed and were willing to seek Christ. Dr. Stephenson always regretted that, after he left the circuit, the chapel and this plot of land were sold. The place on which the Union Jack Club for Soldiers and Sailors now stands, changed hands two or three times, and always at an enhanced price. He thought that to sell it at all was a great mistake, and that if it had been held, it would have given Methodism one of the finest sites for a Central Hall which could be found in London.

In the winter, on Saturday evenings, Mr. Stephenson held 'Newspaper Socials' in the Waterloo Road Schoolroom. Here the chief items of the week's news were read, thousands of the *Monthly Greeting* were distributed gratis, and cheap refreshments were served. Such enterprises began to tell upon the regular congregation. The chapel became popular, and conversions multiplied. One excellent official plaintively remarked, 'We heard from Bolton that Mr. Stephenson would give us chapel-keepers plenty of work, and we know it now.' Stewards and members were surprised to find themselves drawn out of the depths of their pews on Sunday evenings to the service outside. If the new minister made the chapel-keeper work, he worked himself unsparingly. He became Superintendent of the Sunday School, and captain and leader of every enterprise of the Church. Dry bones were stirred and made to live, and new energy was imparted to every branch of the Society's work. The whole place was aroused, and awake with new energy and life.

At the Circuit Chapel, Lambeth, the old London Methodist traditions of worship were maintained, and along with them the old bad habit of coming late on the part of a large number of the congregation, to whom the prayers did not appeal. They aimed at being in time for the sermon, which was due at about ten minutes to twelve. But on one occasion the late-comers were taken aback by discovering that Mr. Stephenson had preached the sermon first, and was now about to read prayers. Nobody took any offence, and some, at any rate, took the broad hint that had been given them. Notwithstanding this difficulty, there was much warmth and spiritual earnestness at that time in the Lambeth Society.

It was, however, the notorious New Cut, with all the courts and alleys opening out of it, and running behind it, that was to give the call to Bowman Stephenson to his life's work. The condition of the children had always made a great appeal to him. Already in Bolton he had been meditating the establishment of a Home for suffering little ones. Of the New Cut he writes, 'I soon saw little children in a condition which made my heart bleed. There they were, ragged, shoeless, filthy, their faces pinched with hunger, and premature wretchedness staring out of their too bright eyes, and I began to feel that now my time had come. Here were my poor little brothers and sisters sold to Hunger and the Devil, and I could not be free of their blood if I did not at least try to save some of them.'

CHAPTER VI

Beginning of the Children's Home—' Praying and Working '—Mr. Horner and Mr. Mager—Condition of outcast children—Cottage taken in Church Street—Inaugural Meeting—' Concerning These Little Ones '—First Committee Meetings—First Christmas at the Home—Reminiscences.

Two young men, who were colleagues as Secretaries of the Clifton Street Sunday School (connected with Studley Road Wesleyan Church), and close friends, had been holding religious services in a Thieves' Kitchen situated in the notorious ' Mint ' in Southwark. The place was known as the ' Farmhouse,' and they had formed a project of buying it, that they might convert it into a Model Lodging-house. They proposed to make an appeal for subscriptions through the *Methodist Recorder*, and they wanted Mr. Stephenson to allow them to give his name as ready to receive contributions. He, however, went to see Mr. Mager, and told him of the friendless and homeless boys he was constantly meeting in the New Cut and its neighbourhood. He would like to take a house, not as a common lodging-house, but as a Training Home, where some of these boys could be taught to live an industrious and Christian life. Would Mr. Mager and Mr. Horner help him ? Mr. Mager wrote to his friend :

'Dear Horner,

'Come round to tea with us. Mr. Stephenson has called to talk with you and me upon a new and interesting subject.

'Yours affectionately,

'ALFRED W. MAGER.'

While these three men are having their tea and talking over their project, we must stop to take some note of the men themselves, and of the England in which they were living.

Thomas Bowman Stephenson was now in his thirtieth year, fresh from his triumphs at Bolton—a man of exuberant energy, courage, and zeal, with a mind that had already been turned towards the needs of the children by his Lancashire experiences. The ignorance and neglect of motherly duties which was fostered by the factory system, and the consequent pitiful miseries of the uncared-for little ones, had led him there to make plans for their relief, which he was not immediately able to carry out. The reading of Fleming Stevenson's book, *Praying and Working*, with its wonderful story of the 'Inner Mission,' in Germany, was also a means by which he was enabled to enter into the inheritance of the saints. He came to Lambeth in 1868, with his mind thus prepared for the service which God had in store for him.

Francis Horner was a young Irishman from Dublin, in his twenty-second year, beginning a business career in London; and Alfred William Mager, who was ten years older, was a native of Bath, where his father was for many years a City Councillor and

Mr. Mager's House in Lambeth.

Rev. T. B. Stephenson, with Mr. Horner (standing) and Mr. Mager, planning the first Children's Home.

[face p. 80.

Guardian of the Poor. Mr. Mager, senior, was an active Wesleyan, and a Sunday School superintendent, among whose teachers was found the late Mrs. Wiseman, of Foreign Missionary fame. Alfred had received a preliminary training for the Law, but had accepted an appointment to a good position in the London and Westminster Bank, the first joint-stock bank established in London. His promotion in the Bank was rapid, being much assisted by his legal training. His first connexion with Bowman Stephenson had been a political one. Immediately after his appointment to Lambeth, a General Election took place, and the young minister was speaking at a great meeting held at the Lambeth Baths, in favour of the candidature of Sir William M'Arthur. Mr. Mager interrupted in favour of Tom Hughes, the sitting member, well known as the author of *Tom Brown's Schooldays*. Mr. Stephenson accepted the correction, and combined the names of Hughes and McArthur. He did not know who his interlocutor was till Mr. Horner told him, subsequently, on the hustings. A few days later he called on Mr. and Mrs. Mager, in connexion with their wishes about the 'Farmhouse,' and talked of his thoughts concerning the poor arab boys and girls around him. He asked Mr. Mager if he would join him in work for the little outcasts, and he agreed to do so if his friend and co-adjutor, Francis Horner, would also consent.

Under these circumstances, the letter referred to was sent, and the gathering of three at the tea-table took place. Mr. Horner writes concerning it: 'There have been big meetings held in the interests of the Children's Home since then, meetings thronged by thousands of warm-hearted friends; but to those, at least, who were present, none can ever exceed in interest that first enthusiastic meeting of three. The "lines" of a life-boat were laid down that evening, which has since then, with God's blessing, saved many from destruction.'

We ought to stop to try to realize the state of things in England with regard to the task they were about to take up. The public conscience had long been exercised as to the condition of the children of the land. Lord Shaftesbury's noble work, first on behalf of the chinmey-sweeps, then of the children in factories and mines, and later in connexion with the Ragged-school Movement, had been a great factor in arousing public interest in questions concerning child-life.

The period itself will stand out in English history as one of the landmarks of progress. In 1869 Thomas J. Barnardo, who was himself a Ragged-school teacher, had been brought to such vivid realization of the neglected condition of the waifs and strays of London, that he had in a tentative way begun the great work that will always be connected with his name. We have seen how Mr. Stephenson and his friends were about to commit the Methodist Church to a similar enterprise. About a year previously a lady had given Mr. Spurgeon £20,000 for the establishment of an orphanage. In 1870, Forster's Education Act was passed, which first admitted the right of every child in England to education, and began in earnest to make provision for it. It was estimated that at the time when the Act was passed, there were at least one million and a half children in the country who were not attending schools, or at any rate not attending schools of any reasonable efficiency.

The condition of the neglected and outcast children of London was most pitiable. The story is widely known which Dr. Barnardo used to tell of his dining with the Earl of Shaftesbury, and being challenged as to whether he could that very night find any number of such neglected boys as he was speaking of. Taking a cab, as they were, the Earl and Mr. Barnardo and two others, went down to Lower Thames Street, where, among one collection of boxes and barrels, no less than seventy-three homeless lads were found, who were brought out of their hiding-places by the offer of a halfpenny each.

Of Mr. Francis Horner we read a similar story in connexion with the beginning of the Children's Home work. 'Shortly before Christmas, he went out one night, when the snow was falling rapidly, in search of veritable street-boys. He reached London Bridge about midnight, and asked a policeman if he could tell him where any destitute lads were sleeping out. Sleeping out! When the keen blast was whirling the snowflakes over the bridge into the dark river below, and when even one of London's busiest thoroughfares seemed deserted. "Sir," said the officer, "come with me, and when I turn on my 'bull's-eye' they'll swarm from their holes like rats from a sewer. I haven't the heart to turn them out such a night as this." He led the way to an open space near the landing-pier, and lifting up a huge piece of tarpaulin which covered some boxes, turned on his "bull's-eye." The lads, who had been crouching beneath some empty boxes, came out, shoeless, ragged, and miserable. Two of them were brothers. They had been deserted by their father, and their mother had been dead some years. "Would you like to be placed in a Home, clothed, fed and taught?" inquired Mr. Horner. The boys' eyes lit up at the word "home" before the poor pinched lips could answer, "Yes." These lads told Mr. Horner that some boys who went to the half-penny coffee-stall to "get a warm," had been telling them about a school which would be opened on New Year's Day. "What school do you mean?" inquired Mr. Horner. "Why, Mr. Gover (of the London School Board) and a lot o' swells have been clubbing together, and a-woting one another hin, and they're a'going to open a school on New Year's Day, when we shall be taught a trade, so as we can earn a living." In the end, the poor lads who had been disturbed crept back to their boxes, the worthy policeman telling them, "I won't turn you out to-night." Before Mr. Horner retired with his rescued outcasts, one lad, thrusting his head from beneath the tarpaulin, said, "Do what you can for us, sir."'

It need hardly be said that Mr. Stephenson and his friends were on fire with the new project. A local habitation and a name were soon forthcoming. The place was a rented cottage, No. 8 Church Street, Waterloo Road. Mr. Curnock describes it as follows: 'A more prosaic place could scarcely be imagined. The street—its name has been changed to Exton Street—is close to the railway arches which cluster around Waterloo Station. It is by no means the brightest street in a not very brilliant neighbourhood. An entry (now figuring as a wide doorway) was the only playground. A stable behind served as a dining-room. Wood-chopping was the

PART OF THE INTERIOR OF THE FIRST CHILDREN'S HOME IN CHURCH STREET, WATERLOO ROAD, WHERE THE FIRST BOYS WERE TAKEN IN.

face p. 84.

only industry. A loft in the rear became a dormitory for the boys. A white mark on the wall of the higher building shows the spot at which the wash-house was erected.

Such was the local habitation. The *name*, although only boys were received, prophetically enough, from the first was 'The Children's Home.'

On July 9, 1869, two boys were received into the Home, and the work was begun. Mr. Callister, who was Mr. Stephenson's co-Superintendent at the Waterloo Road Sunday School, and who lived two doors away from the 'Home,' gave assistance at the reception of these boys which Mr. Stephenson never forgot, and from that time forward has been a warm friend both of the Founder and of the work.

A week after the first two boys had been received, a meeting was held on the premises to promote the work. A record of it exists in the shape of a pamphlet which we reprint in full.

STATEMENT AND APPEAL

ON BEHALF OF

THE CHILDREN'S HOME,

THE OBJECT OF WHICH IS

TO RESCUE CHILDREN WHO, THROUGH THE DEATH OR VICE OR EXTREME POVERTY OF THEIR PARENTS, ARE IN DANGER OF FALLING INTO CRIMINAL WAYS.

'Inasmuch as ye have done it unto the least of these My brethren, ye have done it unto Me.'

JULY, 1869.

Council of Advice and Aid.

Rev. John Hall.
Sir Francis Lycett.
W. M'Arthur, Esq., M.P.
John Chubb, Esq.
Alex. M'Arthur, Esq.
J. F. Bennett, Esq.

(With power to add to their number.)

Committee.

Rev. C. H. Kelly.
A. W. Mager, Esq.
W. T. Whelpton, Esq.
F. Horner, Esq.

Hon. Director.

Rev. T. Bowman Stephenson, B.A.

Hon. Medical Attendant.

T. Brown, Esq., M.D.

In Charge of the Home (' Father ' and ' Mother ')

Mr. and Mrs. Austin.

THE CHILDREN'S HOME.

A gathering of friends of this enterprise, for the purpose of imploring the Divine blessing upon it, was held in the workshop of the Home on the afternoon of Friday, July 16. About thirty ladies and gentlemen were present. Rev. John Hall commenced the proceedings by giving out a hymn. Rev. Simpson Crump read Matt. xxv., and prayer was offered. Sir F. Lycett, Messrs. W. and A. M'Arthur, and J. F. Bennett, were prevented from attending by previous engagements. John Chubb, Esq., was called to the chair. He expressed his deep sympathy with the movement, and believed it was urgently needed. He thought the modest scale on which it had been commenced recommended it, for it was from small beginnings that great movements arose ; and he trusted this would be but the commencement of a movement which should spread very widely, especially among the members of the Wesleyan Methodist communion. For though this Home was not commenced in any sectarian spirit, it was hoped that it would commend itself to the sympathy and support of Methodists, who at present had nothing of the kind especially dependent upon them; and he thought it had a special claim upon Christian people who had gone out into the suburbs to live, and who, now that their personal labours and influence were withdrawn from the centre of the town, ought all the more liberally to contribute their money to aid in the evangelization of the masses of our fellow-countrymen.

Statements were then made by the Rev. T. B. Stephenson and Mr. F. Horner. Addresses were next delivered by the Rev. John Bond, of Wandsworth; Henry Parker, Esq., LL.B., of the Connexional School, Dublin; Henry Avis, Esq., Circuit Steward, of Lambeth; Rev. Simpson Crump and Rev. John Hall. Mr. Hall pointed out that, though this movement had the hearty goodwill of his circuit, it was not a circuit movement, but appealed to a much wider circle. In the course of the proceedings the following statement was laid before the meeting, which will fully explain the object and present position of the Home:—

The object of this Institution is to shelter, feed, clothe, educate, train to industrial habits, and, by God's blessing, lead to Christ, children who are in danger of falling into criminal habits. It is commenced in humble dependence on the blessing of Almighty God, and it is hoped that its daily engagements will be pervaded by a religious spirit. For it is the firm faith of its founders that good citizens can only be found in good Christians, and that Christian philanthropy should aim at nothing less than the conversion of the soul from sin to God.

This Institution is not for orphans only; in some

cases children with both parents living are in a worse condition than if they had none. It prescribes no limit of age or circumstances in the applicants, but the Committee will judge of every case presented to them on its merits. The cumbrous mode of election to vacancies will not be adopted, but the utmost deference will be paid by the Committee to the recommendation of any subscriber.

The necessity of such an institution is sufficiently shown by the fact that, while it is calculated that there are 100,000 children in London who ought to be in some such institution, all the Reformatories, Refuges, and Industrial Schools at present in operation do not provide for one tithe of them.

The immediate occasion of the establishment of this Institution has been the need discovered, in the course of their duties, by some of our Home Missionary and other ministers in London, and especially in the immediate neighbourhood in which the Home has been established. It is believed also that the hand of Divine Providence is remarkably seen in the circumstances which have hitherto attended this attempt to do His work.

The Home will be managed by a Director and a Committee of four other gentlemen. There will also be a Council of Advice and Aid, to which the Committee will present a monthly statement of the condition and progress of the Home, and who will be consulted in any critical matter.

The immediate charge of the Home will be committed to a Master and Mistress, who, however, will be known among the inmates as 'Father' and 'Mother.' The character of the Institution, and the spirit in which it will be conducted, are apparent from the instructions which have been prepared for those who are put in charge. (See Appendix A.)

As far as possible the feeling of independence will be

cultivated among the boys. They will receive wages for all the work they do, which will be carefully saved for them in the Penny Bank. Out of this they will be required to pay some small proportion of the cost of their clothes, and by this means it is hoped not only that habits of thrift and industry will be cultivated in them, but that the expenses of the Home will be somewhat lightened. Still, too much must not be expected from this source, and the cost of the Institution will in the main be defrayed by subscriptions and donations. The premises now rented will accommodate twenty-three boys, and at present boys only will be received. The sum required for ordinary expenses on the present scale will probably be from £250 to £300 per year. And in addition there is the cost of repairs and fitting the house for its present use (£25), and the cost of furniture (up to the present enough for six boys, £15). In many other ways, however, besides the gift of money, the friends of the Institution may render it valuable aid :—

1. By the gift of articles of furniture, school-books, old or new clothing, provisions, picture-books, &c., &c. Old clothing will be valuable, as it may be altered to fit the boys, and will then save a considerable item of expense. Shoes and boots are specially needed. (See Appendix B.)

N.B.—Persons desiring to provide sleeping accommodation for one boy can do so at a cost of 25*s*. At present only six beds are bought, and no inmates beyond that number can be received until additional beds are provided.

(Since the above was written, three additional beds have been given.)

2. Help may be rendered by the purchase of firewood, which will be prepared by the boys, and delivered to order, monthly or oftener, as the buyer may direct. It is hoped that gradually other trades may be added

to this ; but in the present premises the industrial occupations must necessarily be few and simple.

FORM OF ORDER FOR FIREWOOD.

The Manager, Children's Home, 8 Church Street,
Waterloo Road, S.E.

Please to supply me with .... Bundles of Firewood (weekly ?) at 4*s*. per hundred.

Name ....

Exact address ....

APPENDIX A.

INSTRUCTIONS AND ADVICE TO THE FATHER AND MOTHER IN CHARGE OF THE CHILDREN'S HOME.

The object of the Institution committed to your charge is to rescue poor children who, through the death or vice or extreme poverty of their parents, are in danger of being led into a life of crime, and to train them for the service of the Church and the nation.

For this purpose it is believed best to surround them with all the influences of a Christian home. To realize yourselves, and to make them realize, that you all form one family and one home, should be your constant endeavour. He who has revealed Himself as the God of all the families of Israel will surely bless an Institution which truly embodies the idea of a Christian home ; and you, so long as you try, from love to Christ, to supply the place of father and mother to your charge, may surely in some measure count for your own the promises made to the fathers for the children.

You should, therefore, constantly think of yourselves as heads of a family, and endeavour so to act as to lead the boys to treat you with all the respect, confidence, and affection which children should feel for their parents. The titles by which you should encourage the children to think of you, and speak to you, are 'Father' and 'Mother'; and it should be your constant endeavour to act with the mingled firmness and wisdom and love which alone will justify the assumption of such titles.

In performing your duties, it will be well to have special regard to the following particulars:—

1. You will have to care for the boys, to teach and train them rightly, and to correct them if correction be necessary. Any flagrant case you will report to the Director, and will not inflict serious punishments without consulting him.

2. You will have family prayers with the inmates of the Home morning and evening. The Scriptures should be read, and each boy should have his own Bible, and follow the reading as far as he can. After dinner it is desirable that a hymn should be sung; and it would be well to encourage each boy during the week to learn a text of Scripture, to be repeated at family prayers on Sunday morning.

3. On you, with such assistance as the Committee may decide, will devolve the purchase of all articles needed for the Home, as well as the cooking of the food and the making or mending of the boys' clothing.

4. As put in the position of parents to these children, you will sit at table with them. Dinner you will need to take separately, but then one at least of you should sit with the boys while they have theirs. At their meals let them be merry and cheerful, but repress rudeness and boisterous conduct.

5. Each boy should make his own bed and clean his own boots. Help in the housework, in cooking, and in waiting at table will be given by some of the boys,

selected from time to time by the Director. But the duties of such boys must be so arranged as to allow of a proper amount of attention being given to their school duties.

6. Strict attention should be given to the hours for rising, for school-work, and for industrial occupations. They will be fixed from time to time, as circumstances may indicate. In a household like yours nothing can be done without regularity. When the boys are getting up or going to bed, you should take care that a proper time is secured to them all for private prayer.

7. It will be your duty to keep a journal, in which any unusual event is to be recorded, and in which you can report upon the general condition of the Home. It will also be your duty to keep strict accounts of household expenses, of the receipts and expenditure in the industrial department, and of the boys' earnings and deposits in the Penny Bank. The Visitors' Book also should be at hand for entries.

8. Sunday must be observed as a day of rest and worship. The whole family will be expected to attend chapel twice. During the rest of the day you should supply the boys with illustrated books, some of which will be for use on Sundays only; or you might sing hymns with them, or tell them suitable stories; and in the afternoon they should have a Bible lesson. Try to make the day the most attractive of the seven, while taking care that it is reverently observed.

9. In all your dealings with the boys keep a watch on your temper, on your words and deportment. You will have much to try you, many annoyances, and some occasions when firmness alone will save the discipline of the Home. But love will be your greatest strength in all your dealings with the boys.

10. Above all things, give heed to personal piety. The children will be apt to catch your tone in this as in all other things. Be much in prayer for them and

for yourselves. Remember, you are not doing this work for the sake of a livelihood, but out of love for Christ and His little ones. Not in your own strength can you fulfil your task. Ask wisdom from Him who giveth liberally, and seek to be clothed with the Spirit's might. Do not be disappointed if your highest wishes are not met all at once. Labour in faith. Remember that 'bread cast upon the waters' shall be found, even though it be 'after many days.' And if you only act as in the sight of God, and under the constraint of the Cross of Jesus, you shall one day receive a bright crown, as you present yourselves before the throne, saying, like your Master, 'Behold, I and the children which God hath given me.'

APPENDIX B.

LIST OF ARTICLES SPECIALLY NEEDED AT PRESENT.

A Family Bible. Small Bible and Hymn-book for each boy.

Illustrated books, either in volumes or in numbers.

Slates, Primers, and First Reading Books.

Clothing of all sorts.

Bedsteads and Bedding (see above).

Provisions of all sorts—Flour, Oatmeal, Cheese, Butter, Sugar, &c.

A Clock for the dining-room.

GIFTS ACKNOWLEDGED.

Thanks are cordially presented for the following gifts :—

Rev. John Bond.—Bed and Bedding for one boy.

Henry Avis, Esq.—Bed and Bedding for two boys.

H. Buckland, Esq.—Two Butts for water.

Messrs. Scott & Lamb.—Fourteen pounds of Cocoa.
Mr. Medlock.—A Sack of Potatoes.
Mr. Sercombe.—A Large Water Butt.
Mr. T. B. Smithies.—Pictures for the Schoolroom.

FIRST LIST OF SUBSCRIPTIONS.

Sir Francis Lycett	£20
W. M'Arthur, Esq., M.P.	£20
John Chubb, Esq.	£20
Alexander M'Arthur, Esq.	£20
J. F. Bennett, Esq.	£20
W. T. Whelpton, Esq.	£20
Mrs. Phelps	£1

DONATIONS.

Rev. John Bond	£1
Henry Avis, Esq.	£2 1
Miss Pocock	£0 1
Miss Stephenson	£0

Subscriptions are earnestly requested. Larg small sums will be thankfully received. Four boys admitted within the first week, and application admission are being received daily. Shall the ones be refused for lack of funds? Cheques and Office Orders (at Lambeth Post Office) should be payable to Messrs. Stephenson or Horner. The pr address of Mr. Stephenson is 5 Lambeth Ter London, S.E.; Mr. Horner's is 34 Lime Street, Lor E.C.

The following verses, written about this tim Miss Maria Osborn, daughter of the Rev. Dr. Osb were so effective in calling attention to the ne the work which Mr. Stephenson was beginning, that they deserve to be reprinted here :

LITTLE SCARAMOUCH.

Poor little Scaramouch, homeless and sad !
Ragged little Scaramouch, dirty and bad !

Father gone to prison, mother in her grave ;
Vice and crimes learnt betimes ; who is there to save ?

'In the street all day, sir.' Yes, but where at night ?
Where he goes no one knows : somewhere out of sight.

Stupid little Scaramouch, neither reads nor writes ;
Stands up for himself, though, lies and swears and fights.

Lonely little Scaramouch, God cares for you ;
God above is power and love ; Christians, is it true ?

Jesus came to save the lost, thieves and murderers too ;
Helped the vilest and the worst ; Jesu's friends, will you ?

Something from your luxuries, something from your time :
These would save poor Scaramouch from misery and crime.

Six months afterwards, Mr. Stephenson, issuing his apologia for the work he had undertaken, speaks as follows :

'A few months after my coming to London, circumstances occurred which appeared to me an indication of God's will in the matter. At any rate, they forced upon me the duty of seriously considering whether the time had now come for making the long-desired attempt. It implied a considerable responsibility, from which, nevertheless, one ought not to shrink, if the divine will on the matter seemed clear. Several gentlemen, conversant with such matters, were straightway consulted, and their reception of the proposal was so cordial, and their opinion that the experiment ought to be made was so decided, that in the fear of God, I determined to begin at once. The aid of a small committee was secured, and a master and matron were engaged. The course to be pursued was, thenceforth, perfectly clear. The experiment must be made unpretentiously, and allowed to develop itself by a natural and healthy growth. But from the very commencement a definite plan of working must be laid down, which might be maintained with only slight modifications, if any, as the institution grew in size and importance ; and the accounts, though comparatively small, must be kept as exactly as though each pound were a thousand.

'It was resolved, then, to begin upon the "home principle," originated and exemplified by Dr. Wichern at the Rauhe Haus, near Hamburg. Its peculiarity is this : that instead of gathering many hundreds of children into a huge institution, half barracks and half workhouse, it divided them into "families," each family living in a separate house, maintaining its own intimate special relations and interests, and being connected with the other families by the common school, the common worship, and the common superintendence. Many advantages are gained by this plan. It checks, if it does not entirely prevent, the evils so frequently found in very large gatherings of children—evils against which special precautions are needed, when the previous habits and associations of the children have been so foul. It renders the maintenance of discipline possible without crushing the spontaneity and vivacity of child-life. It secures an exactness of oversight and a dealing with individual temperaments according to their special peculiarities, which in other circumstances would not be possible; and it reproduces, as nearly as may be, that home-life which is God's grand device for the education, in the best meaning of the word, of the human race. There are, moreover, economic advantages attaching to this system, very important, but of which I need only mention one. It enables the institution to be established without any enormous outlay for buildings, allows it to grow naturally, and by a succession of comparatively easy efforts, house being added to house, as the families multiply.

'Of course, in our experiment, we could only begin on a small scale—in fact, with one family; but the essential principles of the scheme are being carried out there.

'The admission of the children is determined by the committee alone, after a careful consideration of each case presented. The cumbrous and costly system of election is entirely eschewed.

'The Children's Home is not an orphanage, though several of the children are orphans. Often children with both parents living are more to be pitied than if they were orphans. Nor is poverty of itself a sufficient qualification for admission. Each child must either have already become a criminal, or be in such circumstances as render his falling into criminal ways a matter of the highest probability.

'On the reception of a child, he is first sent to the doctor for examination, and if he be suffering from cutaneous or other disease, he is sent into the hospital before he is allowed to associate with the family. And here I cannot fail to mention the services of our friend Doctor Brown, who has given his most kind and careful professional assistance to the "Home" gratuitously. If the boy passes the medical examination, he is next photographed before bidding a final farewell to the rags of his roving life—and then his clothes are burned, or otherwise disposed of. He has a suit of garments for everyday wear, and one "for Sundays and holidays." We have tried to avoid the appearance of a charity livery, though economy has compelled a partial uniformity in dress. The everyday clothing of the boys is mainly made from cast-off garments, which (in a parenthesis we may say) are amongst the most valuable gifts that can be sent to us.

'Thus clothed, the boy enters upon his life in the Home. He sleeps in a room with some half-dozen others, but he has a bed to himself. He rises at six o'clock in the morning, and from half-past six till breakfast at eight, he works at some employment. For breakfast he has cocoa and bread (milk in London being too expensive). After breakfast and family prayer, he resumes his work till dinner-time. For dinner, he has on three days of the week, meat from the joint, on one day fish, on one day broth, and in each case an abundant supply of vegetables ;

on the other two days of the week, the dinner diet is dumplings and rice.

'At two o'clock he goes into school, and works till five under the charge of the resident teacher—a certificated mistress. Tea is at six. The evening is occupied with drill, with some light occupation, with singing-lessons, with play, or with attendance at some public service or lecture. At nine he goes to bed, but not until he has been instructed in the duty and privilege of privately praying to God. He is not taught to utter any set form of prayers, but to speak to the Merciful Father in heaven just the thought that is in his own heart, in the words that rise naturally to his lips.

'In every possible way the boy is encouraged to feel at home. The doors are not locked; the boy is sent freely on errands; and every appearance of rigid inspection is avoided. Flogging is forbidden, except after report to the Director. We seek to develop the better feelings of the boys, and have found them amenable to kindly treatment. And, accordingly, they are encouraged in every way to exercise the utmost confidence in those who are around them. Nothing like a mechanical discipline is allowed. The boys speak freely the thought that is in them to the master and matron, whom they always call father and mother. They know each other by the Christian name, like the children of a private family. Their birthdays are observed by some little special celebration, and once a week the whole family, including the pastor, assembles for a family gathering, at which good conduct is noted and rewarded. Each boy receives printed tickets for his behaviour and for his work; these are reckoned to be of a small money value, which is given to them, and by them put into the savings bank for purposes of their own. And the purposes for which they have withdrawn the money have generally been such as we would approve, e.g. many of them made little presents to their friends at Christmas, one boy buying a pair of shoes for his crippled sister, and during the recent severe weather another of them bought a pair of blankets for his mother. Moreover, the discipline of the Home is adapted to develop the feeling of honourable pride—some of them being placed in positions of special trust, while idle and disobedient boys are made to sit upon "The Bad Boy's Chair," and watch the rest at work. But the most potent influence in the management of the Home has been earnest, loving conversation with the boys, and prayers for them. When a boy has done wrong, he has been taken aside, and the wrong of his doing has been pointed out to him. Generally speaking, they have not been slow to see and acknowledge the wrong, and in every case persistent pleading for them and with them has softened the heart and drawn forth the confession of sorrow. Some of them have begun to feel acutely the sin and shame of their earlier life, and have voluntarily made confession of wrong-doing, and sought advice as to restitution and reformation. And, best of all, we believe that some of them are learning to love our Father in heaven, and to put faith in the merits and mercy of His atoning Son.'

The Minutes of the first committee meetings are more interesting than is usually the case. We reprint some of them, as they tell the story in the most direct fashion :

Minutes of Committee Meeting held at the Home, 17th August, 1869.

Present—

Rev. T. B. Stephenson, Messrs. Horner and Mager.

1. Mr. Stephenson laid before the Committee the Statement and Appeal on behalf of the Children's Home, of which a copy is appended. He also stated that arrangements were made with Mr. and Mrs. Austin to be master and matron of the Home at a salary of 26*s.* 6*d.* per week. Also that the house, No. 8 Church Street, Waterloo Road, had been taken at a rental of £40 per annum.

2. The accounts of Receipts and Disbursements to date were laid in detail before the Committee, showing Receipts of sums amounting to £114 9*s.* 0*d.* and Disbursements £73 10*s.* 3*d.*

3. It was reported that the following boys had been admitted to the Home since its establishment : George Olliver, Frederick James Hall, Edward John Rayner, Robert Hargreaves Self, Frederick George Willetts, Henry Harris and William Baxter. The particulars of each case are entered in the Application Book.

4. It was then resolved that the action taken up to this date by Mr. Stephenson (all of which has been after consultation with individual members of the Committee) be approved, and all regulations made by him for the conduct of the Home be confirmed.

5. It was also resolved that an account should be opened with the City Bank in the name of 'The Children's Home,' and that the Rev. T. B. Stephenson and Mr. Horner be authorized to draw cheques jointly.

6. Mr. Austin was authorized by the Committee to employ a carpenter to construct framework for circular saw.

7. The account of J. Bartlett, dated 14th August, 1869, was ordered to be paid.

8. Mr. Stephenson was asked to invite Mr. Charles Poulton to join the Committee.

9. It was resolved that the first Monday in every month be appointed for the parents and friends to visit the children at the Home.

10. It was resolved that the Committee sit every Tuesday evening, at 5 o'clock p.m.

SEPT. 7, 1869.

5. Mr. Stephenson made a statement to the Committee as to the regulations and discipline of the Home. The conduct of the lads had generally been good, far better indeed than was to have been expected, from their antecedents and the characteristics of some of them. Still there were cases in which the restraint and discipline that were necessary, as well for the lads themselves as for the orderly carrying out of the arrangements of the Home, were found to be irksome. It was essential that prompt obedience should be enforced, but that could only be done, so as to avoid anything like disturbance, by a firm but kind bearing towards the lads. The difficulty of dealing with the cases referred to had been observed by several of the Committee, and in their opinion it could only be successfully met by wisdom and tact in proposing that which may be required of the boys, and by mingled kindness and firmness in insisting upon those requirements being fulfilled. It was thought that Mr. Stephenson's influence and guidance would operate most beneficially in these cases, and upon the lads generally. He accordingly very kindly undertook to be at the Home as much as possible so that the desirable state of things indicated might be brought about. A room in the house was therefore ordered to be set apart for him, and such articles as be considered necessary obtained, so as to facilitate him in the transaction of his ordinary duties.

The extent to which Mr. Stephenson threw himself into his work at this time may be illustrated by the fact that when there was difficulty about providing accommodation for girls, Mrs. Stephenson and he took the first waif girl into their own house, and cared for her there until a Home could be provided. There is also a story of Sister Dora being recognized in after years by a sturdy young fellow, who, when he was asked if he knew her, replied, 'Know her, sir? why, I have known her since she was a baby; many's the time I have gone from the old Home in Church Street, to wheel her perambulator!'

There also exists a very vivid description of the first Christmas of the Children's Home. As our readers will see, it was written for the *New Zealand Methodist*.

'"My, ain't it jolly!" Such was the chorus of exclamation indulged in by five or six boys as they watched the preparations for the first Christmas in the Children's Home. Poor lads! There was some excuse for the warmth of their demonstrations of delight, for it was the first time that Christmas had brought them any gladness. A few short months before they had been living the life of street arabs, having scarcely known a touch or a word of kindness from the time of their birth. To find themselves in a comfortable home, where they were well fed, decently clothed, and kindly cared for in every way, surpassed the wildest dreams of any paradise that had floated through their little minds in their gutter life, and they might well tuck each other under the ribs and shout, "Ain't it jolly!" and throw somersaults in the exuberance of their joy. Twenty-two years is a goodish space to bridge over in one's memory to that first Christmas gathering in the Children's Home, but I have before me, as I write, the portraits of most of those present that day, and by the aid of these faces that now look up into mine, I must try to picture what I then saw for the benefit of the readers of the *New Zealand Methodist.*

'The Children's Home of Christmas, 1869, is a small cottage in a narrow street that leads out of Waterloo Road. It lies almost under the shadow of St. John's Episcopal Church, the graveyard connected with which abuts on one side of the street. But we forget the dark, dismal nature of the outward surroundings, as we step across the threshold of No. 8, for the Children's Home, always clean and tidy, is now shining with Christmas decorations. Some bits of coloured paper and some evergreens have been skilfully disposed of, and the place, to the wondering eyes of these waifs from the streets, is radiant as with the glory of Aladdin's palace. The boys have got through the roast-beef and plum-pudding previous to our arrival, and we scarcely need the assurance of the "father" and "mother" in charge, that they had attacked what was set before them with a vigour that showed that whatever weaknesses they possessed, want of appetite was not one of them. On the testimony of the "father," rendered in the vernacular, the way in which those boys eat was "a caution." We are here to spend the afternoon and evening in helping to make bright this first real Christmas to these lads just rescued from the perils of the street. Who are "we?" First of all, the worthy Principal, the Rev. T. B. Stephenson, Mrs. Stephenson, and little Dora

Stephenson, who comes with her hands full of spoils for the boys, which she plucked the night before from a famous Christmas-tree in Waterloo Road Chapel. Then there are Mr. and Mrs. A. W. Mager, whose devotion to the Home has been second only to that of Mr. and Mrs. Stephenson. Here, too, is the Secretary, Mr. Horner. My readers, however, will be most interested in these boys who are capering about in all directions, every now and then exploding in their limited vocabulary of delight. "Ain't it jolly!" Let us catch some of them, if we can, one by one, and learn something of the story of their life.

'"Come here, Harry, let us have a look at you." A shock-headed stumpy boy comes forward, with eyes of the peculiar shape which have earned for him the name of "Boss-eyed Harry." The entrance of this boy to the Home was a sight to be remembered; his raggedness was simply indescribable, and he looked as though he had never been washed from the time he was born.

'"How did you pick up a living, Harry?"

'"Selling matches, sir."

'Harry was known in the trade as a timber merchant; he had a home of a kind, to which he was expected to bring fourpence every night, excepting Sunday, when he had to bring two shillings. Failing this, he had to spend the night in the streets, into which, if he dared to return without the money, he was brutally kicked like a dog.

'Here is another lad with the unmistakable air of a gamin still about him.

'"Well, Fred, and how did the pudding go today?"

'"Oh, sir, it was werry good, it was."

'Fred has been a "mud-lark," and a "wharf-rat," getting his living by picking up unconsidered trifles at the river's side. He has been an expert in diving after coins thrown by passers-by into the mud—hence his cognomen "mud-lark." His wits have been preternaturally sharpened by the hard life he has had to live, and he is one of the most interesting boys in the Home.

'"What was the last thing mother read to you, Fred?" I said to him one day.

'"It was all about a cove wot had two kids, and one on 'em was a bad un. He kicked up a row with the old guv'nor and bolted. When all his tin was gone, he got werry hard up, and a cove gave him a job to look after his pigs, and he faked (stole) the pigs' grub. Then he thought he'd go back to the old guv'nor again; and he went back, and the old guv'nor said, 'Well, young 'un, I'm glad to see you, come and have suffin' to eat.' And the young 'un felt prime, and there was lots of carrying on—music and all that sort of thing, and everybody was happy 'cause the bad young kid wot bolted had come home again."

'That was the familiar story of the "Prodigal Son," done into the best English that poor Fred could command. Notwithstanding his shaky English, Fred gave clear proof that he had seized intelligently the priceless truth imbedded in this pearl of parables.

'Here is another lively young customer—the smallest of the lot—little Georgie, who, although not eight years old, has already graduated in the school of vice. The boy has a sweet, clear voice, and he has been hired out by his mother to a brute of a fellow who has taught him a number of low, filthy songs. He was taken round from one public-house to another, and placed upon a table to sing these lewd songs, for the sake of putting a few coppers into his employer's pockets. The rescue of little Georgie came not a moment too soon, for wicked thoughts have already found a place in his mind which it will take a long time to root out.

'Here are other lads—gaunt, pale-faced Charlie, and little Ted—but we must move on, for the nuts, and the oranges, and lollies are on the board, and the most must be made of this Christmas festival. Merrily pass the hours in games and songs; then, when bedtime arrives, all gather round the table for family worship. The Principal goes again over the beautiful story of the Divine Child who came seeking the lost little ones of earth, and whose voice may always be heard sounding in the ears of weary wanderers, "Come unto Me, and I will give you rest." Then, in fervent prayer, the inmates of that Home are commended to the loving care of the heavenly Father, and intercession is offered for the many thousands still left homeless and friendless on the hard streets. A hearty "good-night" is said, and the boys tumble off to bed, tired and happy with their first experience of a Christmas in which they have felt the loving touch of the Christ who came to seek and to save that which was lost.

'Of poor, "gaunt, pale-faced Charlie," Mr. Williams writes later: "To that pale-faced boy, that bright Christmas was the first and the last he was to know on earth. The poor lad had been so cruelly pinched with hunger and otherwise ill-treated, that the utmost care and kindness proved unavailing to do aught else than simply prolong the journey to the grave. He gradually sank until it was evident that the end was not far off. He had been long enough in the Home, however, to take in the meaning of the Cross, and for him death had no terrors.

'"Charlie, you're not afraid to die," said a kind-hearted friend, as the end was approaching. "No," whispered the dying boy, "I'm not afraid to die since I've been told that Jesus died." And then, his eyes beaming with gratitude, he said, "Wasn't it good of Him to die for a poor chap like me?" It was almost his last word; soon after poor tired Charlie was at rest.'

When the Home had been opened about eight months, a Public Meeting was held on its behalf in the Waterloo Road Chapel, on Monday, February 28, 1870, which was reported fully in the *Watchman*. Mr. John Chubb, who was in the chair, quoted the great work that Dr. Guthrie was doing in Scotland, and said that Methodists ought to emulate his example. It is a familiar touch to read that the boys of the Home sang one of their pieces entitled "The Fire Brigade." Dr. Rigg, who was even in those days one of the leaders of the Methodist ministry, gave the enterprise his blessing. When we remember that this was the year when Forster's Education Act was coming before Parliament, it is interesting to find him pleading 'that the State must aid,' but also 'there must be the tender, earnest love of Christian hearts engaged in this most difficult but most blessed work.' Other speakers were Mr. Hugh Wallace, the Rev. G. W. Olver,

B.A., who referred to John Wesley's Orphan House at Newcastle, and the Rev. C. H. Kelly.

'One of his old boys' writes the following very interesting reminiscences of his life at the Church Street Home, and afterwards in Bonner Road:

'I well remember the big square singing-pew in the Waterloo Road Chapel, where for years members of my own family had led the musical portion of the services with violin and other instruments. But when Mr. Stephenson came, the singing-pew was occupied by the first inmates of the Children's Home. Little did I think as I watched those lads that I should soon join them. My father was dead, but my mother still kept the home together till sickness came upon her, and it became evident that she too would soon pass away. Mr. Stephenson, in one of his visits to her, promised that he would look after us, and when the end was approaching he sent his housekeeper, Jane, to remain with her till the last. She brought the message that I was to be received into the Children's Home, and my mother, sitting up in her bed, exclaimed, "Lord, now lettest Thou Thy servant depart in peace, for mine eyes have seen Thy salvation."

'That same day I entered the little Home in Church Street, and Mr. Stephenson became a father, and more than a father, to me. . . .

'He entered into our joys and sorrows, and knew each one personally. On more than one occasion I had the happy privilege of being held in his strong arms when quite a little fellow, and he would take out his watch for me to toy with. He would also enter into our sports, and many a time he might have been seen playing leap-frog in the playground with us, but I never remember being quite able to clear that broad back of his. I generally used to land on the top. It was no unusual thing to find him busy in the carpenter's shop with his coat off and sleeves turned up working away at the bench. When he was getting the house at Church Street in some sort of order, ready to receive his first boys, he did a great deal of the work with his own hands, and often emerged as black as a sweep. He would come into our house, which was only two doors away, in order to have a good wash with warm water, as the dirt and grime would not come off with cold.

'What memories have also grown around those premises in Bonner Road which thousands of us have loved to call home! and still more sacred memories cling about our little chapel. Who will ever forget the sacred times we spent under its roof! And who, that ever heard it, can forget that lovely voice of his, whether it was in the pulpit, the platform, the playground, or the house, or in one of the music-halls in the neighbourhood, where on many a Sunday night he would conduct meetings after the ordinary services of the chapel. . . .

'I remember one lad in Canada, who was amongst the first sent out, who did not forget his voice. The Doctor had gone to Canada to visit some of the lads, and calling at a farm, he asked to see the boy who had been placed there. He was told the lad was away with the farmer at some distance, making a clearing. So the Doctor went in search of him, and failing to find him, lifted up his voice and called out the boy's name. Presently he saw the lad running towards him, and his first words were, "I knew your voice, sir, I knew your voice."

'On one occasion he was holding an open-air service in Vyner Street, Cambridge Heath, when one of a number of men who had stood listening was inclined to interrupt. I heard one of his mates say to him, "Why don't you shut up? What's the good of you trying to argue against him? He knows the Bible all through, he does."'

CHAPTER VII

Early Developments—Second House taken—Wesleyan Education Committee and the Home—Annual Meeting—Sketch from the *Watchman*—Visit to the Continent—Bethnal Green Circuit—Bonner Road premises taken—Opening—Description.

THE need for more room was very soon felt. We find it being discussed at a meeting of the Committee held on September 14, 1869. After much consideration, they made a bargain with the occupier of the house next door to come into possession on Lady Day, on receipt of £10 as compensation. The Rev. Charles Garrett undertook to provide the cost of furnishing, and before long presented the Committee with £105 for that purpose.

Another matter of great import was whether the Wesleyan Education Committee would take up the Home as a beginning of a scheme for establishing reformatory schools all over the country to be conducted in the same spirit as that in which the 'Inner Mission' was doing similar work in Germany. In case the Education Committee would do this, the Committee was prepared to hand over to them the entire furniture and plant of the Institution, and to make over its direction to any authorized Committee that might be appointed. The answer they received at the beginning of January, 1871, was one of warm approval of the work, which was commended to the support of the Christian public, together with a suggestion that some members of the Education Committee should be united with the Committee of Management, and that a Report of the Directors of the Home should be presented to them from time to time.

At the next Annual Meeting, in January, 1871, Mr. Stephenson, who had the title of Honorary Director, stated that during the year 'the money had invariably arrived as soon as they could no longer do without it. The most trying time was about three months ago, when, the mind of the charitable public being engrossed with the needs of the sick and wounded, scarcely anything was received.'

This reminds us that those were the days of the Franco-German war, and that at the very time when this meeting was being held, Paris was strictly invested by the German armies. He goes on to tell 'that thirty-three children had been received into the Home, of whom one had been reclaimed by his friends; another was encouraged by his mother to play truant, and was at last forbidden to return; another had left to become an apprentice to the printing trade, and another had run away. . . . There were now in the house twenty-nine children, several of whom were orphans, and only two or three had both parents living. . . . Some of the boys gave evidence of true religious feeling.' There would probably have been greater success had they not been grievously deceived in two of the masters, but they had now secured a master and matron in whom, after six months' trial, they had complete confidence.

The premises had been a great difficulty, having been taken after long waiting, because no others could be obtained in the neighbourhood. They sheltered the children, but that was nearly all they could say. A change to other and better premises was absolutely necessary, a Home for Girls being needed, and probably £1,500 would be required.

The balance-sheet showed that the total receipts, including a small balance at the beginning of the year of £6, were £588 6*s.* 8*d.*, and the expenditure £551 16*s.* 6*d.*

By this time the Forster Education Act had come into operation, and the 'School Board' had already been elected; and a good many references were made to the kind of action it was hoped it would take.

One speaker congratulated his friend Mr. Stephenson on 'not having seen any difficulty till he got to the "other side of it."' 'If ignorance was the mother of devotion, the offspring had been very rare, so far as his observation went, and he was glad that now intelligence was to be tried.'

Mr. S. D. Waddy was there, not yet Judge Waddy, who told of a little girl he had met whom he had asked where she lived. 'Oh,' she said, 'I live "about" sometimes in one house and sometimes in another.' Her mother had abandoned her, and on asking where her father was, she replied, 'Please sir, it was a watch.'

Dr. Rigg, now a member of the School Board, was present, to 'maintain that the Children's Home was doing work no School Board could ever do, and to plead that there must be a Girls' Department.'

The *Watchman* of February 1, 1871, contains an interesting sketch of the Home:—

At half-past four on Friday afternoon last 'Mother,' 'Father,' and children were unprepared for any visitors; nevertheless they were all actively employed. Some of the lads were at the Waterloo Road Chapel School, some were out at Stockwell and Brixton selling their bundles of wood; but about a dozen were at home nimbly folding magazines, and preparing for the afternoon meal of their brothers. From the rafters of the workshop hung the paper festoons the lads had prepared for Christmas, at which time they had a merry meeting, and better cheer than the workhouse or the gaol ever gave them.

In going through their bedrooms, I find the lads are well cared for. The little beds are neatly made (by the boys), and warm rugs keep out the cold. Some kind friends have given the Home a mangling and a washing machine, and though now and then playful attempts are made by the boys to investigate closely the machinery of one or the other, these machines are very valuable adjuncts to the furniture of the place. In one of the top bedrooms, on the mantelpiece, there is a flute, and though I feel sure there must be a well-treated 'marchioness' below, I wonder who is the 'Dick Swiveller.' 'Father' tells me, in explanation, that Mr. Stephenson has given the lads some flutes and drums, and already a teacher has endeavoured to induct them into the mysteries of the gamut. . . .

On reaching the kitchen, I find good-tempered 'Mother' getting ready her children's afternoon repast. One lad is on the floor, stirring vigorously away at a huge mess of oatmeal, which half fills a good-sized earthenware pan. 'Father' expatiates on the amount of gluten the oatmeal contains, while the lad, with an audaciously near approach to a merry wink, listens with attention to his eulogium ; 'Father,' 'Mother,' and I catch each others' glances, and—forgive us, good Scotsmen—we burst into laughter. Who but a Scotsman could be grave while porridge is being stirred ? And, concerning this porridge, it seems that when it was first introduced (in place of cocoa) the boys by no means took kindly to it. There was a sort of mutiny, and some of the elder lads had arranged, when the porridge was served for the first time, that no one should eat any. Accordingly when it was brought in, the children were very silent, and when 'Mother' asked who wanted porridge, there was no answer. After a short time, one little fellow said, 'Mother, please, I'll try a bit.' Eager eyes watched the porridge disappear, then came a whisper, 'How d'ye like it, Jack ?' Whereupon Jack replied, very tersely, but most eloquently, 'Oh, it's proper,' and then, one after another, the rebels gave way ; and since then, 'porridge' has become so relished that after one good-sized plate has been eaten, many of the lads, like Oliver, 'ask for more.'

When the lads who have been at school return, there is a general smartening up for the coming meal. Hands and faces are washed, vigorous attempts have been made to effect 'partings' in stubbly crops of hair, and 'Father' opens a book, after a bell had been rung, to call over the roll of his 'children.' Each lad answers to a number, and his appearance is checked in the book, one of the lads shouting out for absent '26,' 'He's stirring the porridge, Father.' Then, after an inspection by Father, and a 'right about face' which would please Mr. Hepworth Dixon, the boys march off to their porridge, of which eight-and-twenty, 'Mother,' 'Father,' and I partake, after the lads in cheery ringing tones have sung grace.

In glancing round at the boys, it is impossible not to note how care and misery have left their traces on many of their faces. But, thanks to those who have the lads in charge, these are rapidly disappearing. At the Home they rise early, they are sent to school, employed in various useful ways, and warmly clothed. They are encouraged in good habits, and some little sums saved up for them out of their earnings are often touchingly devoted to pleasing ends, one little fellow buying for his sister, a cripple, a pair of boots ; another giving his mother a couple of blankets ; and one lad proposing to take money out of the bank to pay a poor woman whom he had robbed.

Some time during 1871 Mr. Stephenson appears to have paid a visit to the battlefields of the Franco-German war, and even to have got so far as Vienna. Of this most interesting journey very little record remains, but it is clear from some articles which he wrote to the *Methodist Family* that he had been carefully studying the work that was done by the Brothers of the Inner Mission, and by the Deaconesses of Kaiserswerth in connection with the relief of the sick and wounded during the war. We may well conclude that at this time the knowledge which he had gained of the Inner Mission from reading Fleming Stevenson's book, *Praying and Working*, was increased by actual contact with the representatives of the work itself. He made a special study of the Ambulance work of the Order of St. John of Jerusalem, as well as of the Deaconess work, and he obtained from Pastor Disselhof of Kaiserswerth an account, which he had translated and printed in the Magazine referred to, of how the Deaconesses started for the war.

The visit can only have been a brief one, but it must have done much to consolidate and develop the thoughts that his study of the Inner Mission had previously awakened in his mind.

Going back to the work of the Children's Home, in Church Street, it was soon obvious that even when the next house was secured, these premises could only be regarded as a makeshift, and when Mr. Stephenson was approached with regard to an invitation by the Bethnal Green Circuit, the attention of the little Committee was at once turned to that part of London. Several expeditions were made to the neighbourhood in search of buildings. Places were seen which were thought to be suitable, and lengthy negotiations went on. They were about to come to a settlement, when in a very unexpected manner the Committee learnt that the Bonner Road premises were likely soon to be unoccupied. They considered these to be on the very best spot that could have been chosen, and in themselves to be altogether more suitable than those for which they had been bargaining. In the end they secured them for a rental of £190 a year. In the middle of May, 1871, they sent down a little colony to take possession of the empty buildings, and prepare them for occupation. Soon hammer and trowel were making merry music, and though for want of money not many men could be employed, yet by the June Quarter Day it was possible to move the establishment, which then consisted of thirty boys with House Father, House Mother, and Schoolmaster.

The work advanced gradually; sometimes they had to stop for lack of money; they purchased the materials direct, and only employed labour when that of their own officers and boys was not sufficient.

They never felt at liberty to make contracts, as they did not know 'whether the Lord would send the money with which to pay the contractors.' The officers and boys of the Home most cheerfully lent their aid in every way possible—painting, glazing, laying floors, making drains, putting up party walls, fixing gas-pipes—anything, indeed, which their past experiences or their present wit enabled them to do, they did right manfully.

They began with three houses—Temperance House, which was prepared with money collected by the Rev. Charles Garrett ; the 'Old' House, so called in memory of the humble cottage in which the work began ; and Sunday School House, built by the contributions of Sunday scholars. To these Mary Fletcher House, fitted and furnished at the cost of one lady, who contributed £100 for that purpose, was soon added.

The formal opening was held on Wednesday evening, October 4. Mr. T. J. Barnardo, of the East London Mission, already becoming known for his own great work, told at this meeting a story of his search for wastrels : 'Having six vacancies, he went one night with two of his boys who were "pretty fly," as the saying was, to Billingsgate. The boys led him to the "Green Shades," where were carts and crates of different sizes and descriptions ; they climbed up a very large and high crate, removed a tarpaulin from the top, and endeavoured to wake the boys within, but it seemed impossible until it was suggested by his lads that he should promise them something ; he promised them a halfpenny each. The boys immediately awoke, and he selected six of them, rejecting one of the applicants called " Carrots," a boy about eleven years of age, with hardly a garment upon him. A few days afterwards he met a policeman who had assisted him in his search, and he told him that a porter, in the morning, had endeavoured to remove two boys from a hogshead in which they were apparently sleeping. One of them ran off, but the other did not answer, and the porter presently removed in his arms the dead body of poor little " Carrots." At the inquest a jury returned a verdict, ' Died from exhaustion and undue exposure to the weather.'

The following description of the New Home was given in the *Children's Advocate* :

Wednesday was quite a gala day for the good folks at the East End of London. Gay bunting fluttered in all its brightness from the Approach Road Methodist Chapel, right across the way to the Congregational Church, and the golden sunlight brought out the hues of banneret and flag in such radiance that few could miss the way to the new Children's Home. And a very capital Home it is, too, considering that the buildings a few months ago were simply workshops. However, by dint of hard work and judicious management, these workshops have been transformed into clean, well-ventilated dwellings, capable of carrying out the special principle of the Home.

The ground (about half an acre in extent) may be described as an irregular pentagon, surrounded on four sides by buildings, and these buildings are the more interesting from the fact that they nestle under the protecting wing of the Methodist chapel. They consist of four ' blocks,' with windows overlooking a fine piece of ground, in the centre of which, to-day, a huge pole stands, from whose lofty head a union-jack flutters in the breeze. As you enter the gates, on the right hand is the first block, and here at once you come to the children's schoolroom. Above this is their 'chapel,' which has already the tablets prepared for the Commandments, and only needs some kind friends to furnish fittings to make it complete. Further on, in the same block is the kitchen, furnished with the children's kitchener from Church Street, and likewise some boilers, famous no doubt by this time for preparing that porridge on which the children seem to thrive so well. Above the kitchen are 'Father' and 'Mother's' rooms, many of the children's bedrooms, and a lavatory, playroom, and general dining-room. The second block is to be devoted to the reception of girls. Beneath the upper portion is the covered play-ground for the children, where they may engage in athletic exercises, and where several to-day are swinging to their hearts' content. And I hold with sturdy 'John Ploughman,' who says children do not like 'their prayer-meetings and religious services' any the less because they have their swing or climb the poles. Here, also, are a bathroom and laundry. The third block, which is called the 'Temperance House,' as a grateful memorial of the services rendered to the Institution by the Rev. Charles Garrett, is apportioned, in its lower compartment, to a carpenter's shop, where the lads are taught a useful trade; and in its upper, to the bedrooms of many of the children, with lavatory, &c., as in the first block, which is called the 'Old Home.' The fourth block, to the left hand of the entrance gates, contains offices, bedrooms above for girls, and a few little beds marked off as an infirmary ward. Beneath this there is to be a room fitted up as a printing-office, where some of the most intelligent of the lads are to be inducted into the mysteries of Caxton's craft. And here, besides, is a stable for the 'donkey,' resplendent, on this opening day, in sleekness and a blue ribbon. A much better donkey than Laurence

Sterne ever wrote about ! So, then, here we have the principle of the Institution founded by Dr. Wichern, at the Rauhe Haus, near Hamburg, which divides members of a common home into ' families.'

At about half-past two the proceedings commenced in this way. Many of the lads, attired in smart scarlet jackets, formed a circle, and with fifes and drums struck up a lively tune. This brought the Methodist friends of the Home around them, and kindly glances on all sides fell on these poor lads, who, rescued from their predatory street life, were a living evidence of what may be done by care and tenderness. Then, after a general look round, there was a march to the schoolroom, where the boys, on a raised platform, were put through exercises in the Bible, grammar and geography, in all of which they acquitted themselves singularly well. Indeed, when I thought of some of these lads, who, but a short time ago, were singing out, ' Special, here 'yhar, special Hecho ! ' without knowing what was meant by a line of the bill they flaunted in their hands, I felt how good and kind was the thought to snatch these ' Children of the Stones ' from street life, and shelter them within the walls of this Home. As Mr. Olver in a most beautiful and impressive prayer indicated, many of them were something more than ' orphans.' Blaspheming and drunken parents had driven them on the streets. They hid beneath the bridges by night, and by day were a fearful sight, all rags and misery.

The school exercises over, the lads march out, and then ' the band ' strikes up again, playing, with infinite spirit, Moore's ' Minstrel Boy,' while Methodist ministers, their wives and daughters, glance round at the Home. The ' Children's Band ' wind up, like loyal little subjects as they are, with ' God save the Queen.' Then comes a practical, homely lecture by the Rev. T. Bowman Stephenson, in the playground, on ' Our Buildings,' and some well-executed drill movements by the lads. A march-off to the chapel ensues, and here, going back to the Home, I leave the boys, dressed in comely new clothes, and looking healthy and well, hoping they and all present will enjoy the evening meeting.

Of course, 'Mother' and 'Father' are especially pleased with their new quarters, and so are the lads. I noticed in the boys' general room, where they have little compartments, some touching evidences of their thoughts. Among other matters, a mourning card was nailed to the wall, and not far off, with a few trifles, a paper flower. Then there were a couple of birds, in very poor cages, not worth perhaps more than a few pence each, and yet what to the lads were those birds? Perhaps they told of a home, long, long ago, in a country lane, where the interlacing trees sent dancing shadows on the pathway, and where, from the boughs, the birds throbbed their happy songs up to heaven!

The Home, I should mention, is capable of receiving one hundred inmates, and already thirty-seven boys and six girls are being cared for. It rests only with the benevolent among Methodism to fill the place. And especially should attention be directed towards the outcast daughters of our city. But a few minutes' walk from the old Home in Church Street, one morning, some years ago, a fragile, pale-faced man, with dark haunting eyes, passed over Waterloo Bridge. Near the steps of the bridge, with a group of strangers around it, lay the dead body of a fair young girl. In a fit of mad frenzy, she had sought oblivion in the rushing, moaning waters below. Tom Hood went home, and wrote the 'Bridge of Sighs.'

> Oh! it was pitiful,
> Near a whole city full,
> Home she had none!

To rescue poor girls from such a fate as this is benevolence indeed. It is only to be earnestly hoped the building for girls will soon be filled.

A few words in conclusion. The day's proceedings are over, and the evening meeting has been very successful. The flags are all gathered in, and the little drums and fifes have been laid aside. I pass, in thought, the gates of the Home. There is no moonlight, and in the high arch above the building the clouds are dark and sombre. Suddenly, lights grow about the Home, then the sound of little voices, intermingled with merry laughter. 'Father,' 'Mother,' and 'Children' are preparing for rest. The stars, one by one, come out, and from the sombre darkness twinkling lights gem the heavens. I grow nearer to these rescued children, as they kneel by their little beds, and I hear them murmur, 'Our Father, who art in heaven, hallowed be Thy name!'

CHAPTER VIII

Edgworth Branch—Mr. Barlow's offer—First Visit to Wheatsheaf Farm—Twenty-five years afterwards—Visit to Canada—Emigration Scheme—Hamilton Branch.

ONE of the matters that was causing a quiet excitement among some who were gathered at the opening ceremony at Bonner Road, on October 4, 1871, was the offer of a farm in Lancashire. This had been made by Mr. James Barlow at the previous Conference. It had a most important effect upon the fortunes of the work. It was seen by the Conference that if one of Mr. Barlow's character for discernment and benevolence was willing to give thousands of pounds at this critical juncture, and to pledge his help and sympathy for the future, the Children's Home had assuredly come to stay.

The Revs. William Arthur and Charles Garrett eloquently pleaded the children's cause as a Christian duty and privilege enjoined upon the Church by John Wesley and by One greater than John Wesley. Thus the critics were silenced, and the Conference sanctioned the work so modestly begun. The resolution of Conference was as follows:

'Considering the great number of children who are deprived of suitable guardianship by the death, or vice, or extreme poverty of their parents, so that they are only too likely to fall into criminal ways, and that many of these have a special claim upon the practical sympathy of Methodists ; the Conference recognizes the establishment of the Children's Home, and commends the undertaking to the support of the Christian public, with the understanding that of the Committee of Management at least one half shall be members of the Education Committee, and that a report of the proceedings of this committee be made, from time to time, to the General Education Committee and the Conference.'

The gift of the Lancashire Branch was also welcomed by the Lancashire people. At Bolton, in January, 1872, a great meeting was held in the Temperance Hall. The feelings, the sympathies and imagination of the great audience were stirred by the accounts given of the sorrows of the poor outcast children of the streets ; promises to support a child in the Home were freely given. Dr. Stephenson's Christian experiment became an object-lesson to the public. It awakened the conscience of the Church, and it also, in time, became a model, to some extent, to the Poor Law Guardians for the treatment, the nurture and the training of the neglected and destitute children of our land.

Mr. Mager describes the first visit to the Farm in January, 1872, made by Mr. Stephenson, Mr. Horner, and himself, in company with Mr. James Barlow and his son, Mr. John R. Barlow.

'The hospitality of Greenthorne made our visit very pleasant, and the moorland estate offered to us for our Christian enterprise, then scarcely more than a private venture, filled us with expectation and hope, if not enthusiasm for the future. But the winter climate and aspect of the unfamiliar moorland were certainly not inspiring ; and when past the scanty plantation below, we saw the little farmstead now so well known to us as "Pleasant View" (a misnomer at the time), one of us eagerly inquired, "Is that it ?" but was told, "No, it is higher up, round the shoulder of the hill." Reaching there, a fiercer wind, from along the Entwistle ravine, rushed on us, and from the eminence we saw what happily we shall never see there again. In the midst of a wild and desolate scene was the old wayside public-house, with its dilapidated barn, standing grimly and alone by the unfrequented wayside. The loneliness of that fully licensed inn gave it not a little of its value. It was out of the way of the public, but it was also out of the way of the police, and, therefore, a chosen place for Sunday drinking, dog-fighting, cock-fighting, and such debasing sports. This public-house was in the market, and to Mr. Barlow's benevolent and religious mind, the thought occurred that a double blow might be struck at the devil and his works, by buying the house, destroying the licence (valued at several hundreds of pounds), and devoting the estate and premises to 'the nurture and training of orphan and destitute children.' Therefore he offered it for our merciful work, and invited us to come and see the place. If its appearance was not pleasing, its potentialities, as a training-ground for rough boys, were at least guessed by hosts and visitors. We were twenty-five years younger then, with life and opportunity before us, and strength and courage for the self-imposed task.

Public meetings were held in Manchester and Bolton to arouse interest, and raise the £1,200, which was needed to stock the farm and make the necessary alterations in the buildings. In February the Wheatsheaf Estate was taken over, and Mr. and Mrs. Mager accepted the position of Governor and Matron, and by April they were ready to take possession.

Writing twenty-five years afterwards, Mr. Mager says :

'To return to the landscape and the land. The superficial view called forth by this narrative of many acres of bog, heather, and sour ling, with here and there a swamp, the habitat of snipe and moorhen, will not sufficiently convey to the minds of our friends at a distance an idea of the continuous toil necessary to produce the remarkable change of scene which now attracts so much attention and interest. Much more than the superficial cultivation of the soil was required. It was necessary to go far below the surface, to delve deep into the bog and get below it ; to discover and collect in drain-pipes the springs and percolations of water that kept the bog alive, and made such herbage as grew rank and worthless. The surface was not soil at all, but, for several feet below, a widespread mass of fibrous, living, sponge-like roots, sustained by the water beneath. Cultivation with spade and hoe ; after this draining ; then burning the surface refuse ; afterwards lime and manure, were necessary for conversion of the bog to fertile soil. And not the plough, but slow spade culture, by boys, in yearly succession, was needed to produce the transformation to the firm green sward which makes the place pleasant and profitable now. What obstructions were met with beneath the surface ! Big boulder stones, brought during the glacial period, we suppose, and left by their dead weight, sometimes of several tons, in every depression of the land. These boulders of hard sand grit had to be cut out with wedges and heavy hammers ; and as no crane or windlass could be fixed to lift them, they had to be rolled up and along planks, with the help of strong men, from their slippery clay-bed, to the swampy surface above. No more interesting sight is to be seen at this moorland farm than that of boys engaged in such toil. After their training at the quarry, they know how to go about their task ; they know the grain of the stone, the depth and position of wedge-holes necessary for a straight cut. The weight of hammer required (from fourteen to forty pounds), and a good deal of other technical knowledge is needed in order to sever these big blocks of rock into pieces suitable for window-heads and sills, thresholds and lintels, wallers and coping, and other " dimension stuff " required for building our houses and premises. The boys like the work. It is manly, and obviously beneficial to them. To show their strength, after the flabby period of their early months here has gone by, they will choose the biggest hammer with which to strike the wedges. Such work, like mercy, is twice blessed. It gives stamina and capacity to the youthful workers. It is also of some advantage to the Home that trains them for the world's service. In the moral and material results of this land culture, there is more than the beneficence of the original curse. The reclaimed land is valuable, but the reclaimed lives of the youthful workers are beyond price ; a blessing to society and precious, we believe, in the sight of

Him whose gracious ordination it is that labour should be so abundantly fruitful and beneficial.

'But if this work of land cultivation has been so difficult, it has also, necessarily, been slow. You cannot change sterility into fertility all at once. The land is said to be "honest," but the various processes of nature require time to work their course; and sun and rain, wind and frost, must succeed manual toil ere the increase can be ingathered. We have verified in our experience here the Scriptural statement, "The husbandman waiteth for the precious fruit of the earth, and hath long patience for it." A neighbouring farmer, looking over a ten-acre plot, upon which we had expended years of toil, in draining, digging, liming, fencing, &c., said to us one day, "Yo' han moor pluck nor brass, for aw thowt, first, yon land 'ud break yer pockets, and then aw thowt it'ud break yer 'earts." Happily it has done neither. We kept working away at it, day by day, month after month, and year after year, and what is it now? Not a wet cranberry moss, without bite or footing for a sheep; but a rich, well-fenced rectangular meadow, that will keep eight to ten cows, to produce, say, not less than 20,000 quarts of milk every year. What authority was it who gave us the statement, which has passed into a proverb, "Who makes two blades of grass grow where but one grew before is a public benefactor"? Thank God, our lads have made two blades of grass grow where none grew before, and themselves, all the while, have been blessed in their deed.

'It will be seen that we have been engaged during the twenty-five years past "in a fight with Nature in her most obstinate moods." I well remember our trouble to get horse and cart on to the bog-land, long after it was drained ; and even during succeeding hay-times, when a fair sward had been formed from the seed sown months or years before. A man who knew the ground would precede the horse to indicate to the carter-boy the safe course for the animal with its load ; yet, notwithstanding all care and foresight, the surface would sometimes give way beneath the horse's hoofs ; and the weight of the load would be precipitated on to its back. All hands were then engaged in lifting the load, and releasing the struggling, half-buried creature beneath. Planks were hurriedly procured for placing under the animal, to give it temporary footing ; and ropes and bands were used for lifting it on to its legs. The overturned hay was then re-gathered, and carried by the boys to a safer distance, to be removed from thence to the barn. But difficulties and accidents of the kind were even more numerous and troublesome during the earlier periods of cultivation, before a sward had grown, and whilst the land was still swampy as well as soft. Besides the preliminary liming operation (after draining, lime is the chief fertilizing agent of peaty land, and ten tons per acre are required for an ordinary coating), the manuring process, year after year, was necessary. The land, like many of our lads formerly, was very hungry, and cried again and again, " Give, give." A dressing of two hundred and fifty tons of farmyard compost was required only for one ten-acre meadow ; and all this weight of lime and manure had to be carried on from the road in hand-boxes by the boys, or wheeled in barrows upon planks by them, because no horse could find firm footing, and the yielding surface would not bear the weight of a cart. In the earlier years, too, the tiles and the stones for the drains and the fence-walls around each field and meadow—thousands of tons—were also carried or wheeled by the boys in this toilsome way to their destination. Every acre of meadow-grass seen here to-day is really the triumph of laborious and patient husbandry. The boys, however, generally took an interest in their work, and they were proud of the results of their toil. To thoughtful minds few pleasanter sights could be seen than successive troops of stalwart lads, merrily marching to their work, each shouldering his spade or hoe, prepared by skilful use of the same to show how peacefully fields may be won.'

One great advantage of the Edgworth Home was that it supplied a change of locality and of work. The restless habits engendered by street life made it hard for some lads to settle down to ordinary industry. One of the boys in the Abbé Roussel's Home for Apprentices in Paris, ran away five times, and five times returned through pressure of hunger. Mr. Stephenson had a similar experience in the beginning of his work. He received into his first little cottage at Lambeth a true street arab, known among his companions as 'The Lord Mayor of Chequer Alley.' He was quite independent of all the world, ready to lie about in the sun until hunger drove him to seek food. In the little cottage, with its tiny playground, the 'Lord Mayor' was utterly out of his element. No work that could be given him there exhausted his energies. Three times he stayed for five or six weeks, but then his roving instincts returned. He would be found at Smithfield, or busy assisting some drover with his cattle. At last he altogether disappeared. It was a pity to lose this lad. He was an affectionate, obedient fellow, but he could not endure the drudgery of a cottage workshop. Had the Edgworth Home been available, such a boy would have found congenial occupation.

The problem of the way out of the Children's Home very soon began to press upon the Committee. It was well to take the boys in and train them, but what were they to do as they grew older? We find the Minute of a Committee Meeting, on March 11, 1872, which says, 'The Canadian project was discussed. A House of Reception would be necessary, and a Resident Officer to undertake the oversight of the children. It was considered highly desirable to initiate proceedings while Dr. Punshon was there, and accordingly the following resolution was agreed to: That having respect to the future destination of the children educated in this Home, and having received a communication from the Rev. W. M. Punshon referring to the probable openings in Canada for the employment of such children, and inviting Mr. Stephenson to visit Canada this spring in the interests of the Home; this Committee respectfully request the President of the Conference to sanction such arrangements as shall relieve Mr. Stephenson for a few weeks from his circuit duties, for the purpose of his proceeding to Canada to establish, in conjunction with Mr. Punshon, a Canadian Branch of the Home.'

The President's approval was secured, and Mr.

Stephenson started on April 20, 1872, on the steamship *Scotia*, in company with the Rev. Luke Wiseman, President of the Conference, who, accompanied by his son, was going to visit the General Conference of the Methodist Episcopal Church as Official Representative of British Methodism. At New York Dr. Punshon met them, and the Rev. Alex. McAulay, who appears to have been in New York at the time, joined the party. After a few days they paid a visit to Washington, and returning, stopped at Baltimore and Philadelphia. We find Mr. Stephenson starting off at ten o'clock at night with a New York Methodist minister, a magistrate, and a detective, to explore some of the lowest parts of the city. He hoped he was the means of rescuing one poor English girl, whom he found in a German dance-house.

After a few busy days, attending the Methodist Conference, hearing distinguished preachers, visiting the 'Home for Little Wanderers,' and other similar Institutions, they started off for Niagara, and went thence to Toronto, Guelph, Galt (where Miss Macpherson had recently bought a Farm for training her children), and then to Hamilton.

At Hamilton he was entertained by Mr. Sanford, who became the Treasurer for his Canadian work. Dr. Punshon came over and gave him his powerful assistance in getting matters organized. The Hamilton people arranged to raise £1,000 to buy a house and some land for the Canadian Branch. He was busy completing the organization, and raising this subscription throughout the month of May, and most of June. He sailed for England on June 22. He writes as follows :

'I proposed to myself the following subjects for inquiry and action. 1. Is it desirable that we should send our children, or many of them, to Canada? 2. If so, what method should be adopted for introducing them into Canadian families? 3. What help towards this enterprise may be expected from Canada? Having arrived at a definite opinion on these points, it would then remain for me to take such practical action as might seem feasible and desirable.

'To obtain information on the above points, I sought it from persons of all classes, clergymen, philanthropists, working men, employers of labour, and persons engaged in municipal affairs. I examined also such publications as were accessible; and last, not least, had a lengthened interview with Miss Bilborough and Miss Barber, who have charge of Miss Macpherson's Institutions at Belleville and Knowlton. These ladies, hearing I was in Montreal, did me the favour to call upon me. They exhibited the most cordial interest in our enterprise, and most freely gave me whatever information their experience had brought them.

'1. From all this evidence I came to the conclusion that Canada offers singular advantages for the disposal of many of our children. The tone of society is remarkably moral, and a very large part of the population is under the influence of religion.

'Work is plentiful, and any person who is willing to work diligently with his hands will never lack a comfortable subsistence. I say "with his hands" because it is manual labour in artisanship and farming which is wanted. The supply of clerks and shopmen is more than equal to the demand.

'There is scarcely any feeling of caste in the country; and in the lower middle class, and especially in the farming community, the servants associate continually with the family of the employers, all eating at the same table and occupying the same sitting-room. Children such as ours, if received into a farmer's family, would share with the farmer's own children work and food, school and play.

'The feeling of Canadians generally is highly favourable to our scheme. They do not wish to have the dregs of our pauper population cast into the midst of them, and they deprecate the sending of untrained children to their country; but they hail the idea of well-trained children coming to them, and I was assured on all hands that the only difficulty we should find would be in supplying the applicants who would ask for our children.

'These opinions are confirmed by the fact that at Miss Macpherson's house, at Belleville, there were four hundred applications for children before the last group left England.

'On the whole, therefore, I am of opinion that while we should not refuse eligible openings for the settlement of our children which may be presented in this country, Canada is the field for the dispersion of our trained children, in which we can do this work most readily, and at the same time with the brightest prospects of success for the children in life.

'2. As to the method to be adopted. We must undertake the distribution of our own children. There is no person, or body of persons, in Canada who could do this work in the way we should wish to have it done.

'And we have peculiar advantages for doing it. The reception which I met with amongst the ministers of Canada assures us of their cordial co-operation.

'But in order to do this work thoroughly, we must establish in Canada a Home, ultimately perhaps several. To this Home the children should be sent, under the care of two or three officers for the voyage. Proper oversight during the voyage is of the first importance. At the Home an Agent must reside, who must be a thoroughly intelligent and judicious man. It should be his duty to receive applications for the children, and designate them to suitable applicants. He must also visit the children periodically at their homes, and preserve a bond of union with them. To the Home the children must return in case of sickness or change of situation. In a word, the Agent must be a sort of foster-father to the children in Canada during the whole period of their minority. Such a man may do most blessed work for Christ. He would have access on the friendliest terms to many Canadian farmhouses, and he might address audiences of the neighbours, night after night, in the true evangelistic style. It may not be easy to find a suitable man or woman for this most difficult and delicate, and yet most valuable post; but God, who has given us the work, can give us the agent.

'The necessity of this machinery is proved by very many circumstances. I met with fact after fact which prove that to send children out to Canada without providing this watchful and fostering agency for them is a very dangerous course, to say the least.

'3. As to the help which Canada will give: friends of this movement in the city of Hamilton have contributed 3,500 dollars, and Dr. Punshon and a few friends at Toronto have contributed 1,500 dollars. These together amount to 5,000 dollars, which it is believed will be sufficient to purchase land and house. Friends at Montreal and other cities have promised material help towards furnishing the Home, which will probably cost 2,000 dollars more. It was impossible for me to conclude the subscription for this object in the short time at my disposal, but I entertain no doubt whatever that Canada will give us the Home complete.

'As to the maintenance of the Home, I did not ask for any guarantee from Canada. It is understood that in Canada we shall make our case known, as we are doing in England, and it is believed that very many benevolent persons will volunteer help there as they do here. I am of opinion that if our Canadian Branch is worked vigorously, it will pay its own expenses. It only remains for me to report on the action which I took, to give effect to the above convictions.

'1. I addressed the Conference of the Wesleyan Methodist Church during its session at Montreal, and the following resolution was passed:

'"Moved by Rev. E. Ryerson, D.D., LL.D., and seconded by Rev. S. D. Rice, D.D.,

'"That whereas a statement has been made to this Conference by the Rev. T. Bowman Stephenson, of London, England, respecting the work of God now being carried on in the Children's Home, an institution for the reception and training of orphan and destitute children; and

'" Whereas it is the wish of the Committee and Director of that Institution to establish in Canada a Home, to which these children, when duly trained, may be sent for distribution amongst Canadian families:

'" Resolved, That this Conference expresses its cordial approval of the scheme, and commends it to the sympathy and support of the Christian public of the Dominion.

'" (Signed) WILLIAM SCOTT,
'" *Secretary.*" '

'2. I formed a Committee at Hamilton, consisting of Rev. W. M. Punshon, LL.D., Rev. S. D. Rice, D.D., Principal of the Female College, and Rev. W. J. Hunter, pastor of the Centenary Methodist Church, with Messrs. W. E. Sanford, Dennis Moore, Lyman Moore, Donald McInnes, A. T. Wood, W. V. Muir, and Finley. Mr. Sanford was appointed treasurer for Canada; Rev. W. J. Hunter and Mr. Dennis Moore were appointed secretaries.

'This Committee met, and was duly constituted. We arranged that the property, when purchased, should be vested in trustees, to be managed by a committee, which should receive its appointment year by year from the General Committee in England. A draft of the deed will be forwarded to us for consideration as soon as it is prepared.'

The property at Hamilton was secured in accordance with these arrangements, and the first party, consisting of forty-nine children, was sent to Canada in charge of Mr. F. Horner, about the middle of May in the same year. In September we find Mr. Horner making a statement respecting the distribution of thirty-four boys and fifteen girls, whom he had taken out to Canada in May.

'About two hundred applications for the children had been received, and they were finally placed with forty-five families, of whom thirty-seven belonged to the Wesleyan Methodist Church. In every case the children had been placed in the charge of Christian persons. Of the thirty-four boys, twenty-six went into the families of farmers, two are learning carpentry, two the blacksmith's and wheelwright's trades, two are employed in Mr. Sanford's warehouse in Hamilton, and the two printer boys are engaged in the Methodist Book-room, Toronto. Of the fifteen girls, five were adopted into Christian families, six were engaged as domestic servants, and four have gone into the families of farmers. The wages to be received by the boys for the first year range from three and a half to six dollars per month, in addition to board and lodging; and the girls placed as servants will receive three dollars per month. The savings of the children are to be remitted to Mr. Sanford and placed by him in a bank.'

Mr. R. T. Riley, now one of the most influential citizens of Winnipeg, was appointed the first governor of the Canadian branch. After he resigned that position he has for many years given most valuable assistance to the work, especially by taking responsible charge of difficult cases of boys and girls whom it was thought desirable to send out West.

Mr. Stephenson visited Canada again with a party of ten boys and thirty girls in 1874. In connexion with this visit he writes as follows:

'The Children's Home at Hamilton is a pleasant place. There are about eight acres of good land, which produces grapes, peaches, and strawberries in profusion, as well as the plainer and more substantial vegetables. There is a well-built brick house, and a large wooden house behind, containing dormitory, dining-room, and lavatory, intended for the reception of the young emigrants on their first arrival. The cost of all has been about 11,000 dollars, the whole of which has been, or will be, contributed by Canadians. Hamilton is the heart of the very garden of Canada. Moreover, it is a great and growing railway centre, and, therefore, an admirable place for a distributing "Home." Some thirty miles distant is Miss Rye's Home, at the town of Niagara, and about sixty or seventy miles in another direction is one of Miss Macpherson's Homes at Galt. The Canadians are fully alive to the importance of these institutions, and are quite willing to help to establish them; in some cases by private donations, in other cases by grants from municipal funds. The use of such a Canadian centre is threefold. It is a reception house for the children on their arrival in the country. It is also a house of shelter for any of them who, through sickness or other causes, are thrown out of the situations to which they are sent; and it is a residence and office for the governor or agent, who keeps up a frequent correspondence with the children, and visits them at regular intervals. In any good system of juvenile emigration there should certainly be supervision of the children, and a more or less authoritative guardianship over them for at least three years after their arrival in their adopted land. It is neither just to the children nor to the country to throw them into a land in which they are perfect strangers, and leave them to sink or swim, as chance may decide. The scheme of the Children's Home distinctly contemplates this careful supervision of the children; and this element has secured the warm commendation of many influential persons, including those who are officially connected with the Immigration Department.

'Scarcely had the party arrived at Hamilton before applicants for the children began to appear. Indeed, before we left Quebec offers to receive some of them were made to us; and it is no exaggeration to say that we might have found homes for one-half of them on the journey to Hamilton. But at Quebec I had received intelligence that already 250 good applications had been made in writing for these thirty girls, and therefore all requests on the way were kindly but steadily refused. One respectable woman who, with her husband, was "going West," having purchased a farm with the savings of several years, took a huge fancy to a bright little girl, and almost with tears begged to be allowed to take her, promising to treat her as her own child. Considering that the little object of her sudden affection was only five years old, this offer certainly seemed disinterested; but like the rest, it was declined. At the Home, however, on the morning after our arrival, began a procession of farmers' "spring wagons," "buggies," "democrats," "rockaways," and other extraordinary vehicles, which went on day after day till all the children had gone.

'I want now to explain by what process the

children are distributed. When the time draws near at which a party of children is expected, a notice to that effect is inserted in one or two newspapers; and forthwith each mail brings in applications. To every applicant is sent a printed paper of questions; from the answers to which a judgement may be formed as to his status and character, and as to the sort of boy or girl he desires to have. This application must be accompanied by a certificate of character from a magistrate or clergyman, and preference is given to those who are members of some Christian communion. Frequently other means are available for estimating the character of the applicant; and there is rarely much difficulty in coming to a tolerably correct judgement. To the applicants the children are then allotted, after a careful consideration of each child's character and probable fitness for the situation. They are accepted for these purposes:

'1. Bona fide adoption. This is in the case of little children, not more than five or six years old.

'2. "Raising," which is something less than adoption, but much more than service. Children of eight or nine are received by respectable people into their houses to be treated as members of the family, to receive regular schooling, and to be clothed. In return for this they will do "little chores," little bits of work around the house, such as carrying in a few sticks of firewood, or running to the post-office with a letter, or feeding the fowls, or perhaps opening the gate of the meadow for the cows to come up to be milked. A very warm affection often grows up between such children and their patrons; and in many of these cases the children do not leave the family to which they are sent until they are ready to settle in life.

'3. Service, in which for work to be done on the farm, in a shop, or in the house, a fixed scale of payment is agreed on, varying from three to six dollars per month, in addition to board and lodging. In all cases, the agreement reserves to the representative of the Home the right to withdraw the child if he is improperly treated. There are more applications for girls than boys; but for both the demand is greatly in excess of the supply.'

CHAPTER IX

Death of Miss Camilla Stephenson—Visit of Rev. James Hocart—Excursion to Farningham—Moody and Sankey—Set apart as Principal—Purchase of Bonner Road Premises—Convention at City Road—Mission at Bolton—Life at the Home.

WHILE Mr. Stephenson was away in Canada in 1872 a keen personal sorrow came to him in the loss of his sister Camilla, with whom he had been on peculiarly intimate terms, and whose sisterly friendship had counted for much inspiration and help to him. She died at Manchester on May 25. She had been very warmly attached to the Children's Home from its commencement. She was amongst its earliest subscribers, and one of the last deeds of her life was to send on some money she had collected for the work.

The Rev. David Waller sent him the news.

'MY VERY DEAR FRIEND,

'I have to write you in reference to a very sorrowful event. Sincerely do I wish I could command such language as would in some degree, at least, enable you to receive it in a spirit of true Christian submission. You will hear with deep sorrow that your much-loved sister, Camilla, passed away on Saturday last.

'Her fragile constitution gave way under an attack of bronchitis combined with inflammation of the lungs ; but the particulars of her illness you will learn from your sisters and mother, when they feel equal to the task of writing on so painful a subject.

'Your mind would be somewhat prepared by the news sent a few days ago, and especially as the mail would bring you poor Camilla's unfinished letter. . . .

'We had a long talk about you. She gave me your journal letter to read, and when I had finished it, she said, "I hope I may live till Bowman returns. Poor fellow, he would be so distressed if anything were to happen to me in his absence." Unselfish creature, she thought not of herself, but only of the distress her death would cause others, and especially yourself. From that time I saw her daily. I shall always be thankful that I had the privilege of seeing how nobly and bravely a true Christian can meet death. "It is," she said, "a very serious thing to die." But such was her calm confidence in the Saviour that there was an utter absence of dread, and the fullest assurance of personal acceptance. . . I proposed, as I was going from home till Monday, that I should give her the Sacrament of the Lord's Supper. We had the real presence of Christ with us in the ordinance. It was a season of blessed and holy communion. At the conclusion she was jubilant. . . . My dear fellow, if you had been with us you would, in the midst of your sorrow, have rejoiced in the power of saving grace. You have not lost her ; you know full well you have not. Let us try to give thanks ; for truly she has departed this life in the true faith of the holy Gospel. Your heart will be sorely grieved, but comfort yourself in the thought of her happier lot. . . .

'That God may bless you, and make your visit to America a great blessing, and that you may in due time have a safe return, is the prayer of,

'Yours most truly,

'D. J. WALLER.'

During Conference this year a visit was paid to the Home by the Rev. James Hocart, of the French Methodist Conference. He was so impressed that he gave his daughter to the work. Miss Hocart was the first lady who devoted herself to the care of the children in the Children's Home, and thus may be regarded as the pioneer of the corps of Deaconesses. After several years' faithful service, she was recalled to France by the death of her mother, and the failing health and loneliness of her father. She carried with her the love for helpless children, and found her father's heart in full sympathy with her own. Under their joint care there grew up at Paris-les-Ternes the 'Maison des Enfants'—the Children's Home of France; the first institution of this character which obtained its inspiration from Dr. Stephenson's work. It commenced in 1878, with six little French children, rescued from horrible surroundings.

At the Conference there were some kindly ministers who were so pleased with their inspection of the Home, and the general behaviour of the children, that they collected among themselves £4 10s. 6*d*. 'to be spent in amusement,' and Mr. Moore, of Mill House, Farningham, in Kent, invited the children to spend the day in the grounds of his house. The 'Special Correspondent' of the *Children's Advocate* tells the story:

'I need not describe the journey with its numerous stoppages, till at last Swanley was reached; there our kind host of the day met us, to take on our provisions, and to drive the few unable to walk. Neither need I chronicle the tendency to climb and scramble for blackberries or nuts, manifested by certain of these peaceful, yet excursive, pilgrims, to which their stained cheeks and torn fingers abundantly testified. At the Farningham hill, the van of the procession waited till the loiterers came up; then headed by the band, they marched through the village, past Mill House, through the orchard, over the stream, into the meadow, where the marquee stood.

'Through the grounds the children wandered, or were shown in delighted groups over the mill, the millers with almost parental forbearance very kindly explaining all the "wonders." No doubt the cream and crown of the fun to the boys, and especially to Mr. Moore, was the bathing. One lad had hardly received permission for a plunge, when half a dozen had divested themselves of outward encumbrances and were standing upon the bank of the stream, shivering in primitive simplicity. In and over they jumped, their glad shouts awakening echoes, which at once collected about forty more; these soon "peeled," then ducked, dived, and darted about after each other in merriest glee. Mr. Horner superseded the use of the towel, by chasing them till they were fairly dry. One little mortal, particularly christened by "Director Stephenson" the "cherub," caused him no little effort, and us all great amusement. Our host clapped his thighs and laughed, till he declared he could laugh no more. The girls had gone down the stream under Brother Godley's superintendence, whose skiff was freighted with a joyous crew, crowded near the water's edge. On the banks lively groups were watching the fun, and a few more meditative souls sought the sweet seclusion of a shady arbour on the hill.

'In healthy, hearty games the day wore on. Georgy was found (for he had been missed), with his head buried in the grass, waving his sturdy legs wildly in the air, maintaining (which no one dared to dispute) that it was "proper." '

One of the Committee evidently thought that it was 'proper' too, for at any rate, the daughter of the host afterwards became Mrs. Francis Horner.

The year 1873 was marked by a visit of the great American revivalists, Moody and Sankey, to England. The Agricultural Hall, Islington, was used for their services. More than once, when through some mishap Sankey was not able to sing, Mr. Stephenson took his place, and sang with great power to the crowded meeting. And when the evangelists went away, and the people showed themselves unwilling that the meetings should come to an end, an arrangement was made to continue them for a while, with the Rev. W. Hay Aitken as preacher instead of Mr. Moody, while Sankey's place was again filled by Mr. Stephenson.

By 1873 it had also become evident that the work demanded the whole time and strength of the Principal, and in that year we find the Committee asking the Conference formally to set apart Mr.

Stephenson for the work of the Home; and in the *Minutes of Conference*, after the business of the Education Fund, there is accordingly the following record:

1. The Conference receives with pleasure the Report of the Children's Home, and recognizes with gratitude to God the liberality of various friends in England, and particularly of Mr. James Barlow; and expresses also the pleasure with which it has heard of the generous co-operation of Christian people in Canada in this work, particularly by the establishment of a Distributing Home near Hamilton.

2. The Rev. T. Bowman Stephenson, B.A., is appointed Principal.

He writes to his wife:

'I am glad to tell you that the Conference appointed me yesterday Principal of the Children's Home, with unanimity, and without a syllable of opposition, or even a question. Everybody blesses the work and congratulates me. . . . The Conference received my report, and spent near an hour and a half in conversation upon it. Arthur, Punshon, Olver, Hirst, Shrewsbury, and many others spoke most kindly in support of the work. In fact, it has taken deep hold of the Methodist heart, and is counted fairly amongst the institutions of the Church.

'This is a most blessed Conference. The spirit of unity and power is given to us as I have never before known it. Surely we are on the eve of good days.'

We shall see later that at this Conference Mr. Stephenson brought forward a very important proposal with regard to the constitution of the Conference itself.

During this same summer, that of 1873, negotiations had been going on for the purchase of some property which should be the permanent London centre of the Children's Home. Up to this time the houses occupied in Bonner Road had only been rented. The Committee spent much labour in searching for a suitable site ; one place was especially attractive, for it was the spot where Miss Bosanquet, afterwards the wife of Rev. John Fletcher, of Madeley, had conducted an orphanage, in Methodism's earliest days. Unsatisfactory reports as to the unhealthiness of the neighbourhood turned the Committee's attention away, and in October we find them considering the problem of purchasing the premises at Bonner Road, with some additions. Lengthy negotiations took place, and the premises seem to have been actually purchased while the Principal was away in Canada in 1874. The purchase-money was £4,850, and what was bought is described as 'the premises at the rear of Denmark Terrace, the houses Nos. 1, 2, 3, and 6, Denmark Terrace, and the house at the corner of Albert Road.'

Having bought the property, £5,000 more was needed to make additions, and place the whole in an efficient state ; and the Committee set to work to raise a special fund of £10,000 for this purpose.

The Report presented at Midsummer, 1874, tells us that a Ministers' Children's Gift-House had been erected at Edgworth, with money collected by the children of Wesleyan Methodist ministers, who had raised upwards of £1,100 for this purpose; also a beautiful property at Hamilton had been purchased by Canadian sympathizers at a cost of £2,000. Negotiations were in progress for a suitable building for establishing a Certified Industrial School as a fourth Branch of the Home. The Report goes on to say that £2,571 6*s*. 0*d*. had been raised towards the special Fund of £10,000 for the purchase of, and expenditure on, the property at Bonner Road.

In 1875 Mr. Stephenson acted as Secretary for a 'Convention for the Study of Entire Consecration,' which was held during that year at City Road Chapel. The Rev. Gervase Smith, President of the Conference, lent his support to this movement, and presided at the meetings. The meetings were held on November 2, 3, and 4, and were arranged for the benefit of members of the Wesleyan Methodist Church who were engaged in some definite Christian work. The movement was supported by such ministers as the Revs. George T. Perks, W. Darlow Sarjeant, Marmaduke C. Osborn, Mark Guy Pearse, William Wilson, William Gibson, and G. Bowden; and such laymen as James Smetham, Alex. M'Arthur, W. W. Pocock, J. E. Vanner and W. Vanner, T. B. Smithies and William M'Arthur, M.P., and the meetings were a great blessing to the Church life of the time.

In 1876 we find Mr. Stephenson conducting a great mission at Bolton. Of this mission he writes to his wife:

'On Sunday we had immense crowds; scores were turned away, and last night we had a very large audience. There have been already about one hundred inquirers, and the work is widening.

To-day we had one hundred and twenty at the noon prayer-meeting.'

And again:

'The work here is so remarkable that I feel I must stay another day or two. Last night the chapel was full, though there was a great Alliance meeting in Bolton. Already one hundred and twenty profess to have found Christ, and the interest grows every evening. I have, therefore, promised to stay till Monday night. I only wish you were here, for I don't like being so long away. I am going to have a day's rest to-morrow at the Farm; and on Saturday begin again with two meetings.

'I have no more time now. I have been out with Mr. Barlow, getting some money towards the debt, and service begins in half-an-hour.'

The early years of the Children's Home were the true years of fruition of Mr. Stephenson's life. His own temperament and disposition fitted him admirably for the care of 'these little ones.' While on the one hand he had very high ideals indeed of the importance of duty, of order, and obedience, yet on the other hand there are few men so singularly free as he was from any social pride or caste feeling of any description. The children of the Home were his children, and he never thought of himself as divided from them by any social barrier. He expected submission and obedience, as he would have expected it from children of any class, and as he claimed it from all his assistants in the work.

The combination of these high ideas of authority with the deepest conviction of the Christian equality of all concerned was a very remarkable and striking one, and made him a most incomprehensible man to those people whose notions of authority are based upon class distinction.

When Dr. Creighton, Bishop of London, was taken round the Home, the writer remembers hearing him remark privately to some friends at the end of his visit, that he very well knew how much could be arranged for the inspection of any one in authority like himself. 'But,' he added, with a twinkle in his eye, 'it was not easy to arrange beforehand that children should hang on to a man's coat-tails and claim him as their property as they had done for Dr. Stephenson.'

The five years following the Conference of 1873 form a period during which Mr. Stephenson's connexion with the actual work of the Home was most close and intimate. He took parties of children to Canada in 1874, and again in 1877; but during these years the main current of his energy was expended on the actual life and work of the Home at Bonner Road; and we may perhaps count it the very happiest part of his life.

One of his first workers contributes the following:

'Every one who knew and loved Dr. Stephenson, knew the remarkable charm his personality had for those who came under its influence. There was (if one may say so) an air of romance, of large courtesy, and noble ideals, that made a kind of spiritual atmosphere about him; and the girls of the Home who grew up around him and came into closest touch with him, readily responded to the call. Beauty in life and character began to appeal to them, because they appealed to him, and his courtly graciousness was dimly reflected here and there, colouring and beautifying lives otherwise dull and dim.

'One girl stands out from a group as an illustration of this. A very commonplace story was hers, no romance, no tragedy; but the dull tragedy that is daily lived in almost every back street of our great cities—a drunken, brutal man, a feeble, broken-down woman, and a houseful of half-fed children. A pair of unwanted twins brought a climax of brutality, and on the death of the mother, one of the twins and an elder girl were brought into the care of the Home. The baby was one of the most uninteresting of its kind—dirty, pale-faced, red-haired, and dull. With the wonderful tenacity of childhood she pulled through a severe illness, and started life afresh at the Alverstoke Branch. In those days Dr. Stephenson was often there, spending an occasional week-end, or a few hours of hardly earned rest. There the large-hearted father of his big family became acquainted with this bit of waif life. He never forgot to ask for her, and about her, calling her by the quaint pet name that had been given her by the Sisters.

'It seemed at first as if the child's brain had been so deadened and dulled that if she grew up she might be little more than an idiot. But love works wonders; love, and endless patience and care. By-and-by cheeks grew rosy, eyes grew brighter, brain woke up, and every step was duly reported to "Doctor." "Let the bairn come and stay with me for a bit," said he, and she went. Then began a curious and pathetic friendship; on the child's side it was worship, as far as she knew what worship meant. Every fresh effort of brain or hand was to please "Doctor." The terrible things that were made for his birthday—the odd little crotcheted mat that lay for years on his desk, the fearful bed socks that I believe he really wore, the wonderful Christmas cards, gorgeous and gay; the childish letters with their rows of crosses to show the writer's vast affection,—all these were answered and acknowledged; and to this day among the special treasures of a bright, attractive servant maid, are Dr. Stephenson's letters; while to the girl herself he represented every thing that is highest, noblest, and best in life. Many bright and clever girls have gone out into the world from the old Home, their lives touched into fuller life, and influenced in gracious ways because his life was so full and gracious; but many others unnoticed and seemingly commonplace have been touched and lifted also, and have had their "vision splendid."'

Another friend gives the following picture:

'Crossing the playground, I saw him on the roof, where some alterations were going on; he was smeared and dirty with plaster, but within ten minutes, as I crossed the playground again, I heard him calling, and there he stood on the chapel steps arrayed in cap and gown! A lady who had adopted a baby from the Home had driven up, asking that it might be baptized at once, as she was leaving England; and there he stood, ready for the service, and calling a few of us to form the congregation.'

'As some of the elder boys remember him, he was strong, young, and resourceful. When the Christmas Appeal for the Home had to be got out, he and his many willing helpers would work all day and stay up until early morning three or four times a week, making two or three hours of sleep suffice. The elder girls were perfectly happy if they were allowed to stay up too, and serve the busy workers at intervals with coffee and other refreshments.

'On Christmas Eve he seldom went to bed at all. There was always a grand surprise to be made for the children in the Schoolroom. One year, the end of the Schoolroom was turned into a Canadian hut, large enough to contain several persons ; and also a present for every child in the Home. Another year it would be a great ship, or a monster Christmas-tree ; but labour and time were never spared in making Christmas Day the brightest of the whole year for the children.

Mr. Bottrill, a valued worker in the Home, tells of two occasions when he had to take Mr. Stephenson's place at preaching appointments, because the latter had sprained his foot in playing leap-frog with the boys. He says that often on a fine cold day, when the boys needed warming, he would say to Mr. Bottrill as he left the Officers' Dining-room, 'It's a fine day ; leave your work for a while, and let's have a game with the lads.' At once the boys would scent what was up. The playground would be cleared, and a brisk game of leap-frog would be carried on by the Principal, the workers, and the boys, both big and little ; and a wooden-legged laddie won great renown by sometimes doing better than them all.

'Mr. Stephenson never forgot the supreme importance of leading the children to decide for Christ. Sometimes carefully organized services were planned for this end. The Governor and the

Sisters of the children would give special thought and prayer to their charges in preparation. Then, either Mr. Stephenson himself, or some carefully chosen minister, would conduct special meetings in the evening. The Revs. William Spiers and John Stephenson both left lasting results on occasions like this. The children's own prayers at these services were amongst the most blessed influences of the time. Those who had decided for Christ would be seen individually by Mr. Stephenson, or some experienced worker, before their first Communion. At one such service a Cornish lad was so wonderfully blessed himself, that he had more influence upon the others than even the missioner, and there are some who remember it to this day.

'But he did not depend too much upon these special services. He was always looking for conversions from the influence of the Sisters upon the children in their homes, and nothing gave him greater pleasure than to hear from one and another that Harry and Mary had given their hearts to God, and wished to see him about taking the Sacrament.'

Some beautiful pictures are drawn of his treatment of children newly admitted to the Home. Thus one of the Sisters tells us how she took a little girl who had just been received to have her first interview with 'the Doctor.' He always kept biscuits and sweets for the newcomers, and usually succeeded in making friends with them immediately; but for once (and it was the only time Sister remembered), here was a newcomer who would not go to him. She had been cruelly beaten with a belt, and was absolutely terrified at men. 'Never mind, Sister,' he said, 'she will be all right in a day or two.' But the one interview had really been sufficient, for as the poor little ill-used child was being taken away she inquired, 'Be any more gentlemen like that ? I likes that sort ' ; and when she next saw him, went to him with perfect confidence.

Another says :

'Very often in the evening the organ of the little chapel would be heard, and Doctor would be found playing with a little waif, or home-sick orphan sitting on the organ-stool near him, while he played the sorrow or rebellion out of its young heart. It was his custom, after the music, to tell the child its first Bible story, and many a time he has seen the tears flow as the child has for the first time in life heard the wonderful news of the love of Jesus. Then Doctor and the bairn would be seen coming down from the chapel hand in hand, both very happy, and he would take the newcomer to his or her house and Sister.'

CHAPTER X

Industrial School Work—Education Acts—Member of School Board—Gravesend Branch—Mr. Tyson—Difficulties of the work—Training Ship—Financial Troubles.

ONE of the effects of the Education Act of 1870 was to bring prominently before the public notice the case of those children who had taken to the streets for a living, and were beyond the control of their parents, and defiant of any government whatever. To the public Education Authorities these children were truants; to the police many of them were known as petty thieves; their parents protested their utter inability to bring them under any home discipline, and a movement took place in the country to provide more Industrial Schools and Reformatories for their rescue and training. Charles Dickens had, twenty years before, roused public opinion in the matter; and, largely as a result of his writing, the first Reformatory School Act was passed in 1854. One great flaw of this Act was a provision, not finally removed till 1899, that a short period of imprisonment in gaol must precede reception into the Reformatory. Moreover, another kind of school was evidently needed for children who were not yet criminals. To meet this need the first Industrial School Act was passed in 1856; and although at first it only applied to Scotland, in the next year its provisions were extended also to England.

The provisions of the Education Acts of 1871 and 1876 led to a large increase in the number of children committed for breaches of the law, and to the establishment of Truant Schools and Day Industrial Schools. It was felt by the Churches that Industrial Schools ought to be under distinctly religious management, and to be carried on with a view to the conversion of the children, and their training in the Christian life.

Mr. Stephenson had not been very long at Bethnal Green before it was felt that he was just the man to represent the people on the London School Board; and at the second Triennial Election, in 1874, his name headed the poll for the Hackney Division by a large majority.

The story is told that an ironmonger, who was a great admirer of his, largely assisted in this election by scattering broadcast a large handbill with Mr. Stephenson's portrait, and a picture of a ragged waif, and a second of the same lad changed by residence in the Children's Home. Below was written:

'Vote for the man who changes THIS into THAT!'

His experience on the School Board soon showed him that while the doors of the Home were open to admit those who voluntarily sought help, there was a large class who could not be reached by such methods, and with whom it was much more difficult to deal. The officers of the London School Board were actively engaged in searching for children who were not attending school, in visiting the homes of the degraded and immoral, and rescuing the boys and girls from their evil surroundings, by getting them committed to schools under the provisions of the Industrial Schools Act. It soon became clear to Mr. Stephenson that the Children's Home might well take a part in this work, especially as a large proportion of the Funds would be provided by the Public Authorities.

The Report for 1874–5 says:

The need of our work has not materially lessened. . . . In saying this, we do not undervalue the influence for good of the School Board system, and, least of all, of the Industrial Schools Department of the London School Board. There is a perceptible impression made upon the class of 'Arab' children. Still, the meshes of the School Board machinery will always be too wide to enclose all these children; and there will be multitudes of cases left which no legal provision can cover. In three directions there will be left ample scope for voluntary Christian enterprise:

1. In dealing with the orphan children of very poor Christian people, who have a special claim upon Christian sympathy.

2. In dealing with cases of moral need, which cannot be met by legal provisions.

3. To aid and take advantage of the legal provision, by establishing and managing Industrial Schools, in which voluntary zeal and religious instruction shall be brought to bear on the children who are sent by legal arrangements. About this class of educational enterprise there is amongst religious people no controversy. However controversy may rage around the Primary School system, no Christian man doubts that for children who are shut up for five years in a boarding-school religious instruction and influence are a necessity.

Hence, we report with great satisfaction that during the year we have been able to add to the other branches of our work a new Branch, in the form of a Certified Industrial School for Boys. Excellent premises have been secured, with twenty acres of land adjoining, at a rental of £130 per year, on lease for twenty-one years. They are situate in the parish of Milton, near Gravesend. The school has been certified by the Home Secretary. So soon as certain proposed additional buildings are completed, we shall have accommodation for one hundred boys; and the London School Board has promised a grant of £1,000 towards the preliminary expenses, on condition that we guarantee to them one hundred vacancies during the next ten years. Forty boys are already in residence. Mr. Tyson, who was for some years the Principal's Secretary, has been appointed Governor, and has entered on his work with every prospect of success.

Mr. Henry Tyson, who is named in the Report as having been appointed Governor, was a Londoner, who was brought up with a practical acquaintance with the printing trade. He was already engaged in business with fair prospects of success, when the Children's Home was commenced. As he had a partner who was able to give close attention to the business, Mr. Tyson could give some hours daily to assist Mr. Stephenson with the rapidly growing correspondence of the Home. Ultimately he became wholly occupied as its Secretary. Mr. and Mrs. Tyson entered on their duties at Milton in February, 1875.

The premises that had been secured in the neighbourhood of Gravesend are described by Mr. Tyson as follows:

'The physical aspects of the Gravesend Branch are exceptionally beautiful. The grand old leafy kings which nearly surround the estate and stud the grounds, are not to be surpassed by any in the neighbourhood. Almost every variety of woodland tree is represented, and the rich park-like land which slopes gently towards the house, with the shady drive through the avenue forming a "rookery," renders the place charmingly picturesque. There is also a fine old walled-in garden of about two acres, with fruit trees of various kinds, and a small orchard adjoining. These beauteous works of God's loving hands are attractive and inspiring to the lover of nature; but, alas! the attraction of the portions of estate last referred to has been of an exceedingly mundane character to the majority of our charge. We scarcely hazard an opinion as to how far personal responsibility in this matter is affected by the taste inherited from our first maternal grandparent; but on the methods adopted to gratify the inborn craving, we have had to express very decided opinions, with practical suggestions as to the duty of self-denial. Many a time life and limb have been risked in the accomplishment of their designs upon the apples and pears; topmost windows, narrow ledges, and rain-water pipes being used in the most light-hearted way. I well remember one imperative summons to the orchard. Appreciating the position, I directed officers to various points of vantage, and ordered the bell to be rung for parade. Going myself into the orchard, I could see through the leafy scenery several figures moving about, and securing one by the collar, I demanded the names of the other culprits. I have frequently contrasted to myself that scene in the orchard with the peaceful scene at prayers in the morning. I believe I am the youngest of the four Governors; but if I am the whitest, this can perhaps be accounted for by the size and charm of our garden—not that for one moment I imagine there is any lack of trouble in any of the Branches.'

'I had had nearly five years' experience of the work at Bonner Road; but it was not without feelings of considerable anxiety that we entered upon this new Branch of the work. The fact that the children we had undertaken to shelter and train would be sent to us by the law, and that their associations would savour more or less of the police-court, was a new element in this work of grace. We were familiar with the terms "criminality," "moral and physical impurity," "depravity," and such like, applicable to many of the children already in our hands, but now that we were about to be brought into close touch with collective representatives of the class, it was natural that feelings of anxiety as well as of interest were unnaturally strong. . . .

'The low estimate which we had entertained concerning the character of the future inmates of this Branch was borne out by subsequent experience. As a whole these children are of lower grade than their brethren in the other Branches. This is not surprising when we again remember that in these Schools there is necessarily a gathering up of the worst. It is the boy who will not go to school who sooner or later makes the acquaintance of the School Board officer, and is ultimately committed to a school against his will. The same may be said of the boy who is the known though perhaps the unintentional companion of thieves, and also of the wanderer who has no "home," but becomes familiar with the coarsest ways of life as seen in many of the common lodging-houses.

'These being the social conditions from which, to a large extent, our inmates are drawn, it will surprise no one that their mental and religious state is correspondingly low. The larger majority of children sent to us can neither read nor write—or but very little—while the religious knowledge of some is absolutely nil. On one occasion we attended Divine Service, when a lad was looking much amused at some incident of the worship; and when spoken to by one of the officers, he professed entire ignorance of the purpose for which he had been taken to church, and had never heard of the existence of God. The fact seemed incredible, but subsequent conversation with him confirmed the sincerity of the poor lad's statement.

'Of the vices which characterized the children in those early days—alas! for the matter of that we can scarcely limit the period—perhaps the two which stood out most prominently were lying and theft. With marvellous ease and apparent sincerity was the lie told; and many an anxious hour have we spent with more or less success in endeavouring to elucidate mysteries in connexion with this phase of the art of speaking. And with wonderful obliquity of vision have the principles of *meum* and *tuum* been ruthlessly ignored, or received the most biassed interpretations.

'But I have given enough of the sombre side of our children's character, and gladly turn to the brighter and more genial view of their nature.

One notable and delightful trait is their strongly marked tenderness towards very young children. This has often been shown when a young and small child has been brought into the Home (and we have some as young as three and four years of age), the little ones receiving every mark of solicitude and affection. This may not be much in itself, but it is the "touch of nature which makes the whole world kin," and it at least shows our boys to possess that susceptibility of heart which, with careful training, may develop into love for all that is innocent and pure. As these are but "reminiscences" of our experience, I may repeat an oft-told story relating to a boy who was amongst the first dozen admitted. The lad himself was musical, and would perform on a tin whistle outside public-houses. The mother was dead, and the father, who seemed a respectable working man, could do nothing with the boy. Before the mother died, she impressed upon her husband the fact that the lad possessed a determined will, and hoped that his future would be rightly directed. She thought there would be no medium course in the boy's conduct ; he would grow to be a decidedly good or decidedly bad man. At present the trend was in a downward direction. He was sent to Milton as being "uncontrollable," but had not been here three days before he absconded. Suspecting that he had returned home, we went there, but the brother informed us the object of our search was "not in." This was literally true, for he was at the moment getting over a wall at the back of the house. We ultimately found him with his face blacked, to avoid detection, and his boots off. I booked at Cannon Street for the return home, but what was my dismay, when gathering the change, to find that my charge had eluded me, and disappeared among the crowd. I went back to the neighbourhood of his home, and fortunately saw the brother, who, Judas-like for a bribe, sold his brother, taking me to the place where I could regain the lost one. In due time we reached home, cold, wet, tired, hungry. But now for my point. When I took the lad into the kitchen, where there was a comfortable fire, I asked him if he would like some milk, and I can never forget the quick searching look he gave me as he doubtingly replied, " Yes, please, sir." I suppose the poor boy was expecting very different treatment after the day's trouble. However, I replied, " All right, my lad, you shall have some—would you like it hot or cold ? " And again came that strange questioning look as he faltering said, " Hot, please, sir." Turning to cook, I told her to give him some hot milk as soon as she could. But this was too much for the boy, who broke down completely, and fervently responded, " Please, sir, I will never run away again ! " " No, my boy, I know that ; you and I are going to be good friends, and I shall trust you." It is pleasant to say that he kept his word, and that I had no more trouble with him on that account.'

Mr. Stephenson was disappointed in a development which he hoped to make in another direction. He gave a good deal of time and strength to a project for establishing a Training Ship. A Committee was formed, a meeting held at the Mansion House, very considerable sums promised towards the project, and the Government offered to furnish the ship; but the debt on the Home was growing so heavy that the Committee was finally daunted by the additional expenditure involved, and after some years of waiting, the scheme was most reluctantly abandoned.

This was a period of financial embarrassment, which was never fully relieved until the Thanksgiving Fund in 1878 gave its substantial help to the work. As far as can be gathered from the published accounts, the cost of the various Branches of the Home was met by the amounts raised; but the expenditure at Bonner Road involved the Committee in a debt of between £5,000 and £6,000, with which it was difficult, if not impossible, to grapple. The Balance-sheet for Midsummer, 1875, shows an expenditure on the regular work of the Home amounting to £6,868 19*s.* 6*d.* To this must be added an expenditure on the Green Street Mission, and the Bonner Lane Mission, which were carried on in connexion with the Bonner Road Branch of the Home, amounting to £155 2*s.* 2*d.* This expenditure, however, was met by General Subscriptions and Donations, £5,188 4*s.* 9*d.*; and a new item, destined to grow to great importance, £1,402 8*s.* 5*d.* from the Sunday Schools. Subscriptions received at Edgworth amounted to £564 2*s.* 7*d.*; so that the current expenses were fairly met by the current income.

The Report states, however, that it was not possible in that year to pay off £500 of the money which had been borrowed for the purchase of the London premises. In August, 1876, we are told that £10,000 is required to set the

Institution in its various Branches completely free from liabilities. A resolution was passed, pledging the Committee to refuse all further extensions until either the whole of the above sum was raised, or the whole of the money for any proposed extension had been secured in cash.

These debts burdened Mr. Stephenson very heavily indeed, and, unhappily, for a time caused friction between him and Mr. James Barlow. The two friends did not see eye to eye as to the way in which the accounts should be presented to the public, and beside this Mr. Stephenson was no doubt in a very difficult position when friends offered him money for new work which very much needed doing; because even if the gift offered was sufficient to pay for the new extension proposed, that extension was sure to add to the current expenses of the enterprise; and it was by no means so easy to increase the current income as it was to get people to give money for new objects.

The fact is, that there is something essentially wrong with the Methodist plan of giving. And Mr. Stephenson is by no means the only example of a splendid Christian worker whose life has been made a weariness to him by financial troubles.

There is a pretty little story about one of these Committees that met to deal with the difficult financial situation at the Home, when affairs were critical. The meeting was held in Dr. Stephenson's room at the Children's Home, and strict orders had been sent out that there was to be no noise in the playground, and no visitors could be seen, nor must the Committee be interrupted by anybody. But a little girl, who had been accustomed to report her proceedings to the Doctor from time to time, in order to get a kiss, and had just been absent from the Home for a day, felt it necessary to tell him of her return; so she fearlessly knocked at the forbidden door, and when some grave Committeeman opened it, marched past him, straight up to Dr. Stephenson with a bright smile saying, 'I have just come to tell you I have come back, Doc.,' and held up her face to be kissed. The kiss was given, and the happy child walked serenely out of the room, leaving the Committee to go on with their work in an atmosphere freshened by a breath as from heaven itself.

CHAPTER XI

Training of Workers—Metropolitan Methodist Lay Mission—Deacons and Deaconesses—Sisters of the Children—Willard House—Some well-known Sisters.

One part of the original idea that Mr. Stephenson had in starting his work was not received by his friends and supporters with a welcome such as that given to the Children's Home. He wanted an establishment for training lay missionaries and assistants in orphanages, refuges, reformatories and hospitals. And he desired to establish such a Training Institution for both men and women in connexion with the Children's Home. We find it entered on the *Minutes* for November 17, 1872, that 'while the Committee approved generally of the scheme, it should not seek immediately to carry it into effect, but wait for the indications of Divine Providence respecting it: that when any suitable candidates offered themselves their cases might be considered.'

On March 21, 1873, we find a note that two men and one woman 'have offered themselves to assist in the work of the Home, with a view to being trained for Christian labour, and have been accepted by the House Committee.' One of the men was Mr. Arthur Gregory, destined by-and-by to become the second Principal of the Children's Home.

We find Mr. Stephenson in 1873 taking part in a

Breakfast Meeting in connexion with the 'Metropolitan Methodist Lay Mission,' of which the Rev. John Burgess and Mr. T. B. Smithies appear to have been the Secretaries. Mr. Burgess's speech, which is reported in the *Christian Advocate*, tells us that this was one of the youngest of Methodist Institutions, being only about two years old. 'In order to reach those whom the ordinary agencies could not reach, the Mission employed lay missionaries and deaconesses; the former visited from house to house, preached in halls and the open air, distributed tracts and copies of the Scriptures, and paid special attention to the sick and dying. The deaconesses—"that word was used because it was scriptural, Protestant, simple and descriptive—" did a most important work in house-to-house visitation, mothers' meetings, Bible-classes, tract distribution, &c. The importance of nursing in connexion with mission work could scarcely be understood by those who had not had some experience of it. One of their deaconesses was appointed to a very destitute part of London, where there were not more than five or six houses to which at first she had access; she nursed a sick person in a very dangerous illness, and the moral effect of that act was so great that now five hundred houses were open to her, and she had about eighty members at her mothers' meeting.'

The Rev. T. B. Stephenson is reported as saying that he 'believed the work of that mission, especially that of the deaconesses, was the most powerful anti-Popish agency amongst the poor which could possibly be employed. One of their deaconesses was told by one whom she visited, that it was of no use for her to call on her, as she was a Catholic.

She explained that some years previously her son was dying, and she applied to several ministers, but none of them could come and see him; at last she applied to the Roman Catholic priest, and he came with two Sisters of Mercy, who attended her lad until he died. She concluded by saying, "The Church that I will belong to is the Church that was kind to my boy." They could not do anything in the interest of Protestantism more successful and valuable than setting a large number of their Christian sisters at work amongst the poor. He did not think they ought to work in a spirit of bitter antagonism to any Church, or in a propagandist spirit, but if they were to hold their own against the influence of the Roman Catholic Church, they must have a great increase of that sort of work.'

The references to deaconesses in connexion with the Lay Mission are the more interesting because in the year 1873 Mr. Stephenson published a series of articles in the *Methodist Family* on women's work in the Church, in which he outlined a scheme for the training and employment of deaconesses, which varies very little from that afterwards successfully established.

His plans for the training of men as Christian workers of various kinds did not gain the same permanence, though it would be impossible to say that they were not successful in the face of the fact that the few who did accept the training went on to do such honoured and valued work in the Church of Christ.

In the Report for 1873, he says:

'There is needed in England to-day an army of workers, possessed of and thrilled by the love of

Jesus, who shall go forth to visit the sick, to nurse the diseased, to teach the neglected children, to care for the idiot, to aid in mission work amongst the lapsed masses. There is a vast aggregate of benevolence; but how seldom are philanthropic institutions officered by earnest Christians! How vast a tide of fertilizing influence might be poured upon the wastes of our national life through these channels if only Christian men and women would undertake to do the work, not in the narrow spirit of sectarianism, but in the blended power and gentleness of a simple and sincere love to the Saviour! How would the flow of our national charities be sweetened and purified if the spirit and life of women like Agnes Jones and Florence Nightingale could be reproduced in the workhouses and hospitals of our land! Yet, for all such work, training is needed, and such training as can be obtained only by personal experience in some other branch or branches of the great Inner Mission work. It is the peculiar glory of some of the Continental charities, that they have made their administration a practical training-ground for Christian men and women who have a vocation towards such work. Hitherto, nothing similar has been attempted in England, except in the one department of nursing. If it were the Blessed Master's will we should like the Children's Home to be ennobled by becoming a normal Training School for Christian Workers. In this way it would multiply itself a hundred-fold; and, if God counted us worthy of so great an honour, our influence would ultimately extend to every part of the land; and perhaps it might be given to us to send forth one and another to far-off lands, there to reproduce in new forms this blessed work of Christ.'

In the Report for 1874-5, he writes :

'The value of the Training Department of our work becomes increasingly apparent. The great difficulty in our enterprise has been to secure officers who are suited for their most difficult task. High moral qualities are needed for it. Thorough devotion to Christ is a first requisite, implying such an habitual realization of His presence as will prevent the work ever sinking into routine, but will perforce keep before the mind of the worker the spiritual results which are the great object of our work. And only second to this is needed a complete and habitual self-control, together with a quick eye for peculiarities of temperament ; an almost boundless patience ; and a loving sympathy which no perversity or wilfulness or ingratitude on the part of the children can tire out. Therefore it is a huge mistake to suppose that anybody, who may have proved incompetent in any other walk of life, but who can wash a child's face or sew a button upon a child's dress, is fit for such work as ours. Of all departments of educational work, there is none which makes a greater demand upon the highest moral qualities ; nor is there any in which the breadth and refinement which mental culture only can give may be used to better advantage. Hence, both in its influence upon the future of the Children's Home, which, as it grows, will demand a larger number of efficient officers every year, and in its bearing upon that great 'Inner Mission' in which alone there is a good hope for the purifying of our country from the inbred and inwrought taint of drunkenness, thriftlessness, profligacy and immorality, the Training Department is, perhaps, the most important branch of our work.

'Up to the present time, nineteen probationers have been received—ten young men and nine young women. Of this number, eight young men have completed their period of training; and of these, two are now officers in the Home; one has returned to business life, but is still hoping that his way may open into missionary work; one is a City Missionary; one is in the Methodist ministry in Canada; and one is a student in a Theological Institution. Two others have just successfully passed their examinations as candidates for the ministry, and will shortly leave us to enter college. Of the young women, two are now recognized as matrons in the Home, one has retired for want of health, and six are still probationers. We speak of all these as young women, because we do not know any more respectable and suitable phrase; but we are glad to say that in point of education and manners, several of them may very well claim the conventional title of lady; and we call attention to this fact, because we believe that to such a work as ours, many ladies who have no paramount family claims might devote themselves with immense advantage to the work of Christ, and with no disparagement to themselves.

'In connexion with the Training Department of our work, the Principal has given lectures during the year, with as much regularity as the urgent and wide-spread demands of the work would allow, upon the Science of Education, and the Study of Holy Scripture; and the Secretary has conducted a class for the study of the elements of Christian Theology.

'On this head, it only remains to be stated that we have a deep conviction as to the importance of extending the Training Department of our work, so soon as the funds of the Home will permit.'

In connexion with Bonner Road, and with the training of workers, responsibilities were early assumed for conducting some Missions in the neighbourhood; and the first of these was one that was carried on in the 'British Workman' public-house, Green Lane, Bethnal Green. The Committee agreed to assume the responsibility of conducting this Mission at an estimated net charge upon the funds of £50 a year. A proposal to establish a Children's Mission in connexion with the work of the Home, at the British Schoolrooms, Bonner Lane, was also agreed to, the total estimated expense in this case being £100 a year. These two Missions were carried on for many years, and provided opportunities for the training of the 'Brothers' received into the Home. They also gave the Sisters of the children some outside work which came as a change and relief among their more onerous duties. At these Mission Halls, often chairman, preacher, organist, teachers, doorkeeper, were all of them workers and children from the Children's Home.

An endeavour to develop the Training Department in 1875 failed for want of funds. It is, however, interesting to note an idea which was certainly Mr. Stephenson's own. It was that a minister should be appointed by the Conference for this special purpose; that four small Mission Halls should be worked, in some suitable spheres for missionary effort, and that the working of these Mission Halls should be supplemented by theatre and tent preaching. It was also proposed to form a 'Union of Christian Workers,' who were either present or past Officers of the Home, or had received training there. This, however, never materialized.

A little later, the Rev. Thomas Champness started his 'Joyful News' Training Home, which has since had such a wonderful development at Cliff College. As usual, we find Mr. Stephenson with the mind of the pioneer; only this time the track he attempted to strike out was not destined to be the one finally adopted. The question of cost militated against his project; it is the village evangelist, rather than the town mission worker, whom the Methodist Church has selected to train in this way. And moreover, it is in other spheres than that of the Children's Home that such training has been provided.

Years afterwards, in an address on 'Deacons and Deaconesses,' in 1897, Dr. Stephenson tells us something of what his ambitions had been.

'The Deacon referred to in my title is not either of the officers known by that name in English church life. The Deacon in churches of the Congregational order is a Christian layman fulfilling important duties which very nearly correspond to those of the Methodist steward. In the Church of England the Deacon is a minister in minor orders, corresponding to the licentiate in the Presbyterian Church, or to the preacher on trial in the Methodist Church. The Deacon of my title is very different from either of these. He is, in fact, the male edition of the Deaconess—her brother in the work of Christ, whose life is ruled by the same ideals and devoted to similar objects. In England he does not exist under that name and form. The only men whom I know in this country as comparable to him, are those who have devoted their lives and energies to the work of the Children's Home. In Germany, however, the Deacon is a very considerable institution.

'The extent and variety of the work, as also the severity and loftiness of its aims, are difficult for us to realize in this country. Nor are these Deacons few in number. Large brotherhoods exist in several parts of Germany, and many of them are at work in the mission fields of Africa and India. From this it will be seen that nothing corresponding to the German diaconate for men exists in this country. It may be questioned whether it ever will. If it should be created, it would have to be modified in some degree to meet the English habits and modes of thought, but everybody will admit that here is a noble conception and a powerful instrument. A noble conception; for the Deacon represents the devotion of men to the service of Christ and their fellows in a form in which such service is likely to develop to the utmost the man's power of work. He is a humble man, who is "content to fill a little space if God be glorified." He is a skilled man, having been taught how to do his work in the best way. He is a consecrated man, doing his work from the loftiest and most unselfish motives. He is an obedient man, content to go where he may be needed most, and to stay there until he is sent somewhere else. He is an enthusiastic man, but with an enthusiasm that is persistent and intense, an enthusiasm whose force is the pressure of water, not the explosion of a squib. He is linked with others in a close fellowship, which sustains and confirms all that is good in him. Such a man joined with others in such a federation, and that federation ready to move in a moment, is a power for Christian work similar to the German army in international affairs. And though I cannot now deal at suitable length with the subject, I must remind you that the work of such a marvellous Christian enterprise as the Colony of Mercy at Bielefeld would have been impossible without the devotion of the Christian Deacon.

'Years ago I cherished the hope that in connexion with the Children's Home some such agency might be trained and equipped. My hopes are not so bright to-day. Probably this must wait for another and wiser and stronger hand. Perhaps when I am gone my dream may be fulfilled. For the moment, I must be content to know that in connexion with our work there are men who, without the name and without the organization, do, to a large extent, exhibit the spirit of devotion which is characteristic of the true Deacon of the Lord Jesus.'

The mental and spiritual training, not only of his workers, but also of the elder boys and girls, was always an important item in Mr. Stephenson's work. From the earliest days, there was night-school for the elder children who worked during the day; and in those early years he conducted a fortnightly 'Bible Instruction Class' in his office, for all workers, including those who were responsible for the industrial training of the children. He used to emphasize the fact that the children were with the shoemaker, carpenter, printer, or cook for more hours in the day than they were with the Sisters. It was therefore necessary that all these workers should themselves be good Christians, alive to the higher influences of religion. It meant very much to him that on the 'Day of Prayer' all grades of workers attended and took part in the worship of the day. He never forgot that at Kaiserswerth he had seen a Deaconess, of high social standing, scrubbing the floor of the chapel, and proud to be entirely responsible for its cleanliness and beauty.

The definite training of 'Sisters of the Children' commenced about the year 1878 or 1879, when he made his first 'old girls' into Probationer Sisters. His rule was that they should help in domestic work until 10 a.m., from 10 to 11 o'clock take out-door exercise (mostly a walk in the park), and from 11 to 1 o'clock attend lessons, which were given by an educated lady in a room set apart for that purpose. From this time forward he worked hard to give all his younger women-workers spiritual and intellectual instruction, which, as time went on, became more and more systematized, and took its place as an important part of the week's work.

The Sisters of the Children were from the early days 'set apart' to the work. It was very simply done, usually at the close of a prayer-meeting, or other devotional gathering. One Sister tells us that she was 'set apart' at the end of the children's Monthly Tea-meeting, as Mr. Stephenson was taking the evening Family Prayer. The simplicity of the method, and the significance of the act, would both be dear to his heart. The idea which afterwards developed into the Consecration Service at Convocation was in his mind from the beginning.

In the earlier days of the Children's Home the methods of training had, of course, to be adapted to the necessities of the Institution. Later on, in 1898, Willard House was started for this purpose. It had room for seven students, who did all the work of the house, learnt cooking, washing, the making of children's clothes, and had studies in Bible knowledge, Theology, and Nursing. Past students also tell us that they got through a good deal of profitable reading. They went into the houses of the Children's Home and saw the work, and took charge when the Sisters were ill or had an afternoon off. Willard House was put under the charge of Sister Ruth Northcroft, who gave expression to its soul as follows :

'The Children's Home is a place where no gift comes amiss, and where many and varied gifts are absolutely essential. You must be able to sew and knit and darn, to make and mend and mark. To see when a house or a child is clean, and to show unwilling boys and girls how to produce cleanliness in house and person. To cook a little, to nurse a little, to trim dresses, to make hats. To warn them that are unruly, comfort the feeble-minded, support the weak, be patient towards all men. To answer the children's questions, to read aloud to them, to tell them stories, to pray with them and for them. To improve their manners and their morals, their grammar and their tempers. To enter into their play and foster their ideals. We must be full of the spirit of humour, and know how to touch the sacred fount of laughter and of tears. We must have an unerring sense of justice, or we shall do harm ; a steadiness of will to maintain order and authority, and a definite idea of the value of time, leading to punctuality, and of money, leading to thrift. In a word, we must be full "of the spirit of love, of power, and of a sound mind," and have a body fit to put it in practice. . . . So in Willard House regular hours are given every day to study, to needlework, and to housework. The hours are earlier than in most private houses, though not so early as in the Children's Home. We prepare all our own meals, thus learning plain cookery ; we mend regularly, and make up new garments. The idea is that each student should cut out and make a complete set of garments for a child. And so that the routine of washing shall be learnt, certain simple articles are washed at home each week. All the cleaning of the house is done by the students. A course of lectures is delivered by Dr. Tunstall in the autumn, when an opportunity is given for studying elementary nursing and First Aid. All the year round we have weekly classes, conducted by Mr. Gregory, in Theology and Biblical study. In addition to these, we have some hours weekly for Bible reading and general study, and special attention is paid to reading aloud.

'Besides this, our students visit for an afternoon a week in the homes of the poor in our neighbourhood, so that they may have some idea of the surroundings from which some of our children have been taken, and of the great need of such work as ours. They come into personal contact with these children of poverty, sorrow, and sin ; also at the Ragged School, the Cripples' Parlour, and the Children's Mission. . . .

'How best can you serve a child ? By bringing

yourself down to that child's needs, of body, mind, and soul. Is the body weak, sickly, and deformed? It will need your most loving care, your tenderest touch, your ablest encouragement towards active, healthy life. Is the mind dark, erratic, with knowledge of evil and ignorance of good? Every effort must be put forth to stimulate to thought, to tempt to brain work. And the soul? Here, above all, we say, "Ourselves your servants for Christ's sake." Are they not all His children, from the pathetic little toddler who makes your heart ache by his familiarity with pain, and confidence in going to heaven, to the rough lad who hardly seems to have anything but bad manners and a big voice, but who can be made gentle at once by the sight of a wild flower, and a word about the country? . . .

'We are to be servants to one another. It is a strange fact, but many girls grow up to womanhood without ever having lived on terms of absolute equality with any other woman. They have been with their mothers, an only daughter; or the youngest child, and the pet of the home; or they have been elder sisters, with large families to "mother." Or they have only lived in the society of those much older, and without an equal in age, station and privileges. And they have come to think they could never do it. Yet in the Children's Home, and in our Deaconess Homes, it has to be done, as in all community life. We have to learn to be the servants of each other, to be "true yoke-fellows," willing to give and take, and to bear and forbear; if necessary, to speak a painful truth faithfully and in love, but always to be able to hear one so spoken in a sisterly spirit.'

It is a matter of great regret that it is not possible in this book to speak in detail about the noble group of women workers who assisted Dr. Stephenson from the earliest days, and whose ability and devotion had so large a share in the success of his work. Their names are written in heaven, and they are also treasured in the hearts of many brave and thankful men and women who learned in the Children's Home how to fight and win the battle of life. Names like those of Sister Lizzie Grigg, Mrs. Clements, Sisters Lizzie and Bessie Coster, Sister Lydia Woolcock, Sister Emma Gooding, and many others, are very sacredly treasured in the hearts of those for whom they have cared so well. One name, however, stands out in everybody's thoughts, that of 'Mother McDougall.' Miss McDougall, who came from an honoured Manchester family, and whose brother, Sir John McDougall, has long been regarded as an ideal municipal statesman, entered the Children's Home in 1876, before the Sisterhood was established. She brought with her to the work great force of character, originality of thought, unbounded devotion, and, what was by no means her least valuable characteristic, exuberant good spirits. Her love for the work never faltered, but deepened with the growing years. It was inevitable that she should soon take a leading place among the workers, and without any official conferring of the title, she became known as 'Mother.' The word indicates the relation she held, not only to the children, but to the Sisters.

After she had been in the work a good many years, when she was away on a holiday, a consultation took place as to what could be done before she came back. It was suggested that her bedroom should be changed for a larger, sunny one, which looked out upon the street. The room was cleared and decorated, and on her return it was intended to take her to it as a surprise; but by an accident the door was open, and as she passed it and saw her own chest of drawers there, she concluded that her own room had been turned out for a spring-cleaning, and explanations had to be made. As she looked round and took in the situation, she said, 'Is all this for me?' adding, 'I must be a good woman now.'

A fire in 'Mother's' room from this time forward was the special treat for any Sisters who were not well, and needed a rest; and thither came everybody who was depressed or in difficulties, and all felt that both the joys and sorrows of life must surely be taken to her. If the original design of the Sisterhood was Dr. Stephenson's, it is hardly too much to say that its atmosphere, its tone and spirit, were very largely the result of her personality and influence. Her superior education and mental alertness inspired her fellow workers to familiarize themselves with good literature, and to regard the intellectual training of the children as an essential part of their work. Her influence upon the girls was unbounded. It became the custom to send the most trying and the least hopeful to Jevons House, of which she had the management; she received such children readily, hopefully, and merrily. The comic side of disorder and insubordination was never lost upon her. This was a very real help to her in dealing with the wildest girls. She could dismiss with a humorous rebuke what more strict disciplinarians would have regarded as heinous sins.

No one else could tell a story as 'Mother' told it. 'You might have been an interested witness of the incident, but you never knew the true inwardness of the scene, and were sure to miss the best points, unless you heard the story related by "Mother."'

Such stories naturally grew more picturesque in the course of years, and form now a part of the tradition, one might almost say of the mythology, of the Home.

She was one of the most enthusiastic missionary workers, and it was on her initiative that the first Wesley Deaconess was sent to Ceylon.

CHAPTER XII

DR. STEPHENSON AS A MUSICIAN

BY ARTHUR E. SHARPLEY, B.D.

The Musical Minister—Poet and Composer—Ever a Pioneer—Reverent Evangelism—Musical Lectures—The Singing Parson—America and Africa—Children's Home Music—His best Composition—Methodist Tune-Book—The Coming of the King.

IT was in the year 1869 that Dr. Stephenson made his brilliant entry into my life. As a boy attending the services of old Lambeth Chapel in its palmy days, when my father was one of its active workers, I naturally took a keen interest in the arrival of a new minister; and that of the youngest of the trio was of special importance. One frontal fact was particularly interesting to a youthful mind. The new minister wore a moustache, and this was so serious an innovation at that time that some wiseacres doubted whether sound doctrine could possibly issue from beneath such a worldly adornment. To encourage the minister, the two society stewards proceeded to grow similar superfluities, and my father being one of these bristling heroes, we had a good deal of amusement over the matter. Thomas Bowman Stephenson came to us from Bolton with wonderful stories of the Lancashire cotton famine, during which he, with all his resourceful and boundless energy, had of course borne a yeoman's part in the alleviation of distress. But my earliest memories cluster round his first visit to our home, in which he became at once a most honoured and welcome guest. Our home was centrally situated in the circuit, and after Sunday evening service we constantly had one or two ministers dropping in on their way home as they passed our door. Vivid, to-day, is the occasion when I first saw the beloved minister sitting at my mother's Broadwood, drawing forth tones of muscular power which were most amazing and inspiring, and accompanying them with wonderful singing. Sundays were great days for music in our home, and the remembrance is a blessing to this hour, but the visit of the musical minister made them golden.

We soon began to hear of transformation scenes at Waterloo Road, where he was specially stationed. The space between the chapel and the railing was utilized for open-air services, and a small shelter was erected at the side for the missioner and his harmonium. Great crowds gathered to hear the solos and addresses of the minister who pioneered so successfully in this rich department of spiritual toil. Soon after, we heard of the starting in a small house of rescue work, and lads were seen on the streets with barrows of wood, which they sold to help in the expense of the initial Children's Home. The work rapidly grew, and I remember my boyish astonishment when the cashier of an important bank, which I occasionally visited for my father, threw up his position to join the minister in his enthusiastic work of human salvage.

The story of the Home will be amply told in other

pages of this work, but the musical qualities of Bowman Stephenson formed a rich asset in the early days of that enterprise. The wood-chopping soon receded into the background as popular criticism melted in a glow of philanthropy, and subscriptions flowed in, so that the boys could spend their time in acquiring a training that would fit them for something better than mere elementary forms of labour. When the Home was enlarged, girls were included, and a choir was speedily formed, Dr. Stephenson conducting and accompanying. For this purpose he acquired a Mustel organ which he played with much power and sympathy. The Mustel, as musical readers know, is the finest type of harmonium, and of exquisite tone and power. The cheapest, in those days, cost about a hundred pounds, and only eleven per annum could be produced, as each reed in each instrument was personally blown and finished by the brothers who composed the famous firm.

Dr. Stephenson possessed a baritone voice of penetrating quality and exceptional range. It enabled him, as a speaker, till the very end of his public career, to command any audience : and the tone was produced with effortless ease. As a musical organ, it was equally efficient. He could cover the whole gamut of the musician with perfect comfort. I have heard him ring out the tenor upper A with clarion clarity, and presently he would be singing a rich bass to the children's treble and alto. His singing compass must have been several notes over two octaves, and this in the part of the musical register which gave him equal command of all vocal music. This rich gift of natural musical efficiency he dedicated, first to the service of true Home Mission work, and afterwards to that specialized form of it which we know as the Children's Home.

For these purposes, he wrote music or words as needed. He taught, accompanied, conducted, or sang. His versatile genius would march in any direction, and he knew no false humility in his work. On one occasion, in 1878, he was accompanying his children's choir on a small harmonium at an annual meeting in Exeter Hall. The instrument presently collapsed under his vigorous playing. 'Now you go on singing,' said he, quite oblivious to the opinion of the great congregation as he plumped on to his knees, repaired the collapsed bowels of the instrument, and was soon up again conducting. His amiability and all-round efficiency on that occasion so impressed one lady in the audience that she at once gave herself to the Home as a voluntary worker, and served it with generosity and devotion for more than a quarter of a century afterwards.

The mention of Exeter Hall reminds us that Dr. Stephenson was the first Methodist to hire a theatre for evangelistic purposes. He was also the first to take the Albert Hall for a Methodist gathering, and for that occasion he secured several fine hymns for his choir which have now passed into the treasury of our hymn-book and are among the choicest lyrics of our Church to-day. Such, for instance, is the hymn by Dr. Burton, 'O King of kings,' to Stainer's majestic tune.

While he was to the very core an evangelist in his music, enjoying to the full interruptions of ejaculated hallelujahs, yet Bowman Stephenson had a deep sense of reverence and ritual which he carefully developed in the services of the Children's Home Chapel. His influence lingers still at Victoria Park Church, which was long attended by the children from Bonner Road. Even now, the communion service there is rendered, from a musical point of view, in a manner equalled by few, and excelled, perhaps, by no churches in Methodism. All the responses are musically taken, every member of the choir remains and partakes in the service, and the whole effect of solemnity and beauty renders it deeply impressive.

In his lecture notes, the Doctor gives us his ideals of the kind of music most effective for winning the masses. One lecture, frequently given and well illustrated by specimens which he sang to his own accompaniment, teaching the audience to sing with him, was entitled 'Singing for Jesus,' or 'Music in its Home Missionary Aspect.' He does not seek to discuss the position of music among the fine arts, or even to ask how far it has advanced the interests of religion. His aim is humbler. He desires to ascertain 'what means may be employed for gaining the ear of the masses for the story of the Cross, and how worship may be brought into such shape as to attract the multitude, and bring them under our influence.' In fact, he desires to regard the Home Missionary aspect of music. The opening pieces are, 'I will sing for Jesus' and 'Singing for Jesus,' by Philip Phillips, and a song entitled 'Jesus only.' He then proceeds to inquire why, of the working men of London, only about two in every hundred attend divine worship. Perhaps the place of prayer

N

is too fine for them, possibly the mode of preaching is unsuitable. The panacea, he thinks, would be the right sort of music. From the humblest melody of the infant class to the glory of a Handel festival, all music is available, utilizable, if adapted to the varying congregations. He pleads that in this matter we may be all things to all men, that we may save some. If only the lighter, merrier music will attract the crowd, let them have it.

Listed in the cause of sin,
  Why should a good be evil?
Music, alas! too long hath been
  Pressed to obey the devil.
Drunken, or light, or lewd, the lay
  Tends to the soul's undoing;
Widens, and strews with flowers the way
  Down to eternal ruin.

This plan is then illustrated by singing 'Jesus, the name high over all' to 'Auld lang syne,' and 'Canaan, bright Canaan.' If some object that this is degrading music, he pleads that he is regarding music from the ministerial, not the musicianly point of view, and proceeds to 'outrage musical propriety' by setting to a lively air, from Mozart, his hymn:

We are marching through the desert,
  From Egypt's slavish chains,
And our course is ever onward
  To Canaan's happy plains.
March, march from Egypt's strand,
March till we reach the promised land.

Canaan, it is worth noting, is here regarded as the

type of the good man's portion in this life, a view-point often overlooked by less scriptural writers than our clerical composer. Then to Abt's charming strains of 'When the swallows homeward fly,' follow more words by Thomas Bowman Stephenson:

When my sorrow's waves run high,
  Hiding every glimpse of heaven,
And the short-lived pleasures die
  Which but yesterday were given;
Why, my soul, these fluttering fears?
Why so quickly start thy tears?
Hark! what whispers through thee thrill,
Jesus loves thee, Peace, be still!

The first line is perilously near parody, but none will quite understand the effect of such words to such music unless they heard them sung by Bowman Stephenson to his own accompaniment in the days of manhood's prime.

In Home Mission music, Dr. Stephenson well maintained that the first requisite was a 'taking melody,' not forgetting the value of a 'good chorus,' and he pointed to the music-halls for evidence. Many illustrations might be given to show how our evangelist utilized his gifts in adapting popular melodies to sacred purposes. Did not Wesley say the devil ought not to have all the best tunes? and Stephenson bent his best powers to adapt the favourite, and even rollicking airs, to gospel ends. His musical gifts, coupled with his evangelical fervour, made his services very attractive to the multitude. A working man, standing outside Waterloo Road Chapel at an open-air service, said, 'It's worth half a crown any day to hear a parson sing like that,' and the common people heard him gladly, following him to the Master's feet, as he sang them on the way. He wrote a battle hymn to the music of 'John Brown's body lies,' which was very popular.

I hear the voice of mercy sounding from the sacred
    Word,
It calls to sinners from their sins to turn and seek
    the Lord;
The heart of Christ was pierced by the law's avenging
    sword,
        That we all might be set free.
Glory, Glory, Hallelujah! We all may be set free.

Perhaps one more illustration will suffice of Dr. Stephenson's Home Missionary work from the musical point of view. Probably of all his solos, 'Blind Bartimaeus' was the most effective, though I have seen tears flow, and felt my own, when he sang, 'I stood outside the gate,' and, indeed, so many were attended with soul-converting power that it is not easy to particularize. The familiar plaintive melody of 'She wore a wreath of roses' was the one he wanted to utilize, and he chose the theme of Bartimaeus, ready as ever to write words to music, or music to words, if by any means he might save some. We give the first verse:

Beside life's barren highway
    I lingered, blind in sin,
A beggar from the world, to feed
    The starving soul within;
When lo! the tramp of many feet
    That fell upon mine ear,
And when I asked them Why? they said,
    ''Tis Jesus Christ is here.'

THE PRINCIPAL OF THE CHILDREN'S HOME.

(Taken during his first visit to Canada.)

[face p. 196.

I heard the word, I knew my need,
And loudly rose my cry,
'Have mercy, Son of David,
Oh, do not pass me by.'

The verses followed the gospel narrative, and oh! with what thrilling joy and power the singer sang the closing lines:

The Son of David mercy had,
He did not pass me by.

Music was so large a part of Bowman Stephenson's evangelistic work that it may be said that the history of his soul, sunny, radiant, hopeful, was in his music and the words which he wrote for the music of others. In the Supplemental Hymnary he compiled, which must be referred to later on, he opens with:

Be our joyful song to-day,
Jesus! only Jesus!

and from this keynote of experience down to that swan-song of Charles Wesley, which was the constant consolation of his closing hours, the musical experience of Bowman Stephenson was the utterance of his soul life. His music, in union with his evangelism and his great organizing powers, accounts for much of the best work his busy life accomplished. It also brought him into quick contact with evangelism on the great scale. He sang for Moody during his visits to England, and after Moody and Sankey left, Stephenson, with Hay Aitken, continued the meetings in the Agricultural Hall, London. In 1872 he paid his first visit to America at the invitation of Dr. Punshon, then minister of the Metropolitan Church in Toronto. The Rev. Luke Wiseman accompanied him, and the three mighty men had some wonderful services together. At Chautauqua, in 1877, he was greatly impressed with the camp singing, and brought back to England some of the favourites of that famous gathering, notably, 'Day is dying in the west,' 'Break thou the Bread of Life,' with compositions of Bliss, Phillips, Miss Lathbury, Sherwin, and others. Not only in America did our evangelist's music become helpful. In the year 1882 he preached in South Africa, often through interpreters, and was deeply moved by the religious emotions of the people as great audiences sang simultaneously in five languages, his chorus :

Jesus saves me now,
Jesus saves me now,
Jesus saves me all the time,
Jesus saves me now !

In the early stages of the Children's Home, the musical tours, like everything else, were under the personal supervision of the Principal. He accompanied the children on their journeyings, and accompanied them in their music, singing with them as well as directing them. Incidentally, this work led to the establishment of a music printing department in the Home, of considerable commercial importance, and the hymn-sheets and anniversary music printed for and at the Children's Home became a treasure store from which, for many years, Sunday schools all over the country, and in many parts of the world, drew their supplies for festival uses. Many others have followed where Stephenson showed the profitable way, and have reaped where he sowed; but in this department, as in so many others, he was ever a pioneer.

As the Home grew, the musical work became too much for the Principal, and Mr. Heath Mills, and after him, Mr. F. A. Mann, became the musical directors, following the lines laid down by Stephenson with so much skill and success that the choir of the Children's Home remains quite unrivalled among such institutions. Truly, Dr. Stephenson's music has had much to do with winning the heart of the people to sympathy with the beautiful and Christlike work of the Children's Home. One of these early song-books lies before me, kindly lent by Mrs. Stephenson, who has furnished me with many facts for this chapter. It was known by the children as 'the shiny black book,' and contains the pick of the early songs of the home. It includes 'Break thou the Bread of Life,' by Mary Lathbury, 'Jesus saves me now,' Mrs. Knapp's music to 'The Lord will provide' (a great favourite), Dr. Punshon's 'Listen, the Master beseecheth' to Phillips' music, 'O what can little hands do,' by G. F. Root, and Bliss's last song 'I know not what awaits me.' Later on, a series of handsome volumes in grey and gold, entitled 'The Children's Home Music,' appeared. In the first preface, Dr. Stephenson points out that the music is printed as well as published at the Home. All the children are taught music, while some, specially gifted, are encouraged to attempt more than is usually undertaken by children, and so to add refinement to life.

The favourites of the early period may serve to

recall pleasant memories to some readers. Such are 'Fading like a lifetime,' 'The streets of the City are full,' 'The fierce wind howls,' and 'Standing forth on life's rough way,' always sung for emigrants going to Canada. Some, of course, are humorous and this section was much enriched by Heath Mills. Such were 'The rabbit,' 'The sleigh ride,' and 'The bells,' which have given pleasure to thousands upon thousands of hearers, and won them for ever as friends and supporters of the children's cause. Among the pathetic pieces, not less attractive, are 'Far away where angels dwell,' and the touching duet, 'Home, dearest home,' which, when sung by a couple of orphan children who knew no home till the Children's Home found them, has moved multitudes to deepest feeling. Among these pieces appears 'Hushed was the evening hymn,' to which words by J. D. Burns, Dr. Stephenson wrote a fine tune called 'Hannah.' It is number 876 in the Methodist Hymn-Book. The composer evidently wrote it with his eye on the first verse—most writers have some particular lines in view—but the fine effect he gained by making the accented note, first in the bar, fall on the word 'Hushed,' is unfortunately lost in the Methodist Hymn-Book, where the music is regularized so as to fit the following verses. It is the penalty of writing hymn tunes that unless the poetry is absolutely uniform in point of metre, line corresponding exactly with line in every verse, a special effect secured in one verse is lost in the others. This happens in the tune 'Hannah,' The composer placed the accent on the word 'Hushed' for the first verse, and adapted the music to the following verses, and this ought to have been done in the Methodist Hymn-Book. I dwell upon this tune, because, in my judgement, it is the best piece of music Dr. Stephenson ever wrote. His hymns I will not attempt to judge or characterize, as they are very numerous, and I cannot claim to know them all. The reader may judge for himself from the specimens here given. His poetic faculty, like his other gifts, worked freely and easily. As a fountain pours forth from a living spring, so did his verses flow generously from a heart full of song and thanksgiving.

Dr. Stephenson took a deep interest in the issue of the new Methodist Hymn-Book. He had for some years anticipated this necessity, and in his pioneer way had already cleared a good deal of the ground. His Supplemental Hymnal contained, as he says, many hymns of 'great and permanent value, though they strike a note hitherto seldom heard in Evangelical Churches.' The tunes, too, were, as he adds, not only popular in style, but of great musical merit. His critical judgement was justified by the action of the Committee. He attended the sittings with much pleasure, carrying his Supplemental Hymnal with him. Quite a long list of the hymns in that work were included, far too long to give here, and in a number of cases the tunes also were taken, such as 'Tell it out,' 'O King of kings,' 'Thou didst leave Thy throne,' and 'Crossing the bar.' This point, I think, should not pass without honourable mention, as showing how truly Dr. Stephenson in this, as in so many other things, was in harmony with the spirit of the age, generally a little in advance, in his endeavours to promote the work of God.

It has been said already that the history of Dr. Stephenson's soul was in his music. In his closing years this was very manifest. As a member of the Methodist Tune-Book Committee, he was very much impressed, in common with other members, by Sir Frederick Bridge's reverent treatment of Charles Wesley's hymn, dictated to his wife on his death-bed, ' In age and feebleness extreme.' The musical adviser of the Committee had drawn their attention to the high historical interest of that single verse. He thought the words were of great importance, and should be treated with reverential respect. He suggested that they should be sent to Sir Hubert Parry, who, he said, would be proud to set them to appropriate music. This course was adopted, and the result has been extremely gratifying. Dr. Stephenson thought so highly of the setting that he wrote a vesper verse to the music, so that it might be more frequently heard and enjoyed. In the last year of his life it was constantly in his mind and on his lips. For months before he passed away, he would wander from piano in drawing-room to harmonium in dining-room, to play and sing the pathetic lines to the lovely strains :

In age and feebleness extreme,
Who shall a helpless worm redeem ?
Jesus, my only hope Thou art,
Strength of my failing flesh and heart.
O could I catch one smile from Thee,
And drop into eternity !

The last music he heard was the music of the Children's Home. The electrophone had been installed in his house so that he was able to listen to the music of the Children's Home Festival in Queen's Hall just before Christmas, 1911, and with great delight he heard one of the girls sing 'The Coming of the King.' His last thoughts and last love were for the children of the Home, and they paid him back in full measure. The girl who sang 'The Coming of the King,' at Queen's Hall, also sang the solo in the anthem, 'Blest are the departed,' at his funeral service a few months later in July. The procession of children was joined at the cemetery by a number of old boys and girls of the Home who had gathered there before the cortège arrived from Wesley's Chapel. At the grave, 'Wolverhampton,' F. A. Mann's fine tune, was sung to 'Father, now the day is over,' and quite remarkable was the unexpected richness given to the singing of the children by the tenor and bass of the old boys and choirmen present, all familiar with that favourite tune written by their old friend and conductor. The effect was entrancing, overwhelming, and to those present it seemed as if Heaven itself was welcoming their father and founder with that song, which linked, in common rejoicing, those who had passed to the glory beyond our sunset with those who, in the morning, or noon, or gloaming of life, still wait the Coming of the King.

CHAPTER XIII

Chapel and School built—Opening Services and Festival—City Road Service—Bolton Bazaar—Canadian Visit.

THE building of the chapel at Bonner Road, which took place in 1876, gave further opportunity for the expression of the strong aesthetic side of Mr. Stephenson's nature. In those days there had been considerable financial difficulties, and a resolution had been passed by the Committee that there should be no further capital expenditure unless the money was actually assured for it. A school, however, was an absolute necessity, which must be provided if the work of the Home was to be carried on; and Mr. Stephenson, with his keen eye for building construction, saw that the chapel might quite easily be put above the school. He himself tells how he was talking about it to Mr. Horace Marshall, and was asked how much money it would require. He replied, 'Five hundred pounds,' and in the course of a day or two there arrived from 'a friend' a promise of that amount. The Officers of the Home contributed £106 more for the chancel; and an organ-chamber and a gallery were left to be dealt with later. The foundation-stones of the chapel were laid on January 10, 1877, by the son and namesake of Mr. Horace Marshall, and Dora Stephenson, the daughter of the Principal.

The chapel was opened on April 26, 1877, by Dr. Punshon. In connexion with the opening a great Festival had been laboriously prepared for. On May Day the Right Honourable W. E. Forster, M.P., the Minister for Education, took the chair, and Dean Stanley also came to support the Children's Home. Speaking to a large audience in a tent, which had been erected for the occasion, Mr. Forster said:

'I suppose you wish to get outside persons who have studied the question of education to come and see your method of carrying on the work. I am glad to bear my testimony to the fact that this Institution is doing really substantial work, and takes a prominent place amongst such Institutions. This is one of those works in which a man may feel certain he is doing good by rendering help. I am glad to aid in celebrating the success that has attended you, and I hope you will have still further success in a work that is doing nothing but good. It is very necessary with regard to educational institutions like yours, that we should be quite sure they will not be doing a little harm as well as a great deal of good; but I really cannot see what harm this Children's Home can do, and I can see an enormous amount of good that it may effect. If one considers what ought to be aimed at in any kind of benevolent agency like yours one may say there are three conditions required to be fulfilled: first, that the object is one that is worthy of the exercise of charity and benevolence; next, that it is so managed that the object shall really be attained; and then, that the help should be given in such a manner and upon such principles that there would not be any increase in the evil we wish to remove. As regards the object, what can there be better? Hardly anything so good. You try to take hold of these children who, without your help, must be utterly helpless, and perfectly lost in this great metropolis. You take hold first of the orphan child who has lost both parents and is poor; secondly, of those whose parents are so utterly poor that they cannot help their children; and thirdly, of those children who, unfortunately, have parents who will not care for or help them, or who will help them on the wrong road. What is to become of these children unless they are helped? I do not see how it is possible to expect that they should do anything but fall into poverty and misery. What is before these children but the workhouse? And would you not keep them out of it if you possibly could? Not but that I think our workhouses are a credit to England, and that we should be ill fulfilling our duty if we did not maintain them and try in the best way to manage them; but they must be so managed that we would not send any children there if we could help it. The associations connected with them, and the enormous scale upon which they are conducted, give but little hope for the children compared with such an institution as this. Next we come to those children who have had evil influences surrounding them. I need not detain you to prove how absolutely necessary it is, if we look for a future, to take such children away from their evil surroundings and give them some chance of leading a virtuous and industrious life. A second condition is that, having this object before us, we should take the best means of arriving at it. I think remarkable wisdom has been shown in the management of your Home. In enormous establishments it is exceedingly difficult to keep up a good influence amongst the children. They have no kind of family or home life connected with their early childhood. I am told that you have provided separate houses, and that the cost of your separate houses is not in excess of that of a large institution. Then I think it is a very pleasant and hopeful feature of this undertaking that it is connected with one of our great religious societies, and that it is under what may be called earnest religious control and management, although I understand that there is not the slightest preference given to the child of one religious denomination over another. We have been trying, for the sake of England, to secure that a good elementary secular education should be given to every child in the kingdom. But that work is not for one moment to be compared to such work as this. What has been done, was done to give greater knowledge, greater power; but you are trying to give not only the power and the knowledge, but the motive to use that power and knowledge aright. We know very well, by our own experience and the experience of history, that there is nothing but religion that gives that power.

'Let me say a word or two with regard to special agencies. I do not know that I shall allude to more than one; to what you are doing in Canada. When I was over there a little while ago I came to the conclusion that it was very undesirable for people, at present, at any rate, to emigrate to Canada, unless they were agricultural labourers or domestic servants, especially maid-servants. Canada was then, and I believe still is (though it may soon cease to be), full for every other employment. Therefore, I felt when I was there what an advantage it was that there were some people who would look after the emigrants; for emigrants generally, more especially boys, cannot well be expected to take care of themselves. Now, what have you done? You have established your Training Institution—the Emigrants' Home at Hamilton. At the head of it is a man who seems as if he was made for the work, Mr. Riley; and the object is that every boy who comes out is looked after until he can get good employment. And the farmers are glad enough to take boys from such an institution, and with such antecedents. You find out good masters for the boys, and you have some sort of superintendence over them. I know of one special case, that of a boy who went out with the help of your agency, and came under the care of Mr. Riley afterwards; and I was thus enabled to see, having an interest in him, what an immeasurable advantage it is to such boys to have such a friend.'

Dean Stanley made a characteristically gracious and beautiful speech. He said:

'The object of the Institution had been already stated. It was to gather the children away from the bad circumstances in which they were placed, and to try by education to form new characters within them. Putting that into the language of the Bible, they were trying to convert them, redeem them, and regenerate them. To understand what these words meant, they must consider the words in their original meaning. To convert, was to turn round the whole mind, and that was what was being attempted. Through their misfortunes, these children had been wandering about with no fixed purpose ; and the object of the Institution was to put them in the right way, and to cause them to walk straight forward with a fixed purpose in life. To redeem the children—he knew there was a great sacred meaning in the word—was to deliver them from bondage, into that liberty of being good, to which every Englishman was entitled at least to have a chance. Then, again, to regenerate was to create a new mind or character. That was what they wished to do for the children. This was the greatest of all tasks, even under the most favourable circumstances, and one of very especial difficulty under the circumstances presented by the children before them. They knew that, irrespective of the circumstances in which children were placed, good and evil dispositions, and many intellectual defects were born with them. Could they change these ? Could the grooves of their pathway be enlarged and rectified ? He did not speak of the mysterious workings of a Higher Power. With God they knew that all things were possible ; but could they trace in experience the modes in which the Divine Spirit guided them, and of which they must lay hold ? They would remember Oliver Cromwell's speech to his Ironsides, " Trust in God, and keep your powder dry." They must keep the powder dry in order that it might explode when the spark of divine grace came. There were one or two means that might, in the face of the greatest difficulties, give them courage and hope. A change of circumstances would help them. A child brought up in an atmosphere darkened with filth, loaded with impurity, bristling with curses, and crowded with temptations would surely produce a character taking the shape and colour of the circumstances around it. It was possible that by a miracle of grace a little child in one of these human dens might be preserved pure in spite of the infamy, gentle amidst the cruel, and intelligent amongst the brutes. But what they had to do was to change the circumstances in which the children were placed. Under the influence of evil he had known boys grow up as fierce as wild animals, or as ungovernable as savages, and yet in a few months, when the neglect had been remedied, and the boys were placed under gentle influences, it was as though a demon had been cast out. But it was not enough that the children should be redeemed or delivered from evil; they must have a new influence brought to bear upon them. They must learn what Dr. Chalmers called "the expulsive power of a new affection." And this came with the first thought that anybody lived who cared for them. It was the saying of Jeremy Bentham that he owed everything to this feeling having been excited in his own mind by the kindness of the late Lord Lansdowne: "He took me out of the bottomless pit of humiliation, and made me feel that I was something." When he (Dean Stanley) was in Russia three years ago, he went one day to Moscow to see a small establishment much similar to theirs, and built for the same purpose. The boys were taken there after criminal conviction, and a young Russian gentleman lived amongst them. The good effect produced in that establishment was caused by that young man living constantly amongst them. He could hold no conversation with him, but as he looked upon his face he saw written upon his countenance, not only the Ten Commandments of Sinai, but the eight Beatitudes of the Galilean Mountain.'

Next day the Rev. W. Fleming Stevenson, the author of *Praying and Working* (the book which had first brought the great work of the German Inner Mission before Dr. Stephenson, and had so deeply affected his life's work), was present, and preached on 'The Living Stones of the Temple.'

Services were continued in the Chapel on Thursday by the Rev. A. G. Brown, President of the London Baptist Association, and on Friday by the Rev. Henry Allon, D.D.

A great Sale of Work was held in connexion with this Festival, and the Band of the Boys' Home at Regent's Park, as well as the Band of the Children's Home itself, contributed to the interest of the occasion. Nearly £1,000 was raised to assist the Funds.

The chapel was afterwards enriched and beautified by personal gifts, such as the communion rail, the inlaid floor of the apse, the stained glass windows, the brass lectern and the font. 'H. K.' describes it as 'the little chapel with its pathetic stained-glass windows, and memorial brasses, and sweet organ, and lovely little baptistry, and numberless tokens of love and gratitude.' Though all is most simple and unpretentious, the chapel is really beautiful. This, to be sure, is the firm conviction of the successive generations of children who have gathered there; and it is certain that they have learned a reverence, a love for worship, and especially for worship-song, and a sense of the peace and beauty of God's presence, by means of the atmosphere of the place, and the order of its services, which have had the deepest effect upon the character of very many of them. A Service Book was compiled by Dr. Stephenson, for use in this congregation, having five distinct forms of worship, one for each Sunday in the month, with offices, and hymns and anthems. The afternoon service differed from the morning. The anthem was sung after the first prayer; the Methodist Sunday School Hymn-book took the place of the larger book, the evening lessons were read, and a collect preceded the sermon, which was always preached with special reference to the little ones. If the preacher wished to use a cartoon, a map, or a blackboard, he would find an iron frame behind him, which a touch of the hand would swing into full view. There was never any need to call to order, for a Sabbath calm was on the place.

On July 15 of this year a specially interesting service was held in connexion with the Children's Home at City Road Chapel. It had been arranged that the Lord Mayor of London should officially attend some representative Nonconformist church from time to time, and the previous year the City Temple had been selected. It was a rule that the Lord Mayor should not attend any service in his official capacity outside the City boundaries, but in deference to the unique position of City Road Chapel in relation to Methodism this rule was set aside. The collection, which amounted to £96, was given to the Children's Home, as an object most likely to secure the cordial co-operation of various denominations. The children of the Home attended in a body, and Mr. Stephenson conducted the service. Dr. Punshon, who was the Sheriff's Chaplain for the year, was the preacher; and preached on 'Christian citizenship' to a congregation which completely crowded the chapel.

Another item of this very crowded year, 1877, was a great Sale on behalf of the Home held in the Bolton Town Hall, on June 20, 21, and 22, the net proceeds of which amounted to £1,550. The Bishop of Manchester attended, and gave a most helpful address. 'He wished,' he said, 'to hold out the right hand of fellowship, and from his heart of hearts to ask the divine blessing upon every one, no matter to what particular religious denomination he belonged, who was engaged in that eminently Christian work which the Apostle told them was the highest and most acceptable form of worship to God, namely, visiting the fatherless, the widow, and the orphan, and helping to keep them unspotted from the world. They had been told that this Institution rested distinctly upon a religious basis, and Mr. Stephenson had with sufficient explicitness explained to them what that religious basis was. He was one of those who had long wished that Christians in general would take broader and larger views of the great governing principles of Christ's gospel. We had drawn up barriers where it seemed to him Christ had placed no barriers at all. We had forbidden people to look one another in the face, or to shake hands with one another. To teach these children to love God, to love Him with a real love, as a child loves its parent to whom he owes all; to believe in the Lord Jesus Christ with a real belief, to recognize Him as the Great Teacher, to recognize Him as the Saviour, to recognize Him as the source through His blessed Spirit of spiritual life and strength ; to teach them to love their neighbours, and to do what was right and just and kindly towards every man—surely we must recognize such work as in accord with the great principles of Christianity, whether we be Churchmen, or Nonconformists, or Roman Catholics, or of whatsoever denomination we styled ourselves. We must feel that a building which was being raised upon these foundations must be secure if only it were true to the plan which its architects had devised. . . . When we were told that we were nothing but muscular or nervous automata ; when people acted as though the gratification of human passion was the one thing for which they were to live ; when, in fact, they seemed to say, "Let us eat and drink, for to-morrow we die," he repeated that it was to him an encouraging thing that they, and others elsewhere, religious men and women, recognized that this human life was indeed a struggle for existence, but not in the physical sense in which the weakest must perforce go to the wall. He rejoiced that, notwithstanding the moral and physical sophisms of the day, there were those who had not lost their faith in God and their sense of duty to the poor. If they were helping the helpless, recovering the fallen, training the orphans in the ways of virtue, honesty, and the like, he could from his heart of hearts ask for God's choicest blessing upon the work, and thus encourage them in the doing of it.'

On July 19 Mr. and Mrs. Stephenson sailed for Canada with another party of young emigrants. He received a most cordial welcome from new and old friends across the Atlantic, and wrote home some very merry letters to the children. He had considerable success in many of the meetings held in the interests of the Home, and also in his evangelistic labours. Among other things his presence was a prominent feature in a most notable gathering, a Sunday School Parliament on the Thousand Islands, where he sang improvised verses on the union of hearts between Canada and the States, of which the following is a specimen :

> A line runs through these Thousand Isles
> That stud the river's breast ;
> All northward owns Victoria's sway,
> The Union claims the rest.
> The statesmen say the line exists
> In treaty-parchments fine ;
> But when I hither came to-day
> I did not see the line.

He had the pleasure also of visiting a large number of the boys and girls who had been sent out in previous years, and of making some personal acquaintance with their changed positions and prospects. He often found it somewhat difficult to recognize the boys and girls of years ago in the young men and women who greeted him with an honour and respect which had been won by the redemption of their lives.

In a Report which he made to his Committee on his return, he speaks as follows :

A few, a very few of the children have indeed greatly grieved and disappointed us, yet on the whole there is ground for very high satisfaction. In order to bring the matter to a test, we examined very carefully the cases of all those children who had been for two years and a half in the country. We divided them into five classes :—

Criminal : Such as have violated the law of the country.

Bad : Thoroughly idle, ungovernable, vicious.

Moderate : Good citizens, such as would compare not unfavourably with the average of the working classes, though wanting some elements of stable character.

Good : Satisfactory both in regard to work and character.

Excellent : Distinguished by superiority of character, thrifty, diligent, strictly trustworthy, and in some cases decidedly Christian.

Of forty-seven girls, examined and classified as above, three are dead, leaving forty-four.

Of these—

12	are	excellent
23	,,	good
5	,,	moderate
2	,,	bad
None criminal.		

Of 133 boys trained in the Children's Home in England, and classified as above—

22	are	excellent
73	,,	good
37	,,	moderate
1	is	bad
None criminal.		

He adds that they had extended the advantages of their Emigration Home to some children trained in other institutions. The results among them were not quite so satisfactory, but as he points out, these boys and girls were strangers to them until a few days before sailing, and the representatives of the Children's Home had been unable to exercise much controlling influence upon them after they had reached Canada, but this, he says, 'should only make us the more thankful for the results achieved amongst our own children. Remembering what many of them were; remembering how inferior our processes and arrangements for training were in the earlier history of the Home, and then seeing that out of 177 children none has proved criminal, only three bad, whilst forty-two are marked moderate, ninety-eight good, and thirty-four excellent, surely this is matter for devout thankfulness to Almighty God. That less than three per cent. should have turned out badly is indeed astonishing. To God be all the glory!'

CHAPTER XIV

Tours with the Children—Report of Sunderland *Daily Post*—The Tours and the Children—Deputy-Governor.

THE next year, 1878, saw a new beginning, destined to have great influence upon the personal life of Dr. Stephenson, upon the fortunes of the Children's Home, and upon the Methodist people, so far as regards their attitude towards the lost and helpless children of the nation. The beginning was small. Twenty-six boys, varying from ten to fourteen years of age, who formed the band and the choir at Bonner Road, were taken by Mr. Stephenson on a tour. Their first meeting was held at Grantham on Monday, January 14; the next at Doncaster on the Wednesday; then followed a meeting on Friday at Newcastle, and at Gateshead on Saturday. They went back to Newcastle for a second meeting on the Monday, and the tour ended with one at the Victoria Hall, Sunderland, on Wednesday, January 23. Part of the report given by the Sunderland *Daily Post* will describe what has since become so very familiar to the Methodist people in all parts of the country.

The opening anthem, descriptive of the declaration to the Judæan shepherds of the advent of the Messiah, was sung with singular sweetness and almost dramatic power. In the chorus, 'If you are a dunce,' which has not a little humour in it, the young singers showed themselves fully capable of appreciating the philosophy which inculcates looking at the brighter side of things, and well earned the cordial 'encore' which they received. 'The Sleigh Ride,' illustrative of life in Canada, where the 'Home' has a Branch, was given with a charmingly appropriate bell accompaniment, and was also encored. The expressive cadences of the beautiful 'Come where the sunlight sleepeth,' were productive of genuine intellectual enjoyment to the audience; while 'Kriss Kringle' was rendered with a crispness and merry suggestiveness of the pleasant associations of Christmas which were truly delightful. There was given in 'The News-Boy's Song' a semi-comical description of a phase of juvenile life with which the inhabitants of this town are well acquainted, and it was loudly encored. 'Nellie Lost and Found,' which Mr. Stephenson said might be taken as describing the loss of children in the miseries and vice of our large towns, and their recovery for participation in better things, was sung with exquisite tenderness. The concluding 'Song of the Nations' was a great success. In its rendering, different boys were representative, for the time being, respectively of the United States, Ireland, Scotland, Germany, France and England. Each in his turn rose up, bearing a suitable flag, and, Mr. Stephenson having played an appropriate prelude, sang a verse expressing an appropriate sentiment. In addition to the musical performances, the audience was treated by two of the youngest boys to an exhibition of some wonderful feats of memory, showing the astonishing efficacy of the memory system invented by Mr. Stokes, who has been a good friend to the Institution. Mr. Stephenson, who was supported on the platform by the Rev. W. Brown, Wesleyan minister, made in the intervals a series of short speeches explaining facts and incidents in connexion with the Institution. In conclusion, he expressed, on behalf of the children whom the boys present represented, and on behalf of himself, cordial thanks to their friends in Sunderland for the warm reception they had given them. It might not be known, he said, but it ought to be, that in this trip they did not expend one farthing of personal expenses beyond the mere railway fare. The boys were entertained by kind friends in the various towns they visited. In this town so many kind offers had been made, that very many more homes might have been obtained than were required. This generous hospitality had very much touched him. The singing of the National Anthem closed the proceedings.

By means of this trip a net sum of about £400 was raised on behalf of the Home. A second trip was taken in February and March, and a third later in the year. These meetings were much appreciated, and gave large opportunity to Mr. Stephenson to expound the principles of his work to the people in all parts of the country, and were so financially valuable that they grew to be a permanent feature of the work. Some fear was expressed at first lest the children who were taken on these trips, and were entertained in the homes of people of all classes, should be damaged in character by the attentions they received, and by the freedom from the ordinary routine duties of their life. Mr. Stephenson gave great attention to this matter, and in 1884 writes as follows about it :

'Prudent people sometimes say to me, "Do not these tours tend to unsettle and spoil your children ?" I admit, this is not an unnatural query, and it is, of course, one which occurred to my own mind sooner than to anybody else's, for I had to consider this question before we accepted the very first invitation to visit a country town. And perhaps it may not be too presumptuous to ask our friends everywhere to give us credit for carefully considering the best interests of the children, and for being better able to judge what is for their best interests than those persons can who, however kind and judicious, have not our opportunities to judge of the matter.

'I fully recognize that if a number of children were employed for any large part of their time in moving from place to place, the result would certainly be to lessen the probability of their settling down to the quiet and steady employment of their after-life. But this is not the case with our children. The time occupied by such visits in the course of the whole year is not equal to an ordinary child's Christmas holidays, and even that is divided by periods of several months' steady routine work at home. The tours are, therefore, no more unsettling to them than holidays are to ordinary children. And it should be remembered that our children get no holidays such as are enjoyed by those who are wealthier, or even by the children of the working classes. All work and no play makes Jack a dull boy, and we believe that these very occasional absences from the routine employments of their daily life tend to quicken and brighten them, and render them more valuable in any employment to which they may afterwards be devoted.

'Besides, the kindness that is shown to them in the homes of those who are good enough to receive them on our visits, produces upon our children the happiest effects; and we may be quite sure that it is a great moral advantage to any child to be treated as though it were worthy of respect and kindness. Far more children go to the bad because they feel that nobody cares for them, and, therefore, they care for nobody, than because too much kindness has been shown to them. Wichern felt this so strongly that even when he was dealing with the criminal classes of Hamburg, it was a part of his system to send out his children for a monthly visit to the house of some patron. That wise man knew well that converse with those who were better and happier would tend to elevate the taste and purify the ambitions of those whom he was so anxious to save. The lot of our children in life will be stern and hard enough, and a little sunshine, allowed to break in upon their earlier years at judicious intervals, will only tend to strengthen and invigorate the elements of good which exist within them.

'Besides all this, an ounce of experiment is worth a ton of theory, and our experiment in this particular has now been going on for seven years. Nearly all the children who went on our first tours have left us, and many of them have been for several years out in the world. We are not able to trace in one single case the slightest injurious effect from their experiences in this way. In many cases we are able to trace definite advantage, and it is satisfactory to know that our experience is confirmed by that of the Stockwell Orphanage, under the shrewd and able presidency of Mr. Spurgeon.

'In all this I have not referred to the advantage derived from these tours by the work itself, for no financial or political advantage that could accrue should be set against any moral harm which might come to the children. But knowing that no moral harm does come, it is satisfactory to be able to trace in the minds of multitudes of friends the quickened and deepened interest which is secured by occasional visits of our young people to the towns in which subscribers live. The greater part of our friends cannot see the Homes, or become acquainted with the work from actual observation. Many of these, after seeing the children, and hearing some of their sweet songs, and especially after having entertained them a day in their houses, take an actual and personal interest in our work such as nothing else could give them. On the whole, therefore, we are convinced that, under careful management, our tours will continue to be of great advantage to all concerned.'

There was another misapprehension which arose among some who saw the Children's Home Choir and heard them sing. The children looked so clean, happy, intelligent, and even refined, that some imagined that Dr. Stephenson must be abandoning his original idea of rescuing waifs and strays. His answer is : 'Nothing could be farther from the fact. It is true that we do receive, and have received for many years past, a large number of orphan children of the reputable and godly poor, but we have never ceased to receive the waif children, the outcast children, nor to consider that theirs is the first and strongest claim upon us. There has never been a moment yet in the history of our work when such children did not constitute the great majority. But the truth is that when they come under our care for two or three years, a great and wonderful change passes over their appearance and their manner, and, thank God, their spirit too. When the Choir is present at any meeting, I, of course, feel bound to make no personal reference to any one of them. To do so would be to forget the obligations resting upon one both as a Christian and as a gentleman; but if it were right to tell the facts as they exist in the case of some genteel-looking, bright and intelligent members of our choir, our friends would learn that they belong to the very class of which I have been speaking. We ourselves are amazed as we notice the effect of careful treatment, quiet and steady discipline, and the gracious influence of family life, even upon those children whose lot has been most sad, and whose prospects were once most hopeless.'

To all this we may add that the tours afforded to Mr. Stephenson the opportunity of expounding to audiences full of interest and sympathy the great underlying principles, not only of his work, but of Christian responsibility for the care of childhood in general. It would not be possible to estimate how much was done in the children's cause in this way; but it may certainly be counted that a great and effectual appeal for sympathy, for practical religion, and for faithfulness in the care of the nation's neglected little ones was thus made.

The price that had to be paid was of another character, and perhaps was not anticipated, as any possible perils to which the children might be exposed had been. It is indicated in a set of Instructions and Advices to the Officers of the Children's Home. This document ends as follows:

Since the Principal has to take a general oversight of the Home in all its Branches, as well as to advocate the cause publicly, it is impossible for him to attend constantly and personally to all details. Where the word Principal occurs, therefore, in these advices, it must be understood to mean either him or the Governor of the Branch Home, or in the case of the London Home, the Secretary, who is also Deputy-Governor.

In a word, Mr. Stephenson lost that time spent in living in the Home which had given him close personal touch with the children he loved so well. The corn of wheat had to die in order to bear larger fruit. In order to plead the children's cause to the whole country, he sacrificed that daily intercourse with them and fatherly care of them which had been the very joy of his life. Others must necessarily take his place. It is perhaps not too much to say that he never fully adjusted himself to this change, and that as the years passed on it became a keen pain to him to realize that he could not continue to be in precisely that intimate personal relationship with each child of the Home that had given him, for all its anxiety and burden, the sweetest joy of his life.

CHAPTER XV

Admission of Laymen to Conference—Thanksgiving Fund—Hymn-book Committee—Legal Hundred—Œcumenical Conference—Degrees.

As the work of the Children's Home won the heart of the Methodist people, the Principal grew rapidly in public favour, and his voice became a powerful one in the deliberations of Conference. We have seen him in his younger days, a vigorous and unashamed politician, so far as the great social interests of the nation were concerned, and a strenuous fighter for liberty in the Church. His conceptions of Church life and service were, as we have seen, deeply influenced by his study of the 'Inner Mission'' in Germany, and he developed an intense conviction, which cannot be too much emphasized, that all his social work was not only spiritual in itself, but had, and must have for its purpose and aim, the bringing of the children to Christ, and their development in a life that could only find its full expression in Church membership, and confessed allegiance to the Lord.

The prominent ecclesiastical question at this time was that of the share of the laity in the government of the Church. John Wesley's Society had gathered round the personality of its founder and that of his preachers, and the early Methodist ministers all had a right to feel that it was more true to say that they had made the Church, than that the Church had made them. They looked upon their people as 'those who had voluntarily associated themselves with them,' and considered therefore that the flock they had gathered ought to be willing to accept their government and protection. The politico-ecclesiastical history of Wesleyan Methodism is very largely the story of how the autocracy of John Wesley, continued by his Conference of preachers, slowly, and not always willingly, yielded to the public sentiment of the times, which demanded government more and more democratic in its principles and methods.

The institution of 'Committees of Review' provided, at the time we are dealing with, for some considerable expression of the opinions of laymen on matters of Church government. These Committees were large assemblages in which considerable numbers of the principal laymen of the Connexion met in preparation for the Conference, went through the business of the various departments of Methodism, and drew up statements and proposals on which the Conference could take action. Such an arrangement was obviously only a half-way house, and must logically be followed by the admission of the laymen to the Conference itself.

Here again we find Mr. Stephenson taking the part of pioneer. At the Conference of 1873 he moved a resolution in favour of a Committee being appointed to inquire into the legal aspects of the question of the admission of laymen to Conference, with a view to its favourable consideration. In his speech he argued that it was already being said that changes in this direction must come before long. The Conference had for a long time admitted lay influence in all their proceedings; only making an exception of purely ministerial affairs. In District Meetings, and in Preparatory Committees, laymen already took part in their business. Under these circumstances, he held that the admission of laymen into the Conference itself was now purely a question of expediency. He contended that there was no reason to fear any legal difficulty. The present system was a costly and cumbrous one, and a bar in the way of steady progress. Moreover, as a matter of fact, it really gave undue power to the laity, because the Conference deferred so much to the opinion expressed in the Committees of Review, whereas, if the laymen were in the Conference itself they could be met in equal debate. The existing system also unduly favoured wealthy laymen. He thought that admission to Conference would bring among them a number of quiet, thoughtful men, who were hard at work, and who, if they had not great fortunes, and could not offer them very large gifts, could give advice and judgement which would be exceedingly valuable.

Moreover, the time was a time of profound peace, and it would be much wiser to deal with the question while it could be amicably settled, than to postpone the matter to troublous times, when they might have to act under great pressure.

The Conference did not at once listen to Mr. Stephenson's proposals. The 'previous question' was carried, and all that was done that year was to appoint a Committee charged with the duty of reporting on the constitution of the Committees of

Review, and the regulation of their business. However, the matter had been set in motion, and next year a larger and more important Committee was appointed, on which Mr. Stephenson's name appears.

On receiving this Committee Report in 1875, the Conference resolved that the time had come when a comprehensive plan should be devised for more direct and adequate representation of the laity in the transaction of the business of the Conference. Two. Committees were now appointed, one of ministers only, and the other of ministers and laymen, to give further consideration to the whole subject, and obtain legal advice. Mr. Stephenson served on these Committees, and worked actively in favour of the change, and when their Report was brought into the Conference of 1876, he again spoke in favour of the scheme.

In a private letter he says:

'I spoke this morning, and got a good hearing. Towards the end of the morning we got Osborn to speak (on the other side); he spoke for an hour and twenty minutes, but he produced little effect. I think we are sure to get a vote in favour of the scheme, but by how many of majority I cannot guess yet.'

Later on in the week, he writes (after the vote had been taken, the majority proving a very large one):

'The impression made by the vote of yesterday is very profound. . . . This is a great mercy, because there will be no contention during the year.'

The Resolutions carried in 1876 were referred to the Districts, in accordance with the provisions of the Constitution—that all new legislation shall have this further consideration before being finally passed. They were adopted in 1877, and brought into operation in the Conference of 1878. They provided for two Sessions of the Conference, one called the Pastoral and the other the Representative Session. The Pastoral Session met first, and consisted of ministers only. The subjects referred to it were all questions concerning doctrine and discipline, whether of ministers or of members ; and the final decision in all cases of ministerial appointment. It also retained the right of electing the President and the Secretary. The Representative Session, which met a week later, had to do with all business concerning the Committee of Privileges, Home and Foreign Missions, Chapel affairs, the Children's Fund, the Worn-Out Ministers' Fund, the Theological Institution, Education, &c. This arrangement has since been subject to two alterations. The inconvenience of having the Ministerial Session first was soon felt, and led to the Representative Session being sandwiched between two sittings of the Pastoral Session, and when that plan also proved unsatisfactory, to the present arrangement, by which the Representative Session meets first.

It is significant, both of the trend of public opinion and of the effect of the disasters of 1849 and the succeeding years, that this change was carried out 'without the loss of a single minister or the alienation of one member.'

The great leader of the Conference in making the change was the Rev. James H. Rigg, D.D., who was chosen to preside over the first Conference that met under the new conditions—the Bradford Conference of 1878.

It was resolved to celebrate this peaceful and happy solution of a long-standing difficulty by the raising of a great Thanksgiving Fund, and Mr. Stephenson was appointed one of the General Secretaries. The Fund came at a time when it was peculiarly welcome to him, because of the exigencies of his own work. As we have already seen, the development of the Children's Home had been seriously hindered by constantly recurring debts. In this it was only in the same position as many of the great Departments of the Wesleyan Methodist Church. In particular the Foreign Missionary Society was compelled to adopt a distressing system of retrenchment, at the very time when the world was everywhere opening the door for the gospel. The Conference authorized the summoning of a large and representative body of ministers and laymen to consider the proposal. Dr. Rigg, as President, made a great speech, outlining the scheme. It was proposed to deal with debts on the various Funds amounting to £58,000; to provide £25,000 for the Theological Institution, to be used for the erection of a new College at Handsworth, Birmingham; and to devote £121,000 to the promotion of various schemes of Extension.

The first meeting to promote the Fund was to be held at City Road. The Report of the Thanksgiving Fund tells us:

After the first explanatory statement by the President, very little was said about the particular objects which were included in the Fund. But much was said as to personal obligation to God; much as to the preciousness of Christ to the soul; and instead of there being any difficulty in securing the subscriptions, there seemed to be a loving and gracious competition all through these services in laying some offering, whether larger or smaller, at the feet of our Lord and Master. That meeting sent a thrill of holy excitement throughout the Connexion, and under God did very much to secure the success of the entire scheme.

The Children's Home, under these first proposals, was to receive £5,000, £4,500 of which was needed for the payment of debt. Before long it became clear that a very considerable amount of money would be raised beyond what was provided for in the original scheme. 'The first new claim upon the expected surplus arose from the most generous proposal of Mr. Solomon Jevons, who has for some time cherished the hope of assisting to found, as a new development of the work of the Children's Home, an Orphanage for children of Christian, and especially of Methodist, parents. He, besides subscribing £1,000 to the general Fund, offered to give £9,000 towards the foundation of such an orphanage on condition that the Connexion would provide £10,000 more for the same purpose. To so noble an offer there could be but one response. The Committee, with great pleasure, resolved to recommend the Conference to accept it, in the hope of seeing this Institution speedily rise up to dignify and delight our Church.'

The actual amount raised by the Thanksgiving Fund was £297,500.

Mr. Stephenson had been appointed one of the four General Secretaries, and during the five years in which this Fund was being gathered, he laboured abundantly in its interests. He took charge of the Office, and was specially responsible for London, and the South and West of England. He writes about it :

'It was indeed a heavy burden, the more so because trade was greatly depressed, and some of our most generous people could not at the time do what their hearts prompted. . . . But the tide was rising, and our people many of them felt something of the glow and enthusiasm which marked the first centenary of Methodism. The movement was helped greatly by a series of letters to our papers, contributed by Mr. T. P. Bunting, who had a more intimate acquaintance with the great fund of 1839 than any other person then living. Many people of varying financial ability gave to the Fund donations which implied much self-denial. A high note was struck by the gift of Mr. James Wood, who died only a few years after seeing the conclusion of this great effort.'

During the years while the admission of the laymen to Conference was being debated, a Connexional matter of a very different kind had arisen, which also appealed very strongly to Mr. Stephenson. Wesley's hymns had, as they still have, a very strong hold of the religious affections of the Methodist people ; but it was already felt that there was now a great treasury of praise outside this collection, and the people were demanding that they should be allowed to sing the new hymns along with their own much-loved old ones. The matter was made more urgent because of some question as to the continuance of the copyright of the book, which had been originally published by John Wesley in 1780; and the London Book Committee, of which the Principal of the Children's Home was a member, proposed to the Conference of 1874 that a new book should be forthwith prepared. The Conference thereupon appointed a number of ministers to act with the Book Committee in its preparation. Mr. Stephenson, who had already begun to form his own remarkable collection of Hymn- and Tune-Books, shared the conviction of Immanuel Wichern, of the Rauhe Haus, as to the great spiritual value of hymn singing, and moreover was himself a composer both of hymns and tunes. He, therefore, threw himself into this work with great earnestness. The hymn-book produced under these circumstances, and published in 1876, was obviously an attempt at compromise. The old volume of Wesley's Hymns was left very nearly in its previous condition; and a Supplement of nearly equal size was added to it. After the hymn-book thus formed had been used for nearly twenty-five years, the Conference of 1901 appointed another Committee of Revision. This Committee, upon which Dr. Stephenson also served as a very active member, entered upon its work with more thoroughness, and published in 1904 the Hymn-book still in use in the Wesleyan Methodist Church.

It contains two hymns composed by Dr. Stephenson: No. 765, a hymn for Deaconesses, 'Lord, grant us, like the watching five,' and No. 922, 'Fading like a life-time.' It is matter for regret that a place was not also found for the most popular and successful of all his hymns, 'Jesus saves me now.' This hymn was composed and sung by him in connexion with some great Revival Services at Brighton, held by Moody and Sankey.

It should be noted here that he himself prepared and published several Hymn-books and Service Books for the use of the Children's Home, and of young people generally. His knowledge of existing hymns and tunes was very extensive, and his taste good. In his earlier days, as we have seen, he had himself made singing a very powerful part of his ministry, and in the Children's Home he used it as a great means of religious and social discipline.

There is one honour given by the vote of the Wesleyan ministry which is very frankly prized by every one to whom it comes. Election into the Legal Hundred carries with it no special privileges, except that of a permanent seat in the Conference. When John Wesley appointed 'one hundred preachers of God's Word' to exercise those rights and privileges in connexion with the government of Methodism which had been his own, he wrote a letter which was read after his death in the first Conference, beseeching the hundred men to whom he had thus given power never to separate themselves from their brethren. They at once resolved that they would not do so, and from that day to this the Legal Hundred have held their power as a trust. All decisions are arrived at by the Conference as a whole. The Hundred never hold any separate discussion, and never take a separate vote on any matter that may arise, except for the purpose of giving legal validity to what has been done by the whole Conference. When the meetings of the Conference come to a close, its proceedings are solemnly ratified by a vote of the Hundred, which does not attempt to revise or correct them in the slightest particular. To elect a minister into the Legal Hundred is, therefore, to trust him with preserving the liberties of his brethren, and it is an honour of which men are unashamedly proud. Mr. Stephenson was so elected at the Conference of 1880; his activity in connexion with the admission of Laymen and his services in connexion with the Thanksgiving Fund no doubt having their influence upon the vote, as well as the great work he was doing at the Children's Home.

We have noted the interest Dr. Stephenson took in drawing together the branches of American and British Methodism. So far back as 1876, the General Conference of the Methodist Episcopal Church of the United States, sitting in the city of Baltimore, had taken action towards the calling together of a representative body from all the various companies of Methodists throughout the world. By 1878 the project had taken shape sufficiently to be brought before the English Wesleyan Conference, then assembled in Bradford, under the presidency of Dr. Rigg. Communications proved satisfactory, and an Œcumenical Conference was arranged to be held at City Road Chapel, London, in 1881. There were to be four hundred delegates, one half chosen by the Methodist Churches in Europe and their Missions, to be called the Eastern Section, and to have as its head the President of the Wesleyan Methodist Conference; the other half to be chosen by the Methodist Churches of America with their Missions, and to be under the presidency of Bishop Simpson.

On Wednesday, September 7, 1881, they assembled. They represented twenty-eight different denominations. 'They came from England, Ireland, Scotland, France, Germany, Italy, Norway, Sweden, Switzerland, Africa, India, China, Japan Australia, New Zealand, Polynesia, and from all sections of the United States, from Canada, Nova Scotia, New Brunswick, South America, and the West Indies. They belonged, for the most part, to the Teutonic and African races. The Latin races were not unrepresented, but their numbers were small. Numerous first-fruits of various races, to whom the English tongue is strange, were praying for the Conference in thirty or forty languages, and the hearts of missionaries in the assembly were often turned towards those absent brethren in hope that future Œcumenical Conferences would witness the presence of many a nation and race not now represented.'

Such a gathering as this was to Mr. Stephenson a time of the fruition of some of his largest hopes, as well as one of great inspiration. His Canadian tours had made him acquainted with a considerable number of the leading representatives from the American Churches, and he had already become deeply convinced of the great advantages to be obtained by closer union.

His own contribution to the Conference was an Essay on 'Methodism and its work for Orphans, for the Aged, and generally for the Dependent Classes.' In the course of this paper he gave an account which may be taken as a very clear and good statement of the principles of his own work, as he himself understood them:

'Now, there are three classes of children for whom in different ways the care of the Church is needed. First, there are the orphan children of its own godly poor. These have a most sacred claim upon us. Let me illustrate by a case to which I can bear personal testimony: a local preacher whose wages have never amounted to a pound a week is stricken down by fever; in a fortnight his wife dies also. The relatives undertake the care of five out of the seven children, but two are left for whom there is nothing but the workhouse. Have not these children a claim upon the care of the Church? The day ought to come when the orphan children of all our poor who have died in the Lord, and whose relatives are unable to undertake their maintenance and education, shall be folded to the heart of the Church, and cared for with a mother's love.

'Secondly, there are various classes of children for whom legal provision is made. The management and control of the institutions in which such children are to be trained is very largely given to local authorities, Boards of Guardians it may be, or Committees of Management. . . . I cannot believe but that our Church, through its most intelligent members, ought to take its full share in the doing of such work for the nation. There are defects, not to say abuses, in the management of some workhouses, which would surely cease if, in large numbers, Christian men would consent to serve upon the Boards, and bring to this service of the public and the children, Christian conscience, Christian principle, and Christian tenderness.

'There is yet another class of children for which the liberality of the Church is specially demanded. They are the children of vice; children who may be orphans, or who may not; but if they are not orphans, are more to be pitied than if they were. . . . Now, for those children the Church can do what the law cannot. The Church can deal with a child on the one ground that the child's soul is in peril. The Church may do, and ought to do, that which the political economist, or the secular statesman as such, would not feel himself justified in doing. There is many a child in this city, many a child in New York, who does not actually want bread, who will manage to keep alive, at least for some years to come, either by honest or dishonest expedients, about whom the Christian man, as he looks at him, is compelled in his heart to say, "The parent of that child is not fit to be trusted with him; the law cannot interfere. The law, if it did interfere, could not make that parent do his duty, because it could not give him the moral qualifications which alone could fit him to do it. The child, if left where he is, will certainly drift into evil, and become, morally, a wreck. For the sake of Him who took the children of the streets into His arms and blessed them, I will take hold of that child, and though it cost me labour, cost me money, cost me pains, I will try to bring the heart of that child to Jesus, and so win the life of that child for society. . . .

'In all our great populations, after our educational systems have been brought into most effective working, and our reforming agents have been set into the fullest movement, there will still remain a large number of children for whose rescue Christian love can alone suffice.

'These three classes of children are all cared for in the system of Institutions which is the most recent outgrowth of British Methodism. During the last twelve years, nearly 1,200 of such children have been received and benefited.

'I will suggest what are the three great principles which lie at the foundation of all such work.

'First, Religion—earnest, heartfelt. For whatever may be our views and theories as to the place of religion in popular education, none of us would be disposed to question that in an institution which must be to the children resident in it a home as well as a school, religion should be the controlling element of the daily life. And it is this deep and far-reaching principle which justifies the Church in doing this work. In truth, because the work must be religious, it is emphatically Church work, and for the same reason, only the Church can do it.

'Secondly, I believe the best means of accomplishing it is by the adoption of what is becoming known as the "family system," that is, the separation of children into groups, living in separate houses, in which the children, with the officers in charge, constitute separate families. In this way, the utmost personal oversight and individual dealing is secured, together with the largest allowable amount of freedom and happiness to the child.

'Thirdly, such institutions should be industrial. The children should not only be taught in an elementary school, but they should be trained by systematic employment to a certain skill of brain and finger, and to the habit of steady and systematic work.

'Give a child these three things—the fear of God, the love of home, the habit of steady industry—and you put into the hands of that child capital which, if he will but use it, will be sufficient to provide for all his needs through life.'

At the close of the Œcumenical Conference of 1881, the Grant University, U.S.A., bestowed upon Mr. Stephenson the Honorary Degree of LL.D. This was followed in 1888 by an Honorary D.D., from the Victoria University of Toronto. From this time forward he was known by the title which has grown so familiar to many of us—Dr. Stephenson.

CHAPTER XVI

Mr. Pendlebury—Princess Alice Orphanage—Mr. Durley—Ramsey Branch—Tour round the World—Decisions of Committee.

WHEN Mr. Stephenson found it necessary to appoint a Deputy-Governor to the London Branch of the Children's Home, the man marked out for the work was ready to his hand. Mr. John Pendlebury was a Lancashire man, born at Radcliffe, near Manchester, and had been brought up to a business life, which however was most repugnant to him. Although he had not many early advantages, he was of a thoroughly studious disposition, and taught himself, so as to obtain considerable familiarity with Latin, Greek, French, and German, besides devoting much time to the careful study of Hebrew and Syriac. In 1886, the University of Ohio gave him the Honorary Degree of Master of Arts. Through the influence of Mr. James Barlow, he had been received as a worker by Dr. Grattan Guinness and Dr. Barnardo, who were at that time associated in the East End of London. In their Training Institute for candidates for missionary work, he was given duties with the young men, and accompanied them in their visitation of the poor and the lodging-houses, and in their work of preaching in the streets and in the Mission Halls. Mr. Barlow had also written to Mr. Stephenson about Mr. Pendlebury, and after a year with Dr. Barnardo he came to Bonner Road, in

1874. He studied the various phases of the work thoroughly, and for many months took duty in one of the houses, so as to understand practically every detail of the inner life of the place. When Mr. Tyson went to take charge of the Gravesend Branch, at the beginning of 1875, Mr. Pendlebury succeeded him in his office at Bonner Road. It was a great blessing to the work that the services of a man so devoted in his love to the children and so competent in his care of them were thus early secured; and when it became necessary that the practical duties of Governorship should pass out of Mr. Stephenson's hands, it made the change all the easier that so competent and much-loved an assistant was ready to take them.

Mr. Pendlebury's long term of service was interrupted by one serious illness in 1889. On his recovery, he went for a long tour in the East, of which he wrote some very attractive descriptions in the *Highways and Hedges*.

We have already mentioned the magnificent offer of Mr. Solomon Jevons of £9,000, to assist in building an Orphanage in connexion with the Children's Home, on condition that the Thanksgiving Fund also provided £10,000 for that purpose. It was intended that this Branch of the Home should be of a somewhat different character from the others. It was called an 'Orphanage' rather than a 'Refuge,' because it was intended to receive chiefly the orphan children of Christian parents; whilst the original establishment in London, as well as the noble developments at Edgworth and Gravesend, were intended for children who had to be plucked out of the hand of cruelty and neglect. By permission of Queen Victoria, to whom Dean Stanley represented the case, this new Branch, which was situated at New Oscott, near Birmingham, was named the 'Princess Alice Orphanage,' in memory of the Princess Alice, who lost her life through kissing one of her own children when suffering from diphtheria. With the distinction above-mentioned, the Princess Alice Orphanage was intended to reproduce the essential principles on which the other Branches of the Children's Home had been developed.

Dr. Stephenson's ill-health rendered it impossible for him to take any active part in the arrangements for the commencement of this new Branch, and he was absent on a long tour in the Southern Hemisphere when the foundation stones were laid. The Rev. G. Osborn Bate, who took charge and responsibility of the work during Dr. Stephenson's absence, writes a very graphic description of the stone-laying :

'The weather was as deplorably bad as it could be—violent rain, with cold north-east wind—but the attendance was large, and indicated that considerable interest is excited in the locality by the movement. Every speaker spoke under trying and unfavourable circumstances ; but poor Dr. Rigg was suddenly "shut up" by a violent downpour of rain, which so came through the marquee canvas that umbrellas were opened by almost everyone, and Dr. Rigg found below him only a mass of umbrella tops ! The situation was so ludicrous that almost every one burst out laughing, and Dr. Rigg at once concluded, a few words only being said by F. W. Macdonald before the collection was made, which you will see amounted to a considerable sum. The table-cloths were then removed from the plates of cake, &c. (It had been necessary to screen them from the rain.) After tea, Dr. Rigg and I went to Mr. Jevons' house, and we had a good talk with him.'

An efficient Governor for this new Home was found in Mr. Thomas Durley. He was a Buckinghamshire lad, who had been trained as a school teacher at Westminster College. He had married the sister of the Rev. H. J. Piggott, so well known in connexion with Methodist work in Italy; and after some years' good work in England had gone out to Italy, and for seven years had conducted a missionary school for boys and girls of the middle class at Padua. Once again the Children's Home was exceptionally fortunate in the discovery of a man specially fitted for the work. Some years later, Dr. Stephenson writes about him:

'A considerable estate had to be laid out, a large amount of taste, skill, and fidelity were necessary, and Mr. Durley's various qualifications have been of the highest value in the development of the property. In the meantime, he has directed with firmness and skill the still more important mental and spiritual development of our growing colony there.'

The Ramsey Branch, the 'adopted child' of the Home, came into the family about the same time as the Princess Alice Orphanage. In 1880, after considerable negotiation, the Children's Home Committee resolved to take over the property and work of a Children's Home at Ramsey, Isle of Man, which had been conducted by Miss Susannah Gibson, of Newcastle-on-Tyne. Miss Gibson had a friend in Ramsey, named Mrs. Spencer, who had begun a Ragged-school there, which grew into an Industrial School. At her death, Mrs. Spencer left all her work as a legacy of love and confidence to Miss Gibson, whose father was, at that time, in business in Ramsey.

For some years after her father's death, Miss Gibson lived in the Industrial School. Her health failing, her aunt, Mrs. Gibson, of Newcastle, well known for her liberal gifts, bought the house now known as 'Ballacloan,' with a considerable piece of land adjoining. For the children, she built the 'Cottage,' as the annexe was formerly called, and her niece lived in the original villa. Some time before her death, Miss Gibson was in communication with Dr. Stephenson. Both she and her aunt greatly desired that he should take the Ramsey branch under his fostering wing. At her death, 'Ballacloan' was made over to the Children's Home.

The average number of children resident at 'Ballacloan' is about thirty-six. It is situated in an exceptionally attractive position. It overlooks the artificial lake known as the 'Mooragh,' and beyond it the beautiful bay. It provides all the delights which the seaside affords to children.

When the work was taken over, Miss Hurley, who had been associated for many years with Miss Gibson in it, remained as Superintendent of this branch of the Home. There was sent to her as an assistant, Sister Ella Macpherson. She was the child of a godly family of honourable repute in Jarrow-on-Tyne, and had been received into the Home when the death of her parents left her unprovided for.

A lady had wished to adopt her, and she lived with her for some time; but when about seventeen years of age, tall, delicate, and in danger of consumption, she was taken back into the Home, and trained as one of the Sisters of the Children. On the occasion of her being sent to Ramsey, Mr. Pendlebury writes of her as 'a youthful officer, who has nevertheless lived long enough to win the respect and esteem of all who know her. Her promotion by the Principal to the office of Sister is a recognition of her character and worth.'

In the course of these pages we shall meet Sister Ella again in another capacity.

The close of his labours in connexion with the Thanksgiving Fund found Dr. Stephenson exhausted in body and mind. In his own words, 'it became necessary that he should put a wide distance between himself and his ordinary anxieties.' It was resolved that he and his wife and his daughter should spend the best part of a year in travel. Under these circumstances, he says,

'I chose to visit some of the principal English Colonies: for it seems to me that to any thoughtful Englishman the British Empire is, next to the Christian religion, the greatest fact of these latter days. No man, who desires to measure at their true value the great social and moral forces which are making the world of the future, should neglect an opportunity to see that greater Britain which lies all round the globe, where men of our own blood, our own speech, and our own religion, are reproducing this dear old England, with a freedom and elasticity which is not possible to us at home. I am a great believer in the future of the world. I do not think it is dying. I do not look upon it as a sinking ship, out of which it is the function of Christianity to snatch a few saved ones, whilst the great mass go down into the gulf. Rather, I believe that the morning cometh ; that there shall be a new world, wherein dwelleth righteousness ; that God will be the conqueror in the great fight between right and wrong ; and that science and art and discovery, and even the complex strifes of the political world, are by His great power being made to work together for the good pleasure of His goodness. And I believe that in the accomplishment of His great purposes the Anglo-Saxon race is, and is to be, the most potent factor. I felt, therefore, wishful to see how the young and strong communities, which have seized so many of the fair lands of the world, are forming their character, and thus determining their destiny. So I determined to take my way through the British Colonies.

'In some of the Colonies a good many of the old boys and girls of the Children's Home are living, and to me no mere traveller's pleasure could be so great as that of seeing one of my young friends, prospering and living worthily. No old stone in an Egyptian pyramid has to me half the interest which belongs to a living stone hewn out of the quarry of sin and neglect, and, by God's grace, shaped into the beauty of holiness ; nor even the Taj Mahal, though it be a very dream of loveliness, has to me the attraction of some sweet life which I can contrast with the past of hardship and shame from which it has been rescued. And so I wanted to see as many of our boys and girls as I could.

'For such reasons our decision was taken to visit the southern world, and our journey was by way of Cape Town, Natal, the Australian Colonies, Tasmania, New Zealand, and thence homeward by way of the Pacific Ocean and the United States.'

They sailed from Dartmouth on May 12, 1882, and the first person to greet them at Cape Town was an old Children's Home boy, who had found employment there as a printer.

Dr. Stephenson held a good many meetings in Cape Colony and Natal on behalf of the Children's Home and its work; and received some very generous contributions towards it.

He writes:—

'I had several opportunities for preaching the gospel to the Kaffirs. Of course, I preached through an interpreter. I had had some previous experience of preaching through interpreters—to a Dutch audience in Amsterdam, for example, and to an Iroquois audience in North America. But I never enjoyed preaching through an interpreter as I did in Africa, especially in the native church at Port Elizabeth. That is a building which, in elegance and arrangement, would do no discredit to any English watering-place. It holds seven hundred worshippers, and has been built entirely by the contributions of the natives—a few gifts only being volunteered by white Christians. The pastor of that congregation was a Kaffir, and the officers of the church were all natives, and the contributions of the people pay all the expenses of their own church. The minister is a very quick and ready interpreter, and by the time I had been speaking five minutes, he and I were running together like a pair of well-matched horses. The reverent behaviour of these sable worshippers would have shamed the flippant disorder of many an English assembly; and the eagerness with which they listened to the words of life seemed to speak of the comparative novelty of the message to them. But most notable was the singing. There was an American organ—played by a Kaffir girl—and a choir of Kaffir women and men, possessing voices which I have seldom heard equalled for compass and quality. They sang the full harmony, and specially remarkable were the rich, deep voices of the men, basses rolling thunderous at the bottom of the chord. There was about their singing something of the weird and pathetic quality which distinguished the Jubilee singers; and I have seldom been more moved by the grand effects of our great orchestras than I was by the mighty singing of these so lately rescued from heathendom. . . . A startling incident was to come before the service closed. The white minister in charge very much wanted the people to give me something for the Children's Home, and though I protested that I had not come with any such idea, I could hardly without churlishness refuse his offer. So I had to tell as well as I could of the poor children in England who were often so hardly treated, and then I said to them that as England had done so much for them in sending them the gospel, it would perhaps be a nice thing if they would make a collection for those poor children in the London streets. To my astonishment, every man present got up and went out of the church. I looked with amazement into the face of my white friend, and he said, "It is all right, wait a bit,'' and in two or three minutes they began to return, until there were as many as had been present before this startling break, and then the collection was made; for, unlike the English people, these native congregations do not come to church with a small assortment of threepenny and sixpenny pieces, but having heard the cause and considered what was reported to them, they all went home for their collection money and brought it back, in proportion, I suppose, to the degree in which the service had moved them.'

Gold had not yet come to be the great dominating interest in South Africa, but the following incident shows that, at the time of Dr. Stephenson's visit, coming events were casting their shadows before. He writes:

'Whilst I was staying at the house of Mr. Topham (in Natal), he brought to me one day a handful of what seemed to be merely pieces of metal, rough and dirty. He said to me, "Do you know what that is?" I could only answer "No." He said, "It is gold, and has been sent to me from up country, and this in a few years will make South Africa another land."'

From South Africa they sailed to South Australia, where they were going to visit relatives and personal friends. From Adelaide they proceeded to Melbourne and Sydney. The political prospects and social life of the English people in Australia interested Dr. Stephenson very greatly, and he discussed them at length in the lectures on his Travels, which he gave on his return. Tasmania was next visited, and then New Zealand, which he declared to be the finest country on the face of the earth. New Zealand scenery (and especially the celebrated Pink Terraces, which, alas! have since disapppeared), New Zealand climate, and above all, New Zealand political and social life, appeared to him to be an improvement upon anything he had yet met. He writes:

'It was not without a tear and a pang that we left that goodly land, even though we were homeward bound.'

Returning by way of the United States, they called at a happy moment at Hawaii.

'The king, who had reigned several years, was to be crowned with as much of the pomp of European monarchs as the Islanders could command. In fact, Kalakaua wore European clothing. A few years previously he had paid a long visit to the various Powers of the world, and had been received with so many salutes and flying flags and ceremonies, such as monarchs love, that he could not be happy without being formally crowned. The white population is not large, and it seemed somewhat doubtful whether an assembly worthy of so great an occasion could be got together. To help with this point, the incoming mail making for California was awaited, to give the first-class passengers an opportunity of seeing the performance. A palace of some dignity had been erected; in front of this had been also prepared a semi-circle of seats, and a platform run out from the front door of the palace, on which the officiating personages could take their stand. When we had been comfortably placed in our seats and a great crowd of the Hawaiians completely covered one side of the circle, the king, the queen, and some two or three members of the royal family came out upon this platform. There followed some men who wore something corresponding to court dress. The officiating minister was also in attendance. The most beautiful and unique thing on the occasion was a long cloak worn by Kalakaua, made of yellow or golden feathers, of such a deep and brilliant hue as I never saw elsewhere. These feathers had been collected during many, many years. They were part of the plumage of certain birds, on each of which there were but two of these feathers. They, however, were now formed into a mantle which fell from the king's shoulders and reached to his ankles. It was certainly worth going to see. The service proceeded with due decorum, and at the end of it there was a salute of so many guns.

'It was a little odd that in the evening of that day (for our ship waited till the next morning), the king himself came down to pay a visit to the boat. He was received in the captain's cabin, and there saw several people to whom he had taken a fancy, including my own daughter—then a school-girl.

'On the whole, our visit to Hawaii was well worth remembering. Kalakaua died soon after this, and the one remaining member of the royal family has now to be content to live after the fashion of American ladies.'

Landing at San Francisco, he stayed there for two days, and then went direct the long journey to Hamilton, where he found himself again in touch with the work of the Children's Home.

Some of his letters to the children of the Children's Home, written during these travels, must have given great delight to their readers.

On Tuesday, the 20th of March, 1883, after an absence of more than ten months from England, the party arrived in Liverpool, and on the evening of the same day reached the Home at Bonner Road. Mr. Pendlebury describes the home-coming as follows :

'In consequence of the late arrival of the train at Euston, the evening was advanced when the party arrived at the Home ; but the young and eager inmates were too excited to go to bed without first seeing the long-expected friends. About 9.30 the Principal presented himself in the quadrangle of the Home, which was brilliantly illuminated for his reception, when the band immediately struck up "Home, Sweet Home" ; and as he marched through the ranks of the children, as they stood conveniently arranged in open order that he might readily see their faces, and they his, a loud ovation from hundreds of hearts rang through the air—an ovation that might have made a monarch proud in the consciousness that so many young hearts loved him as their benefactor. And, indeed, we may venture to say in passing, that there are but few men in the world who can lay claim to so large an empire of hearts as can the Founder and Principal of the Children's Home. Long may he live to exercise loving rule in his domain of the hearts of Orphan, Neglected, and Destitute Children! Though late in the evening, a welcome meeting must be held—at least every one felt so. Accordingly, all the officers, children, and workpeople met together in the schoolroom, and a very pleasant meeting was greatly enjoyed by all, and a hearty welcome given to the Principal and his wife and daughter. The travellers appeared to be in excellent health and spirits, and the Doctor was obviously very much better for his recent voyage.'

A second meeting was held in the schoolroom on the following evening, when Dr. Stephenson gave some account of his travels. Subsequently, he visited the Milton, Edgworth, and Ramsey branches of the Home, where similar enthusiastic meetings were held, and equally hearty greetings expressed.

During Dr. Stephenson's absence, the Rev. G. Osborn Bate had undertaken, with the approval of the Committee, to conduct the business of the Institution, and to take some oversight of the Children's Home in his place. Upon taking up this work, the condition of the finances caused Mr. Bate some anxiety. The Thanksgiving Fund had not only provided £10,000 towards the Princess Alice Orphanage, but had in addition fulfilled its original promise of £4,500 to pay off the old debts connected with the work. Mr. Bate was alarmed to find that after this was done, there was still a very large overdraft at the bank; and the Rev. George Olver, who was also a member of the Committee, pressed for an investigation into the financial arrangements. The Committee felt some hesitation in undertaking this in the absence of the Principal, but finally resolved to do so; and with the able assistance of Mr. Pendlebury, a small sub-committee made a thorough examination of the whole subject. They found that the debt shown by the accounts for the years 1878 and 1879 was £2,276 in excess of the grant from the Thanksgiving Fund. This state of things came to pass, firstly, because a sum of £835, which had been promised and counted upon, was for various reasons never paid; secondly, because the Committee had changed its method of computation, being of opinion that certain amounts representing plant and stock, which had been formerly treated as assets, should not continue to be so recorded. The Committee also found that since the payment of the Thanksgiving Fund grant, the indebtedness of the Funds had again risen, because of a considerable excess of expenditure over income in the years 1880-1882. Most of this excess had been expenditure that really belonged to the capital account. They estimated the probable debt on the Fund on March 31, 1883, the end of the financial year, at about £5,000.

They proposed that all legacies received should be devoted to the reduction of debt, and that an effort should be made to economize on the ordinary expenditure, so as still further to reduce it; and they re-organized the financial arrangements of the Institution with a view to economy. The Annual Report tells us that:

'The income of the year shows a very healthy increase on that of its predecessors. The ordinary subscriptions and donations show an increase of £765 18*s.* 2*d.* The subscriptions from Sunday Schools also show an increase of £239 14*s.* 2*d.* The Birthday Society, which has now got into vigorous operation, has produced £655 10*s.* 6*d.* And a sum of several hundreds of pounds has been already received on account of yet larger sums which will accrue from Dr. Stephenson's visit to the Colonies.

'It would have been possible to have reduced the debt materially but for the necessity of completing several additional buildings in London, Lancashire, and at Gravesend. Several handsome sums have been contributed for these specific objects. Thus the debt remains just about the same as at the beginning of the year. Considering that during this period, owing to Dr. Stephenson's absence, there has been scarcely any public appeal on behalf of the work, this result is very gratifying. And in reference to the special items of expenditure already mentioned, the Committee would remind its friends that the Home has grown up through successive years without any large Establishment Fund. The development of the work has demanded from time to time extensions of premises, which have been accomplished either out of the current income, or by means of moneys specially raised for these purposes. The Committee are of opinion, however, that on the existing Branches of the Home such expenditures have very nearly reached their extent.

'Some desirable things remain to be done, when funds shall permit, at the London Branch, and in Lancashire there is space for several additional houses, the erection of which would enable us to make fuller use of the great advantages which that Branch presents for training the children. Since the conclusion of the financial year extensive repairs have become necessary at the London Branch, owing to the defects in the foundation of one group of buildings. But when these are effected, the premises throughout may be said to be in thoroughly good working order.'

CHAPTER XVII

The Tours—Founder's Day—A Corps of Honour—The Gravesend Holidays—Gordon Hall—The 'Maiden Tribute'—Canada revisited—The Jubilee Fund—Alverstoke—Death of Mr. James Barlow—The First Workers' Conference.

THE eight years beginning with Dr. Stephenson's return from his tour round the world in 1883, and ending with his election to the Presidency in 1891, formed a period when his life settled down more than at any other time to something like a routine of strenuous labours. The tours with the children became a regular and somewhat exacting part of his ordinary duties. They gave him the opportunity of bringing his work before the people in all parts of the kingdom. The great attractiveness of the interesting musical programme which the children gave drew large crowds, and he used the opportunity to lay his work before them as a part of the gospel of Christ, always keeping in the foreground the great idea that its final purpose was to save the children. The deepened compassion for childhood, and the awakened sense of the duty of the nation and the Church which is visible in English public life, owes much to his work on these tours. At home he was always inventing something fresh that would add interest and life to the work.

The annual observance of Founder's Day was commenced in 1883, to commemorate the beginning of the Children's Home, fourteen years earlier, in Church Street, Waterloo Road. He writes:

'Fourteen years have passed, and almost as many hundreds of children have received the aid of the Home. Assisted, first and chiefly, by the blessing of God, and supported by the faithful sympathy of many helpers, we have survived our early difficulties—have outlived the criticisms of "small friends"—and have been able to place our work on a large and stable foundation. To God be all the glory!'

'Several hundreds of our children have gone forth to situations at home and abroad. Of these, many are now married and settled in life. We have always endeavoured to keep up communication with them, so far as the pressure of our work would permit, but we have long felt that something more systematic and regular was demanded. As a first step, it was decided to hold an Annual Festival, especially for the Old Boys and Girls, to be known as Founder's Day. We did not invite the public, as it was deemed that this should be a sort of family gathering. The invitations were therefore restricted to the Committee, former officers, and old boys and girls. An invitation was sent to every former inmate of the Home. Very many who were across the seas we could not expect to come, but they were asked to send letters which might represent them on the occasion. A pretty little pamphlet was prepared, containing the programme for the day, together with a few leaves for autographs and memoranda. . . .

'Our beautiful little chapel never looked more beautiful than when, at 11 o'clock, it was crowded by a deeply interested congregation. Many of those present saw, for the first time, the stained-glass window, representing Charity, which was presented by Dr. and Mrs. Stephenson as a token of thankfulness for the preservation of themselves and their daughter in their journey round the world. Another object of special interest was a neat memorial brass, which has been placed in the Chapel to the memory of Miss Emily Newsome, known to many of the children as "Sister Emily," who recently died in South Africa of consumption. She was the first child of the Home to be promoted to be a helper in the work. After the service, it was pleasant, indeed, to see the greetings of many who had not met for years. Prominent amongst the excited groups was the first boy who had been received into the Home, now grown into an intelligent and skilful mechanic, nearly twenty-seven years old. After a good hour spent in salutations and recognitions, an adjournment took place for dinner in the schoolroom. In the afternoon the band, conducted by Mr. R. Heath Mills, gave a performance. The playing of the Band gave great pleasure, and none the less because many present could remember the small beginnings of our musical efforts, when drums and fifes were the height of our ambition. Sports, which were greatly appreciated by the younger portion of the company, commenced at 3.15. In the evening, an immense circle was formed around the Quadrangle, which was lighted by three blazing torch fires, and the Farewell Song uprose to the melody of "Auld Lang Syne." Thus ended a memorable day. To those who, like the Principal and his wife, or Mr. Horner, Mr. Mager,

INTERIOR OF BONNER ROAD CHAPEL.
(The most sacred spot of the Children's Home.)

face p. 260

Mr. Tyson, and Mr. Pendlebury, have been engaged for many years in the work (some of them from the very beginning), this gathering had a meaning that stirred the heart to its very depth. Here were represented, personally or by letter, nearly 800 young people, all of them rescued from want and suffering, very many of them snatched from degradation and infamy. And now they assembled, a company of intelligent, well-dressed, well-behaved young men and women, many of them having already risen far beyond the average of their class—not a few of them "walking in the fear of God"—and all of them gratefully recognizing their obligations to the Old Home. God be thanked for the world of evil that has been prevented, and the world of good accomplished, through the Children's Home.'

A 'Corps of Honour' was inaugurated on this first Founder's Day, to encourage excellence of conduct among boys and girls who had left the Home and were doing worthily in life. Awards were to be made, beginning at the age of seventeen. The first year the reward was to be an Album, with suitable inscription; the second, a Bible; and the third, a Badge—a silver plated brooch, embodying the badge of the Home, and bearing the words, 'For Honour,' to be accompanied by a Certificate, signed by the authorities of the Home. These prizes were intended, not as pecuniary rewards, but as certificates of character and conduct, which should encourage and dignify those who obtained them, and assist them in obtaining situations of profit and trust. Four elements were to be taken into account:

1. Keeping up communication with the Home.

2. Keeping situations, and not giving notice to leave them without consulting the Principal or Governor of the Home.

3. Honesty, truthfulness, industry, sobriety, cleanliness, civility, and faithfulness.

4. Attendance at some place of worship.

Soon afterwards, the officers and children of the Home showed their appreciation of the Badge of the Corps of Honour by presenting a Gold Badge to the Principal himself. Mr. Pendlebury wrote :

'This badge will remind you, as you wear it, of your privilege and responsibility in your life-mission in the Lord's Vineyard. Allow it also to remind you of fifteen hundred children who have been rescued, clothed, fed, trained and religiously educated by means of the Institution which, through divine grace and guidance, you have been permitted to found, and give God the glory. Let it remind you that you are surrounded by many warm friends, co-labourers in your toil, who are bound to you by the best of bonds—those of Christian love and Christian toil. Let it be to you always a fragrant souvenir of every blessing realized by the Children's Home, and when your mind and heart need comfort, good cheer and inspiration on the way, may this simple badge, by the hallowed memories and suggestions that it will call forth in your mind, be a silent messenger to minister the comfort and blessing you need.'

What this 'Corps of Honour' meant may be illustrated by the following story :

One year on Covenant Sunday, the first Sunday in January, everybody had gone to the evening service, but a boy who was being trained as an engineer was left behind to look after the taps, which were in danger of being frozen. One of the Sisters, whose room looked out over some leads, had left a fire burning brightly and the blind up. When she returned she found the window open, the dressing-table overturned, the looking-glass on the floor, and some other marks of disturbance; but some small change she had left on the chest of drawers still remained there untouched, and her watch and chain were also in their place. She at once called the Governor's attention to the state of her room. He went outside the window, and found on the frozen snow on the leads the print of boot-nails, which he promptly copied. Then going to the house to which the boy in question belonged, he asked to see his boots, and, as he anticipated, found that the nails corresponded with the prints in the snow. He went up to the bedroom and asked the boy what he had been doing, and on his attempting to stammer out some excuse, forbade him to speak, but told him to get up at once and come and see him at the office. When the lad came, he begged him not to tell lies, but to confess what had really taken place. Breaking quite down, the boy told him with sobs, that he had passed that window on his way to examine the taps, and saw the money lying on the drawers inside. He had got in through the window, and was about to put his hand on it, when something said to him, 'If you touch that money you are a thief,' and he had turned round suddenly, sprung on to the dressing-table, kicking it over in his haste, looking-glass and all, and fled as for his life. It was his victory, and the beginning for him of an honourable Christian career.

The annual Summer Holiday at Gravesend was also enlarged this year. It was arranged to spend a Sunday there, and connect the visit with some popular religious services.

The Home at Gravesend was formerly the residence of a 'county family,' and was surrounded by about fifteen acres of land which was formerly the Park. In this enclosure there were some of the finest trees in England, and altogether it was a place of singular beauty. The services proved a great attraction. In the afternoon, not far short of 2,000 were estimated to be present, and in the evening a much larger number. The hymns were led by the band of the Home, and it was an inspiring sight indeed to see that mass of human beings listening eagerly to a simple statement of gospel truth and love.

For many years, the Gravesend holiday was one of the great features of the life of the Children's Home. One who shared in it writes as follows:

'Preparations for this holiday begin immediately after the New Year! There are two landmarks in our year; and as soon as Christmas is a thing of the past—when stockings are empty, and plum-puddings all gone—then the children's thoughts go forth to "Gravesend."

'Toys and treasures, hair ribbons, tuckers, and even *pins* are hoarded up for "Gravesend." Even the Sisters are infected with the craze; for we find them begging for pinafores, overalls, hats, and any little finery that may have been sent in, and we know that these treasures will all be hidden away in some secret and secure place "for Gravesend."

'As summer advances the excitement runs higher, and at last the eventful day of departure draws near. Then what a cleaning and scrubbing goes on! that all places may be left clean and tidy; and then one evening, all the small fry are packed off early to bed, though not to sleep, so *they* say!

'On this night the rule against talking in bedrooms is suspended, and so for a while there is eager chatting, and excited laughter, and hot tossings in the little beds. But by-and-by Mother Nature strokes her kindly hand over the bright eyes, little lids droop and droop, soft cheeks grow rosy, bonnie hair, golden or dark, grows damp on foreheads, and at last our household is quiet, held in the sweet embrace of sleep.

'Next morning the bell rings as usual at six, and for once every bed is vacated with a hop, skip, and jump. There's no difficulty about getting housework done this day, for every one is good-tempered and obliging. Breakfast is soon over, for most are too excited to eat after the fashion of other days; then comes the "washing up," and a last tidying, blinds are pulled down, doors locked, and for the first time for twelve months the houses are left desolate.

'The roll is called in the playground; then heads are bared and bowed, whilst the blessing of our Father is invoked on our holiday; and finally, the eager and happy tribe troop out of the big gates, and off to the railway station, whilst a wagon-load of lame and halt and tiny brings up the rear. And—

> We're all off to Gravesend,
> To spend a happy week.

'Meanwhile, other preparations have gone on at Gravesend, and the boys there are also all agog with excitement. But real work has to be done there, for three hundred extra people have to be taken in and done foı, and that means work. The schoolroom and workshops are made into bedrooms for Gravesend and London boys; the beds are just big sacks of straw, clothes rolled into a bundle make a capital pillow, and a blanket rolled round and round is ample bedding for an August night.

'Three big tents are pitched to serve as dining-rooms, another tent makes a big washroom for the girls, who, sleep snugly enough in the beds vacated by the Gravesend boys. One boys' dormitory becomes a bedroom for eight Sisters, and I verily believe there is more racket there than in any other corner of our hive at "Gravesend."

'Our Sunday at Gravesend is an event for the town, for, weather permitting, we have camp-meeting services in the grounds, and half Gravesend comes. A platform is erected, which is occupied by the choir, the Mustel organ, and the Doctor. In front sit the band, who lead the service of praise, and then by companies upon the green grass sit our boys and girls of the Home. Rough seats are improvised for some 1,500 visitors, but beyond these there stand some hundreds more, and many of these, we are told, make this their one worship of the year. More than one, we know, has left all and followed Christ, because of the message of warning or invitation given at these open-air meetings; and that not only among our own circle, but among those outside. There are always a lot of soldiers present; and I remember how, years ago, a big guardsman, a gentleman-ranker, heard God's voice under the trees, and then and there began the new life. One of our officers got into touch with him. I believe they still correspond; and when we last heard of him, he was wearing the King's colours humbly and bravely. . . .

'At last we troop back to the station, being once more played off by the band. Here and there is a cloudy face, here and there a tearful one, as the new-made friends feel separation near, and partings are painful. And the Gravesend boys, who have little of the companionship of girls, and *who do like them*, as they naïvely tell us, are saddest of all!

'But the rain soon ceases, and the clouds break, and the sun shines forth again, and the eager voices chatter on and on, and tell all the wonders of the past. And presently, we are back in Bonner Road, and the houses and the cats look pleased to see us once more; and while the bigger children and older folk settle things generally, the little ones, too tired to play, chat in the playground, and plan more wonders and delights still for next "Gravesend."'

Another development belonging to these years was the taking over of Globe Road Chapel in 1883. The nation at that time was mourning the loss of General Gordon, who had fallen at Khartoum, and the sense of his Christian heroism was in all hearts. The old chapel started on its new career as a Mission room with his name, as 'Gordon Hall'; and the next year Dr. Stephenson applied to the Conference for an assistant to take charge of this branch of the work.

The work at Gordon Hall was at first a very great success. A local choir was formed, and if the singing was not as finished as Dr. Stephenson liked it to be, it was, at any rate, immensely popular with the factory girls and rough young fellows who packed the Hall to suffocation, and evangelistic work of the best kind was done among them.

The late Mr. James Wood came and saw the work, and advised the enlargement of the building, and provided the principal cost of it himself. The interruption of the services, however, scattered the congregation. The local choir was dismissed, and a Children's Home Choir from Bonner Road was brought in, but, great as was the improvement in the music, it was never so popular as before, and the success of the enterprise in its new form was only moderate.

At the Mission room at Bonner Lane, not far away, Mr. Frank Hills carried on a very interesting Sunday evening meeting, with a sort of Ragged-school audience, and did a great deal of good.

One motive which promoted such enterprises as this is stated by Dr. Stephenson as follows:

'The great danger of such work as ours is lest it should sink into routine, and lose its evangelical glow; but the fact of its connexion with evangelical enterprises here, there, and yonder, tends constantly to maintain and deepen the religious fervour which is essential to the highest style of philanthropic and educational work.'

The Rev. Daniel Heaton was appointed in 1886 as Assistant to Dr. Stephenson, to take special charge of the work at Gordon Hall ; and next year the Rev. Nehemiah Curnock, whose connexion with the *Methodist Recorder* made it desirable for him to remain in London, willingly accepted the position for a year.

About this time, by the publication in the *Pall Mall Gazette* of the articles by Mr. W. T. Stead, on 'The Maiden Tribute of Modern Babylon,' the national conscience was stirred as never before on any such question. A useful amendment of the law was secured, and a marked impulse given to all activities for the rescue of the lost, and the security of the innocent.

In connexion with the work of the Children's Home, it was determined to put a carefully worded placard of warning into the lobby of every chapel and school where permission to hang it could be obtained. This placard, in addition to the usual warning, stated that, 'Any respectable girl or young woman who finds herself belated and without shelter for the night in London, may come to the Children's Home, Bonner Road, Victoria Park, E. (near Cambridge Heath Station, G.E.R.), at any hour of the day or night, where she will obtain safe shelter at a small charge, or, in extreme cases, for nothing.' A Girls' Helpful Society was also formed, and a Servants' Free Registry.

The Conference of 1886 was held at City Road, and advantage was, of course, taken of it to have a great gathering at the Home. This Conference appointed Dr. Stephenson as its representative to the Canadian General Conference, and he took advantage of this visit to attend to the business of the Children's Home at Hamilton, and in the North-West. One special feature of this journey to Canada is the trouble he took to collect and narrate interesting stories of Canada and its history for the sake of the children. The *Children's Advocate* for the year contains many letters and articles which witness to his skill in selecting and telling such tales as would widen the minds and enlarge the horizon of his boys and girls.

During these years the burden of debt was still resting upon the work. An effort to raise a special Fund of £10,000 to clear it was begun in 1884, and a considerable sum, though not the whole sum required, was got together.

The Jubilee of Queen Victoria in 1887 afforded the occasion for the starting of a Jubilee Fund, which was more successful. In connexion with it a great Jubilee Festival was organized and held in the Albert Hall, on Wednesday, May 25. The Earl of Harrowby was in the chair; the President of the Conference, Archdeacon Farrar, the Right Honourable H. H. Fowler, M.P., and other distinguished names are on the programme. The Band of the Grenadier Guards, and a powerful Orchestra, including the Crystal Palace Band, were present, with a Chorus of one thousand voices, which sang Choral Hymns, specially written, and tunes composed for this occasion. Dr. Stainer and Dr. Bridge were at the organ; Miss Mary Davies and Madame Antoinette Sterling were the soloists, and a very unique and successful gathering was held. Before the year was ended, nearly £10,000 had been raised for the Jubilee Fund.

In 1887 a piece of land at Alverstoke, with useful buildings upon it, was presented to the Children's Home by Mr. Diggle, to serve as a Home for little children who would be likely to thrive in the country air, and as a Convalescent Home for sickly ones. It was also occasionally used for workers of the Children's Home, of whom there had now grown to be a large number—'Governors, Sisters, teachers, mission workers, and laundresses, craftsmen and craftswomen of many kinds'—who were any of them in need of rest and change.

On August 16, 1887, Mr. James Barlow, of Bolton, whose abounding generosity had been such a help to the work from its beginning, died. He had given the Home the property at Edgworth, and large sums of money in addition. He himself lived within a mile of the Edgworth Home, which he constantly visited. His presence there was always welcome, and was coveted by all. Especially on Sunday afternoons, it was his custom to visit one or more of the houses, and 'as he sat with a child on each knee, and a little crowd of them clustering round his chair, it was a means of grace to see that good, grey head shining amidst the group of brown and black, and to see his expressive face indicating the emotions of pity, sympathy, affection, hope and thankfulness, which his intercourse with the children never failed to call forth.' To Dr. Stephenson his death came with all the force of a personal bereavement. For more than twenty years he had been his wise and generous adviser and helper, whose assistance was all the more valuable because often they did not see eye to eye with each other, and Dr. Stephenson therefore had the advantage of being able to consider the same problem as it appeared to another faithful Christian man, with a very different outlook, especially on the business side of life.

Mr. Barlow's funeral on August 19 was attended by more than ten thousand people. His employés unanimously declared that 'better master never lived.' Mr. Thomas Walker, of Bolton, wrote to the local papers suggesting that no mere monumental stone or bust would have approved itself to Mr. Barlow's mind as a memorial of him, and calling attention to the fact that 'at the Home he had established there were tablets recording the munificence of others, but no material memorial of Mr. Barlow's own great gifts.' He proceeded to say that he found that Mr. Barlow had set his mind upon a further necessary development there. Proper workshops were wanted for teaching practically the handicrafts of the joiner, smith, bootmaker, clogger, &c. Mr. Walker suggested that a Barlow Memorial should take the form of workshops and dairy at the Edgworth Home. A representative Committee, formed in Bolton of men of all shades of religious and political opinion, to give effect to the suggestion, resolved to build as a Barlow Memorial a Model Dairy, Workshops, and Swimming Bath.

The Memorial consists of two blocks of buildings, covering an area of five hundred and fifty square yards. On the ground floor of the first block are the dairy, conservatory, and a room for knitted articles, and on the first floor the caretaker's room and the knitting industry ; whilst the second block includes workshops for tailoring, clogging, shoemaking, and carpentry. At the south end of this block is the swimming-bath. The buildings, which cost about £2,600, were opened free of debt, at a Fête held at Edgworth in September, 1889. Other ceremonies included in the day's proceedings were the opening of the Jubilee House, and another one erected by the Rev. J. S. and Mrs. Haworth, in memory of a beloved child ; also the unveiling of a tablet to the memory of the late Mr. Alderman Moscrop, J.P., who had bequeathed £2,000 to the Children's Home. The Barlow Memorial Buildings were opened by Mr. Barlow's son, Mr. John Robert Barlow, B.A., who said that the form which the Memorial had taken was one thoroughly consonant with their own feelings as a family, and one which had been also thoroughly consonant with the needs of the Children's Home. It supplied just the one element which was wanting to make the Institution complete. His father and himself had often spoken with Mr. Mager and Dr. Stephenson of the necessity for those various additions which the generosity of their friends had placed in the hands of the Trustees and the Committee of the Home.

It is a great satisfaction to record that Mr. J. R. Barlow has continued the family interest in his work ever since. He accepted the office of one of the Treasurers of the Lancashire Branch, which for many years he worthily filled, and is now one of the General Treasurers of the Institution.

The year 1888 saw the assembling of the first 'Workers' Conference,' destined afterwards to grow into the annual 'Convocation,'—a name of happy import to Wesley Deaconesses, as well as the workers of the Children's Home.

The first annual Conference was held on the day previous to the gathering of the old boys and girls for Founder's Day. It was preceded by a Sacramental Service, and time was given to a review of the work of the Children's Home.

Next year more time was taken for the Workers' Conference, which was held on September 30, and the two following days. The Governor, Sisters, and some other officers from each Branch were present. The Communion Service was followed by an address by the Principal on the Nature and Importance of the Work. A course of Lectures on First Aid, given by Dr. Tunstall, the medical officer of the London Branch, formed an interesting feature of the proceedings. Mr. Thomas Durley, the Governor of the Princess Alice Orphanage, read a most able paper on the question, 'How can we best use the Bible with the Children ? ' and at other meetings papers were read by Mr. Tyson of the Gravesend Branch on 'Reformatories and Industrial Schools,' and by Mr. Mager of the Lancashire Branch on 'Neglected Children.' The aim of the proceedings evidently was to lead all the workers connected with the Home to careful and intelligent consideration of the essential principles underlying their work ; and this aim has been successfully maintained in the long series of Convocations that have followed.

CHAPTER XVIII

Connexional Work—Committee on Church Membership—Order of Sessions—Methodist Union—Missionary Controversy—Separated Chairmen—Death of Mrs. Stephenson—Centenary of Wesley's Death—City Road Chapel.

DURING the years we have been reviewing, Dr. Stephenson not only administered the affairs of the Children's Home, now grown so large and important, but he did much valuable service in relation to the Connexional affairs of Methodism. Most of this, however, was Committee work of a kind in which it is not easily possible to distinguish the separate contributions made by individual men.

One very important Committee on which he served was that on Church Membership—a subject upon which the Conference of 1913 has spoken what many hope will be a final word. The Committee was appointed by the Conference of 1887, 'to inquire into the cause of decrease in our Societies, and also generally into our mode of Church membership, with a view to extend and consolidate the same, and to secure greater uniformity in our administration.' The Report of this Committee, which was accepted by the Conference of 1888, approved by the Synods, and finally passed by the Conference of 1889, was drawn up by Dr. Stephenson. It contains a very full, able, and clear statement of the vital relationship of the class-meeting to both the ecclesiastical structure and the spiritual life of the Wesleyan Methodist Church. Subsequently, however, this part of the Report has been passed over as something to which everybody agreed, and therefore, to which nobody need attend. One sentence of the Report has had a very different fate. It is as follows: 'It must be understood that there exists no rule which requires a minister to refuse a ticket solely on the ground of irregular attendance at class.' That sentence touched the centre of the difficulty, and from that day to this, nobody seems quite able to find words which will say clearly that the mind of the Church is that the class-meeting shall be maintained as the normal expression of its spiritual fellowship, and yet that those who are unwilling to share in this particular form of fellowship shall not, on that account alone, be excluded from membership. There has been a great fear lest, if this indulgence, which nearly everybody is willing to grant on its merits, should get formally stated as part of Wesleyan Methodist Church law, that statement would be taken to mean that it is generally no longer necessary for members of the Methodist Church to attend the class-meeting, and we should soon get a membership which has departed entirely from the old Methodist ideal of talking together about God's dealings with the soul.

The situation seems to resolve itself into the question whether there exists among us any important body of people who so desire to change the basis of our membership that they would use *any* words making concession on this point for the purpose of introducing radical changes in our doctrine and practice. Forms of words that would

AN EARLY GROUP OF OFFICERS.

[face p. 275.

be quite safe if no such purpose existed, may be dangerous if it does exist.

Dr. Stephenson, as we have seen, after affirming in eloquent and forceful language the vital significance and central importance of the class-meeting, was prepared to take this risk.

Another series of Committees which he attended was on the 'Order of Sessions.' We have already noted his connexion with this subject, which arose out of the admission of laymen to the Conference.

'Methodist Union' was a subject which he had made specially his own, and he toiled for it wherever, in Conference or Committee, he found an opportunity of doing so.

The unhappy Missionary Controversy of 1889 and 1890 did not involve him immediately, though private letters remain which show that he was consulted by the principal leaders in the controversy, and that he did his very best to bring the different parties together, and to preserve the peace and unity of Methodism.

A later question, and a hotly disputed one, in which Dr. Stephenson took an active part, arose from a proposal that Chairmen of Districts should be 'separated,' that is to say, set free from ordinary ministerial appointments, in order that they may give their time to the oversight of the work of their Districts as a whole. It is possible that the suggestion originated with him. It was warmly advocated both by Dr. Rigg and the Rev. Hugh Price Hughes, two men who did not often find themselves on the same side. Mr. Robert Perks, however, suspected it of being a development of ecclesiastical domination, and succeeded in raising such an opposition to it that the resolution was lost by a rather narrow vote at the Birmingham Conference, and it was so manifest that it divided the opinion of the Methodist people, that, notwithstanding the obvious administrative advantages involved, the proposal has never been revived.

In October, 1890, Dr. Stephenson lost his wife. She had been of a very quiet and retiring disposition, and the publicity and restlessness of his career was at first a great difficulty to her. She would have been entirely happy as the wife of a quiet circuit minister, who trod the path of duty faithfully from one ordinary appointment to another.

She came from a home where she had been trained in the simple and somewhat austere Puritan piety of earlier Methodism. Her father was a man of high religious character, highly esteemed by all around him. From her childhood she had been taught to visit and relieve the poor with that tender personal care and financial liberality which sometimes meets with scorn from those who essay to make charity scientific. Residence in London was not welcome to her, nor indeed, well suited to her health ; and the frequent absences of her husband were much against her wish. The sudden changes, the anxieties and risks of his enterprises were hard for her to bear.

She had given him much assistance in his work in the circuit at Bolton ; and when the Children's Home had its first beginnings, she gladly consented to take the first little waif girl into her own home until the House for Girls could be provided, and for many months cared most tenderly for the little one.

Gradually the Children's Home took strong hold

of her heart's affection, and although she always shrank back from publicity of every kind, she gave the children faithful and loving care, and bestowed much time and thought upon their clothing and other such domestic arrangements. Besides giving a good deal of time to a Mothers' Meeting, of which for many years she took the management, she used to conduct a weekly religious meeting for the girls of the Children's Home. For some years before her death she had been in bad health, and had been compelled to live an invalid's life.

Her daughter Dora was able to do much to mitigate her father's loneliness; and, as in all his times of sorrow, he found comfort and solace in the home of a lifelong friend, Mrs. W. O. Quibell, of Newark.

The demands of the Methodist Church left him little time for grief, and the task which called for his energies and took away his thoughts was one which appealed to many of his tastes. The Centenary of the death of Wesley was drawing near, and it was felt that it would be an entirely appropriate method of observing it to restore the Chapel which was so closely associated with his name, and whose graveyard contains his mortal remains.

Among Dr. Stephenson's minor interests in life was a great liking for building operations and improvements; and one of his greater spiritual interests was the drawing together of the various branches of the Methodist Church in England and America. Moreover, he was a convinced believer in the soundness of the doctrinal and ecclesiastical position of Methodism. The idea of renovating City Road Chapel as a Centenary Memorial, in association with all the Methodist Church, was, therefore, from every point of view, a very attractive one to him, and he gladly welcomed the suggestion that he should accept the Secretaryship of the Committee appointed for that purpose.

City Road Chapel occupies a unique place in the affections of the Methodist people. John Wesley's work in London had for its first centre the Foundery in Moorfields, but his tenure of this place was only leasehold, and towards the close of his life, after about forty years' use, it had to be given up. The City of London granted a lease of the ground at City Road for the erection of a new chapel.

In John Wesley's Journal for March 1, 1776, he writes: 'As we cannot depend upon having the Foundery long, we met to consult about building a new chapel. Our petition to the City for a piece of ground lies before their Committee; but when we shall get any farther, I know not.'

Under August 2, of the same year, we read: 'We made our first subscriptions toward building a new chapel; and at this, and the two following meetings, above a thousand pounds were cheerfully subscribed.'

He further records that 'Monday, April 21, 1777, was the day appointed for laying the foundation of the new chapel. The rain befriended us much, by keeping away thousands who purposed to be there. But there were still such multitudes, that it was with great difficulty I got through them, to lay the first stone. Upon this was a plate of brass (covered with another stone), on which was engraved, "This was laid by Mr. John Wesley, on April 21, 1777." Probably this will be seen no more by any human eye; but will remain there, till the earth and the works thereof are burned up.'

Of the opening services on Sunday, November 1, 1778, Wesley writes: 'Many were afraid that the multitudes, crowding from all parts, would have occasioned much disturbance. But they were happily disappointed: there was none at all: all was quietness, decency, and order. I preached on part of Solomon's Prayer at the Dedication of the Temple; and both in the morning and afternoon (when I preached on the hundred and forty and four thousand standing with the Lamb on Mount Zion), God was eminently present in the midst of the congregation.'

The Conference of 1890 appointed a Centenary Memorial Committee, with the Revs. Dr. Stephenson, F. J. Murrell, and T. E. Westerdale as Secretaries. This Committee at once started to raise the necessary funds; but in October, as we have already seen, Mrs. Stephenson died, and Dr. Stephenson was unable to assist in this part of the work. Later on, however, he threw himself into the work of restoration and improvement with all his accustomed zeal.

Largely at his suggestion, an appeal was made to the sister Methodist Churches. The response to it was most ready and generous, and a series of seven beautiful marble pillars given by them now adorns the chapel. The scattered members of the great Wesleyan family were thus drawn together in celebrating the Centenary of the death of their great leader.

Without departing from the original plan of the buildings, they were put into a worthy condition, and arrangements made so that the large number of people from all parts of the world who make a pilgrimage to them shall find that all that is connected with their sacred memories is reverently cared for.

The following record, which was drawn up by Dr. Stephenson, for an inscription on the walls, tells what was accomplished.

'NOT UNTO US, O LORD, BUT UNTO THY NAME BE GLORY.'

WESLEY'S CHAPEL, CITY ROAD, LONDON.

The Foundation Stone of this Chapel was laid by the Rev. John Wesley, A.M., on Monday, April 21, 1777. It was dedicated to the worship of Almighty God on Sunday, November 1, 1778. In the adjoining house John Wesley died on March 2, 1791, and in this Chapel, near this spot, his body lay in state whilst thousands of mourning visitors looked on his face. His mortal remains were buried in the rear court yard. The Chapel was enfranchised, thus becoming the property of the Methodist Church for ever, in the year 1864. It was seriously damaged by fire in the year 1879. In 1891 the Centenary of Wesley's death was commemorated by a series of services held within these walls, in which eminent representatives of all Christian denominations took part, including the Presidents of all the Methodist Churches in Great Britain and Ireland. Immediately thereafter, the foundations were made secure, the roof was raised, and the Chapel was restored and refitted, its ancient characteristic appearance being jealously preserved. This was done as a centenary memorial by the grateful offerings of the Methodist ministers and people. The Statue in the fore court was erected at the same time by the children of Methodism.

President of the Conference:
REV. W. F. MOULTON, M.A., D.D.

The SEVEN MARBLE PILLARS supporting the Gallery in this Chapel were contributed in the year 1891, in token of grateful reverence for the memory of John Wesley, and of the essential unity of Methodism, by the following Churches, which have all sprung from this the Mother Church of the Methodist World :—

THE IRISH METHODIST CHURCH,
by the Rev. Oliver McCutcheon, Vice-President of the Conference.

THE METHODIST EPISCOPAL CHURCH, U.S.A.,
by the Rev. E. G. Andrews, LL.D., one of the Bishops.

THE METHODIST EPISCOPAL CHURCH, SOUTH, U.S.A.,
by the Rev. J. C. Keener, D.D., the Senior Bishop.

THE METHODIST CHURCH OF CANADA,
by the Rev. John Potts, D.D., Secretary for Education.

THE METHODIST CHURCH OF AUSTRALIA,
by the Rev. W. Kelynack, D.D., President of the General Conference.

THE METHODIST CHURCH OF SOUTH AFRICA,
by the Rev. Samuel Evans Rowe, President of the Conference.

THE METHODIST CHURCH OF THE WEST INDIES,
by the Rev. George Sargeant, President of the General Conference.

March, 1891.

When the Conference assembled this year at Nottingham, Dr. Stephenson was elected President, at a younger age than that at which any other living man had received that honour. But his presidency calls for a new chapter, and meanwhile there is another important subject concerning which there is much to tell.

CHAPTER XIX

Deaconess Work—Pastor Fliedner and Kaiserswerth—Deaconesses in England and America—In the Wesleyan Methodist Church —'Concerning Sisterhoods'— Wesley Deaconess Institute—Mewburn House—Preliminary Prospectus—Bowman House and Calvert House—Varieties of Deaconess Work.

DR. STEPHENSON'S studies of the 'Inner Mission' had made him very familiar with the German ideal of the Deaconess. This ideal had been mainly formed by one man—Pastor Fliedner, of Kaiserswerth-on-Rhine. He had gone back to the New Testament, and to the records of the early Church, and had carefully noted the evidence that from primitive days the Church had set apart women for services, many of which only a woman could do. The deaconesses of the early Church had been given a more or less definite ecclesiastical status. They had received the episcopal benediction, and were counted as part of the official ministry. Pastor Fliedner had also visited England, and had seen the beautiful work of Mrs. Fry, who had obtained access to the prisons, and was caring for lost women wherever she could get into contact with them. He felt the need that there was in Germany for such rescue workers, for trained nurses, and for teachers, who should all of them regard their work as essentially Christian service. The story of his great Deaconess House at Kaiserswerth, and the marvellous growth of its work, deeply impressed Dr. Stephenson's mind; only as an English Methodist, he realized that in addition to the forms of service which German opinion allowed women to render, there was much work of a more directly evangelical character which the English Methodist Church would gladly take from carefully selected and well-trained women.

The influence of Pastor Fliedner's work had already made itself felt in England. We have seen how, in his Bolton days, Dr. Stephenson was already speaking of 'Our Deaconess.' Earlier than this Florence Nightingale, who had been trained as a nurse at Kaiserswerth, had by her splendid services in the Crimean War brought the value of such training home to men's minds. In 1860, the Rev. W. Pennefather started a Missionary Training College for women at Barnet. After a few years it was removed to London, where it has grown into the well-known Deaconess House at Mildmay Park. The Mildmay Deaconesses are employed in London parishes, and whilst co-operating with the clergymen in the activities of the parish, their work is superintended from the Deaconess Home. They also have Nurse Deaconesses in charge of hospitals and other similar Institutions. In 1861 Archbishop Tait, then Bishop of London, set apart Elizabeth Katherine Ferrard as a Deaconess of the English Church; and she founded a Deaconess Institution in North London under the supervision of Bishop Tait. After this other Anglican Deaconess Institutions were begun at Bedford and Chester, in 1869, at Canterbury in 1874, and Salisbury in 1875. 'Principles and rules suggested for adoption in the

Church of England' were drawn up in 1871, and signed by the two Archbishops and eighteen Bishops. These recommendations, however, have not been formally adopted by the Church of England. They hold good only so far as they are accepted.

This movement inside the English Church, however, had probably less effect upon Dr. Stephenson's mind than what was taking place in the Methodist Church both in England and America. At the Conference of 1887, the West London Mission was launched, with the Rev. Hugh Price Hughes as its Superintendent, and in November of the same year Katherine House was opened as a residence for the 'Sisters of the People' connected with the Mission. These Sisters do not use the name of deaconess, though their work is of the same character.

'The honour of practically beginning the deaconess work in connexion with the Methodist Episcopal Church in the United States belongs to Mrs. Lucy Rider Meyer, of the Chicago Training School, who during the summer months of 1887, aided by eight earnest Christian women, worked among the poor, the sick, and the needy of that great city, without any reward of man's giving. In the autumn the Home opened in a few hired rooms, and Miss Thoburn came to be its first superintendent.' The Rock River Conference, within whose boundaries the Chicago Home is situated, memorialized the General Conference, asking for Church legislation with regard to deaconesses. Dr. J. M. Thoburn, afterwards Missionary Bishop to India and Malaysia, presented to the same General Conference a Memorial from Bengal, also asking for the institution of an Order of Deaconesses, with a special view to Zenana work. In response to these memorials the General Conference which met in New York City in May, 1888, took action, formally constituting deaconess work as a part of its officially recognized Church life.

Dr. Stephenson was personally acquainted with Mrs. Lucy Rider Meyer, and with Bishop Thoburn; and this American movement deeply influenced him.

The needs of the Children's Home provided a great impetus to the ideas that were passing through his mind. He must have there a body of women trained in the care of little children, and also trained to teach them the Christian religion, if his work were to conform to his own ideal of it. From the first he was very determined to secure the most efficient biblical and other training that could be obtained in order to make the Sisters of the Home competent for their highest spiritual work; and he also recognized from the earliest times the value of definitely 'setting apart' to this work those who after due probation had proved themselves in all particulars fit for it.

The two main elements of the deaconess idea were thus plainly visible. She was a trained worker, recognized by her Church as efficient, and devoted by the solemn act of her Church and herself to her sacred calling.

It must be remembered that the Children's Home at Bonner Road always had a good deal of evangelistic mission work connected with it. This gave opportunity for the exercise of other gifts besides the more domestic ones required for the care and training of a houseful of children, and some of the

Sisters proved themselves to be richly endowed with those gifts which are most valuable in the direct work of the Church. The Deaconess-Evangelist soon showed herself among them, as did also the mission worker, the Sister with a strange power of taming wild and uncontrollable girls, and the one whose pastoral instincts found expression in loving care and sympathy given to the busy mothers and elder women of the neglected classes.

Moreover, the high character and competence, together with the gracious womanliness, of many of the first helpers in the Children's Home work, had created an ideal of the true deaconess in Dr. Stephenson's mind, which being, unlike many ideals, based upon actual experience, guided him well in giving form and direction to the new Order he was about to form.

There was a call for such workers in the Methodist Church at large, as well as in the Children's Home. We have seen how the West London Mission had started with a great Sisterhood, whose story is perhaps the noblest of its triumphs. The Rev. Peter Thompson, at the East End Mission, had gathered a company of women workers, who did deaconess work, though they refused the name and the uniform. A few years later the Rev. S. F. Collier also formed a Sisterhood at the Manchester Mission; and in many cases Churches and Missions that were anxious to take part in the 'Forward Movement' did their best to follow by setting apart women for this work. Mr. George Clegg, of Halifax, opened a Home for the training of women for evangelistic work; and, not long after, under the auspices of her father, the Rev. Thomas Champness, Miss Mary

Champness opened another at Rugby. Dr. Stephenson started the 'Wesley Deaconess Institute' only just in time to prevent something like chaotic confusion with regard to this most important branch of service. His genius for order saved the situation; and the fact that to-day the Wesley Deaconess Institute is a fully recognized department of the activities of the Wesleyan Methodist Church is due to his sense of the great importance of authoritative church government for such a work.

The Deaconess, he held, must be chosen by some responsible and competent body, acting in the name of the Church, after careful and exhaustive inquiry. She must be trained under the same auspices, and should only be set apart for the work after due probation, and by the solemn and deliberate decision of the Church acting through its trusted representatives. All this is not to be taken as in any way ignoring the fact that the vital matter is that she should be called to the work by God Himself. It is just because it is so important that the Church should be assured of the reality of this call, that its own work of selection, direction, and ratification should be solemnly and faithfully done. There were many good women called to Deaconess service who began their work without any regular authorization owing to the spontaneity and informality of the Forward Movement in its earlier stages. The West London Sisterhood recognized from the first the vital importance of the discipline and organization referred to; and to-day for the most part the Methodist Churches and Missions are recognizing the value of these principles in their deaconess work.

It will be easily seen that a work planned on lines such as have been indicated immediately required a home of its own.

In a little book, *Concerning Sisterhoods*, which Dr. Stephenson issued in May, 1890, he discusses the question of women's Church work very carefully, beginning with the early Church, going on with the Béguines of Cologne and Belgium, and then telling of Dr. Fliedner's great institution at Kaiserswerth. The High Church Devonport Sisterhood is next carefully and adversely criticized, and the deficiencies of the 'Biblewomen's' movement are pointed out. He lays down as the essential ideas of Deaconess work :—

1. There must be vocation, though no vow.
2. There must be discipline without servility.
3. There must be association, not excluding freedom.

The question of uniform is dealt with as follows :—

'Twenty years ago I had a strong feeling against the wearing of any particular garb, but what I saw on the borderland between Germany and France during the Franco-German War greatly modified my impression. And much experience in England has confirmed my later view. . . . The accumulated experience of many years leads me to believe that as a practical matter uniform is greatly preferable to a miscellaneous mode of dressing.'

The actual beginnings of the work of the Wesley Deaconess Institute are recorded in a letter which he had sent to the religious papers, and reprints in this book.

'For some years past the subject of women's work in the Church has been creating much interest.

The attention excited by the accounts of the work of the Sisters of the People has quickened and deepened that interest. It is known to some of my friends that for many years I have felt a deep concern in this subject ; and it has been one of the hopes of my life that I might be permitted to aid in the establishment upon a secure basis of an association of Christian Sisters in connexion with our own Church. Indeed, there has long been such an organization in connexion with the Children's Home. For fifteen years we have been steadily and quietly developing one great branch of the Female Diaconate, namely, that which deals mainly, though not exclusively, with the ministry of women to the spiritual wants of children and young people. The "Sisters of the Children" pass through a stated period of probation, and their work is systematized and regulated. But in connexion with our recent evangelistic enterprises another phase of woman's work has attracted attention and curiosity, and the time has become rapidly ripe for some definite organization by which women of suitable character might be trained for the service of Christ and the nation.

'I was not aware that my friend Mr. Hughes was about to make a proposal through the *Methodist Times* for the establishment of a Training House in connexion with the West End Mission, but he was aware that twelve months ago I had received a promise from our friend, Mr. Mewburn, of £500 for the commencement of such a work. It is clear, therefore, that there can be no rivalry between the two proposals.

'About a month ago I received Mr. Mewburn's cheque. The money necessary for the furnishing of the House and for starting the scheme is, therefore, now in my hands.

'Any such scheme must, of course, be of a private character, and must depend for its public acceptance upon whatever amount of faith is put in its promoters. Before any large and general scheme could be established and developed, the Conference would have to give its judgement, because any such scheme must touch our Church organization at a great many points. The relation of the "Sisters" who might go out to work in the various circuits to the Circuit authorities, and to the Church at large, must be carefully defined; and the Church must make up its mind upon the preliminary question of whether the employment of such agents on so large a scale is desirable, and, if so, whether it be possible, considering all that it must involve. The true way to prepare for the employment of such an agency is that the experiment should be tried upon a small scale. A little experience in such a matter is worth a vast amount of theory.

'But I felt that before even so modest an experiment were tried, it was desirable to have the opinion upon it of some who would be most likely to sympathize and best able to judge. On Wednesday last my friends, Mr. Mewburn, Mr. James E. Vanner, and Mr. James E. Clapham joined me in inviting some thirty ministers and laymen to an informal conversation upon the subject. About twenty were able to attend, including Dr. Rigg, Mr. Olver, Mr. Clapham, Mr. Walford Green, Mr. Simon, Mr. Nettleton, Mr. Short, Mr. Arthur Gregory, Mr. Bond, Mr. W. D. Sarjeant, Mr. William Vanner, Mr. Peter F. Wood, Mr. S. Budgett, Mr. Munt, Mr. Francis

Horner, and Mr. J. McDougall. Letters of regret at their being unable to be present, but expressing a general sympathy with the proposal, were also received from a number of other gentlemen. I did not ask the meeting to pass any formal resolutions, but the feeling that such an effort ought to be made, and made at once, was generally acknowledged. The following gentlemen have consented to form a council of advice :—

Rev. J. E. Clapham.	Mr. W. Mewburn.
,, A. E. Gregory.	,, J. E. Vanner.
,, Walford Green.	,, J. McDougall.
,, G. W. Olver.	,, J. Calvert Coates.
,, J. S. Simon.	,, W. O. Quibell.
,, T. T. Short.	,, R. W. Perks.

Mr. Perks has consented to act as Treasurer. I had the pleasure also to inform the meeting that my friend, Mr. James E. Vanner, had promised to contribute £50 a year for three years towards the necessary expenses.

'The scheme, so far as I am able to state it within the limits of this letter, is, in rough outline, as follows: A house will be taken within convenient reach of this spot, capable of accommodating ten or twelve Probationary Sisters. They must be women of good education as well as of fervent spirit. It is not intended, however, to exclude persons of exceptional force and spiritual gifts, even if they have not had the advantage of a complete early education. Applicants must be members of a Methodist Church, unless in exceptional cases. It is hoped that some will be able to pay their own expenses, but board and lodging will be provided. Three months' preliminary trial will be required; then a further period of nine months' training. The second year of probation will be spent in actual work. Instruction in Bible subjects will be given, also in such medical subjects as would be likely to be useful in the after work of the Sisters; and a portion of each day will be spent in practical work.

'I need hardly say that no vow will be required or received of any Sister; but it is expected that candidates will be moved by a deep conviction that God has called them to their work, and that they will intend to spend at least a considerable number of years in it; otherwise the labour and expense of training would be thrown away.

'Three great fields of usefulness lie before the Sisters.

'1. Moral and spiritual education, in connexion with orphanages and industrial schools, both at home and in the missionary field.

'2. The ministry to the sick, especially the sick poor. The noble vocation of the nurse is not open, as it should be, to Nonconformist girls. It is hoped that, if not immediately, yet after a time, arrangements may be made for an Hospital Training Branch of the Institute.

'3. Evangelistic visitation, in connexion with circuits, with congregations, perhaps with groups of village congregations, and certainly in connexion with mission centres. This is such work as is being done by the "Sisters of the People," and by Mr. Thompson's and Mr. Clegg's workers, and to some extent by our "Sisters of the Children."

'Here, then, is work to be done, and the means provided for commencing it. But two important matters arise.

'We must have a woman of high intelligence, of wide sympathies, and of fervent devotion, who will take charge of the Training House as the Sister-Superintendent.

'We must also have some reasonable prospect of being able to meet the necessary expense. If we could see our way clear to about £500 a year for three years, the experiment would be safely tried. £100 of this is already provided by friends. It must be distinctly understood that the funds of the Training Institute must be quite separate from those of the Children's Home.

'In this work I believe there is a force which will go far, if providentially guided and developed, to enable our Church to do her share of Christ's great work for the salvation of the masses of our countrymen.

'T. B. STEPHENSON.'

The contribution of £500 by Mr. William Mewburn, which has been already mentioned, was used in securing a house, situated first at 7 St. Agnes Terrace, and afterwards at 84 Bonner Road, which was named 'Mewburn House.' It was opened in July, 1890, with Sister Rita Hawkins and one probationer. *Highways and Hedges* for October, 1890, says: 'There are now resident four Probationer-Deaconesses,' and tells how the biblical instruction was undertaken by the Rev. A. E. Gregory, and the medical lectures by A. C. Tunstall, Esq., M.D., F.R.C.S.E., and also that the Sisters were hard at work in those practical experiences without which all theoretical training would be useless. Two of them were attached to the Rev. Samuel Wilkes' Mission in Hackney Road. Two others diligently worked in a large district belonging to the Bethnal Green Circuit.

In November, 1890, Dr. Stephenson writes:

'It would have been easy to fill Mewburn House five times over. But the persons who, having the needful qualifications, physical, mental and spiritual, for the difficult and trying work of the Deaconess, are free to devote themselves to such work, are by no means so numerous as might be supposed.

'I wonder whether I ought to apologize for daring to establish and organize this Sisterhood. It is true that I became a sinner in this way a long time ago. Years before Mr. Hughes's Sisterhood was thought of, ours was organized and in active operation. But in the West London Mission Report just published, my vigorous and eloquent friend asserts roundly that 'no man ever organized a Sisterhood.' Well, they don't know everything, even in the West Central Mission. For the above statement is almost as far from the fact as it is possible to be. If my friend had said, 'No woman ever organized a Sisterhood,' he would not have been right, but he would not have been so far wrong. It is sufficient to mention two instances. The first and greatest modern evangelical Sisterhood, the mother to a great extent of all others—that at Kaiserswerth—was organized, not by a woman, but a man, Theodore Fliedner. The Tottenham Sisterhood, the only evangelical one in England, which undertakes the nursing of two great hospitals, as well as much other work, was organized and is managed by a man, Dr. Laseron. On the whole, I think I will not apologize; but quickly go on—wishing all success both to Katherine House and to Mewburn House.'

A preliminary Prospectus was issued in June, 1890, and was as follows:

1. The purpose of the Methodist Deaconess Institute is to train Christian women for the service of Christ's Church:

A. In the care of children, in orphanages, asylums, &c.

B. In the care of the sick, in hospitals, convalescent homes, &c.

C. In mission work: (a) In connexion with Circuits or congregations. (b) In connexion with Mission Centres, &c. (c) In villages, or groups of villages. (d) In Foreign Missions. (e) Generally, as Providence may open the way.

2. Candidates must be approaching twenty-three years of age; of approved Christian character; and members of some evangelical Christian Communion. Ordinarily they will belong to one of the Methodist Churches, but if not, they must be willing to conform to the religious services of all kinds recognized in the Institute, during their residence.

3. They will be received, after proper examination, for three months' preliminary trial. If this should be satisfactory, their training will continue for nine months, thus completing a year. A second year of probation, spent in actual work, will be required before their full recognition as Sisters.

N.B.—In all cases, the right is reserved either to shorten or extend the periods of probation and training, as may appear desirable.

4. Candidates must be women of good education and address; but others will not be excluded, if they possess exceptional spiritual and mental force, though they have not enjoyed equal educational advantages.

5. Board and lodging will be provided when necessary during the period of training, and, in exceptional cases, a small allowance may be made for other necessary expenses. But it is hoped that many will be able to pay even for their board and lodging.

6. During the course of training, all candidates will be required to take:

(1) A course of Practical Biblical and Theological teaching.

(2) A course of Medical Instruction.

(3) A course of Reading in Christian Biography and Philanthropy.

7. They will all be required to spend certain hours daily in gaining practical experience in their work.

8. They will all be required to wear a simple uniform dress when, at the expiration of their three months' probation, they become Deaconess-Probationers.

9. On the conclusion of their period of probation the Sisters will be set apart for their work in a suitable service.

10. No vow will be taken by any Sister; but it is expected that those who seek admission will have considered carefully and with prayer the step they are taking, will feel themselves called of God to this work, and will enter upon it with the full purpose of devoting some considerable term of years to it. Nevertheless, any Sister will be at liberty to retire, and will be liable to dismissal if thought unsuitable for the work. And if any one should marry, or from any other reason retire from the work, within two years of completing her training, she will be expected to repay the cost of her training.

11. On the termination of the period of training, each

Sister will be expected to accept any post of duty to which she may be appointed.

12. Certain subordinate regulations affecting the daily life of the Sisters and Probationers in residence will from time to time be made, with which compliance will be expected.

At this time the Rev. John Gould, Chairman of East Anglia District, was doing much to hearten and encourage the Methodism of Norfolk; and was able to open another Training House, capable of holding five Deaconesses, at Norwich, in September, 1891, with Sister Hilda Rich as Sister-in-Charge.

Calvert House, Leicester, came next. The Conference of 1891 had appointed the Rev. Joseph Posnett to the Leicester Bishop Street Circuit, but had also elected him a representative to the Œcumenical Conference held at Washington, in October. Mr. Posnett came home from America under a great inspiration, and commenced a movement in Leicester which did wonderful things for the Methodism of that town. He also turned to the new Deaconess movement for help. The writer very well remembers the difficulty of getting an interview with Dr. Stephenson, then President of the Conference, in order to arrange things. At last, however, it was found that he would be travelling North by a certain North-Western train, and representatives from Leicester boarded this train at Rugby, travelled with Dr. Stephenson as far as Nuneaton, and returned to Leicester with a definite proposal for the establishment of a Deaconess House there. The late Mr. John Coy, a man full of love and of good works, took up the matter. His daughter Mary joined the Deaconess Order, and, as Sister Dorothy Coy, was put in charge of a third Training Home in Highfield Street, Leicester, which received the name of Calvert House; Sister Ruth Northcroft and Sister Sylvia Pryce-Jones being the first Deaconesses to take up residence and begin the work.

Dr. Stephenson calculated that these three Training Homes would between them be able to send out something like ten trained Deaconess-Probationers every year, and the demand for the services of such workers was so great that the Training Homes were always full.

The work of the Deaconesses was already showing signs of differentiation. In the Preliminary Prospectus which we have quoted, the classification had been: (a) Care of children, (b) Nursing, (c) Mission work. This last was sub-divided into Circuit work, town mission work, work in villages and groups of villages, Foreign Mission work, and a fifth category was provided for any new department that might offer. The work of the Deaconess-Evangelist had evidently not yet marked itself off as a specific and distinct branch of service; although we already find Sister Freer appointed in 1892 to evangelistic work in East Anglia, and Sister Louie put down as 'Singing Evangelist.'

In September, 1894, Sister Alice Hull is put down for 'Special Missions,' to reside at Mewburn House; while Sister Agatha Mandall receives a similar appointment in connexion with Bowman House, Norwich. The name of Sister Jeanie Banks, followed by the words 'Evangelistic Work,' appears on the appointment list continuously from the year

A Group of Deaconesses.

face p. 300.

1896; but the title, now so familiar, was not printed on that list until in the year 1901, the record is as follows: 'Warden's Office, Ilkley. Sister Jeanie Banks, Deaconess-Evangelist.'

At first the whole enterprise rested upon the sole responsibility of Dr. Stephenson himself. He associated with him a Committee of Advice, but had to bear the financial responsibility alone, mainly because of the difficulty of finding others willing to share it with him. Moreover, it was felt from the first that financially this enterprise must be kept absolutely distinct from the Children's Home, although it was desired that the two should work in the most cordial and close relationship with each other. The Sisters of the Children were recognized as Deaconess workers belonging to the same Order as those sent out from the Training Homes to work in the circuits and missions of the country; and for years they met together in Convocation, and were set apart for their work at the same annual Consecration Service.

Looking back at the work after twenty-two years, it is astonishing to note how definitely Dr. Stephenson had formed his plans, how faithfully he adhered to the principles on which they were based, and how little necessity for any kind of change had arisen.

When it is realized that Mewburn House was opened in June, 1890, that September, 1891, saw Dr. Stephenson elected to the Chair of the Conference, that in the autumn he was called upon to attend the Methodist Œcumenical Conference in Washington, and that throughout the year of his Presidency he was, as we have seen, exceptionally full of Connexional work; and when it is also remembered that the demands upon the Ex-President are only second to those made upon the President himself, it is marvellous that he was able to carry this additional burden, and launch this enterprise so skilfully and successfully.

CHAPTER XX

Presidency—Inaugural Address—Order of Sessions—The Nottingham Conference—Dr. Stephenson as President—Official Sermon—Excitement at the Home—A Notable Sermon—Œcumenical Conference—Speech at New York Reception—Methodist Union—'The Words of a Year.'

WHEN the Conference met at Nottingham in the year 1891, there were only two names that were discussed at all in connexion with the Presidency, that of Dr. Rigg, who had already been President in 1878, and whose name was suggested for a second term, and that of Dr. Stephenson. When the vote took place, Dr. Stephenson received two hundred and forty-eight, Dr. Rigg one hundred and forty eight, and the next in order, who was Dr. Randles, twelve votes.

It was customary that a President of the Conference, in his inaugural speech, should make some reference to his own career. Dr. Stephenson said:

'Dr. Moulton, I thank you for the cordial words that you have spoken to me, and it is to me a very great satisfaction that I receive from your hands the insignia of the office to which the brethren have been good enough to elect me. I think it is nearly forty years since I made your acquaintance, when my father and your father were colleagues together in one of our circuits, a good circuit, but not one of the very best. I remember, too, that your father bought for me my first copy of *Virgil,* and that when I looked ruefully upon it because there were no notes, he told me he desired I should read it without crutches. I have thought of that more than once of late, and have very much admired you for making your way to a most distinguished position by the force of your own abilities. I hope that in some humbler measure I may assume that I also have reached without the aid of crutches the position now given to me by the too great kindness of my brethren. I have tried to walk upon my own feet, and to go my own way. I am thankful to the Conference for the vote with which it has honoured me this morning. To tell the truth, there have been a good many years of my life in which I have felt that all expectation of such an honour as this was entirely out of the question for me ; because the special work to which you have referred, sir, has taken me somewhat out of that beaten track of a Methodist preacher's duties and responsibilities which most frequently and properly leads to Connexional honour and recognition. I have had to sacrifice (if, indeed, sacrifice it were) a good many ambitions in the course of the last thirty years. When God's Providence laid upon me the care of helpless children I found I must choose between the scholastic and literary aspirations of earlier years, and a complete devotion to the work thus put into my hands. I am the more grateful to the Conference because it seems to me the vote of this morning is a recognition that the work to which I have given my life, is not unsuitable for a Christian minister, but may properly be considered a part of the true work of the Church of God. Although it is a great happiness to me to try, with such abilities as I may possess, to serve the Church of my fathers, yet I confess that the recognition of the special work of my life by the Conference this morning is, to me, the dearest and best element in this vote. May I refer for a moment to my father and mother? I am not going to inflict on the Conference any lengthened speech, but we may talk to each other as brethren in a happy family reunion, without the formalities which belong to more public utterances. My father was, as many of the older ministers will remember, a faithful Methodist preacher, who, if not of the front rank, did most valuable work; and I remember with a gratitude I cannot express my dear mother's great love for her children, and the efforts she put forth in order that we might receive that education to which, I believe, I personally owe any success that has attended me in life. My father and mother had what was considered a good circuit, but their income was only £120 per year, and I remember how my mother was compelled to contrive, and pinch, and save. I seem to see her at this moment, going to the market, because no one could make money go so far as she could. I do not know whether we can quite appreciate the spirit of devotion and heroism which was exhibited by our fathers and mothers in those years. If I refer to one part of the social work with which we are charged, I am sure those who have known my life will excuse the reference. I am thankful to take the chair when we are giving to the temperance movement a new and more vigorous effort. I owe a great deal as a Methodist preacher to the fact that I have been a total abstainer. Our temperance propaganda recognizes the co-operation of brethren who do not hold my views on that particular point, and I think this is wise and salutary, but at the same time I am quite sure I should be unfaithful to my own deep convictions if I did not thank God publicly for the safeguard which the total abstinence pledge has been to me, and if I did not take the opportunity from this place of commending, especially to my younger brethren, the practice of total abstinence. I have never known my position as an abstainer prevent me from doing service to the Church, but I have known many cases in which it has helped me to do what I could not have done under other conditions, and I believe that this habit which I have been able to practise for so many years, will hurt no brother, but will often safeguard him, and indeed, very much help him.

'I am glad to be called to the chair at a time when Methodism is adapting itself in the most earnest manner to the great work of missions to the masses. I venture to hope there may not be any dead uniformity in mission work. It is by adaptation of our methods to varying needs that we shall be able to do our work best. But do we not all rejoice in that spirit of godly daring and heroic enthusiasm which, more than in some former years, is showing itself in attempts to elevate the people ? Where the spirit of enterprise is wanting there is deadness and decline. Some do not like the phrase " Forward Movement." I dare say some things may be included under that phrase which do not command the sympathy of many here. I am glad, if we must have such a phrase, that it is the "Forward Movement," and not the forward party. There is no party in Methodism, and I pray God there never may be. It would be a calamity if any section of the brethren were to arrogate to themselves a monopoly of earnestness, zeal and enterprise, or were so to glory in their own special success as to seem to treat lightly the labours and successes, however different in character, of their brethren. Do we not all need a forward movement along the old lines; more courage, more prayer, more self-sacrifice, more wisdom, more of the old spirit of which our fathers used to speak as travailing in birth for souls? I do not remember any year in which the call has come to us so loudly, "Work while it is called to-day; for the night cometh, when no man can work."'

The Conference over which he presided was the first in which the 'sandwich' arrangement of the Sessions was tried. The Pastoral Session met first to deal with appointments and other business which affected the Representative Session, and then adjourned for a week while the latter did its business, after which it was resumed, and continued till the Conference closed.

The Conference began with a particularly sad piece of news from China. There had been serious riots at Wusueh, in the course of which Mr. William Argent, a *Joyful News* Agent, who was working there, had been murdered, and the ladies of the Mission establishment had been brutally ill-used by the mob.

Among the principal subjects discussed by the Conference under Dr. Stephenson's presidency, were the enlargement of the Leaders' Meeting; and the repeal of some legislation on Home Mission affairs, the effect of which had been to hamper the operations of the central Home Mission Committee. Arrangements were also made to give up the 'Yearly Collection' in the classes on behalf of the Home Mission Fund. There was a great full-dress debate on the three years' limit of ministerial appointments. A case in which gambling had taken place at a fête in Horncastle, part of the proceeds of which were given to the Wesleyan Day-schools, created a good deal of excitement. The Bermondsey Settlement was started by this Conference, and a re-arrangement of the Committee managing the Book-Room was made.

By universal consent, it was recognized as an 'unprecedentedly happy Conference.' The physical conditions had been very comfortable, and it was felt that the President's administration had been very gracious and kindly, as well as effective.

An estimate of his ecclesiastical position was given by the *Methodist Recorder*, at the beginning of the Conference, in its Appreciation of the new President. It runs thus:

Dr. Stephenson's position in regard to what may be called Methodist politics is rather that of a mediator than a partisan. His convictions are strong, and his opinions are usually expressed with great clearness, but his Liberal tendencies are balanced, or very nearly so, by Conservative leanings. He is not the man to advocate change for its own sake, or to show contempt for the old because it is old. No one need fear that he will go to unwise extremes, and none need for an instant doubt that he will give, without fear or hesitation, all the influence of his high office to the cause of truth and righteousness and charity.

At the close of the Conference the same newspaper speaks concerning the spirit in which he had conducted the business of the Conference :

Dr. Stephenson has been so closely identified throughout his life with the homeliest phases of Methodist life and work that people have naturally been curious to know how he would take to the new position. . . . While not losing in the least his brotherliness or arrogating airs of authority or putting on a pomposity quite unnatural to him, Dr. Stephenson maintains the dignity of the Chair. He is courteous, impartial, mindful of all points of procedure, and anxious to allow the fullest expression of opinion consistent with the rapid transaction of business.

The naïve confession of this appreciation is interesting because of its surprise at Dr. Stephenson's dignified conduct. Evidently some of his brethren had yet to learn that the man who played leap-frog with his boys at Bonner Road, and had done such remarkable things in the way of popularizing evangelical services, had the grand air, and could, with the most perfect naturalness, behave with all the dignity which was called for by the great position to which he had been elected.

His official sermon on 'Our Gospel ; shall we Preach it Still ? ' was a very noble and timely statement of the evangelical position as contrasted with the sacerdotal theory. He describes this latter theory as beginning with the thesis that the spiritual life must be nourished mainly upon the Holy Sacrament of the Lord's Supper. Having made the sacrament necessary to the soul, the theory proceeds to make the priest necessary to the sacrament, and the Bishop to the priest. The Methodist gospel is described as the gospel of heartfelt experience, of a salvation which is conscious, direct and instantaneous. It is also a full salvation, and a witness-bearing one, and finally a democratic one, which is 'declared by the people, to the people, and for the people.'

'Great was the excitement in the Children's Home when it became known that "Doctor was President." A holiday for the children was at once announced, and straightway the Governor was interviewed by detachments of elder lads, bare-armed and in white aprons, from the printing department, the carpenter's, and the engine room, all anxious to know, if on this unprecedented occasion, they might not lay aside their work also, and join in the general rejoicing. Girls from the laundry, folding and sewing-rooms followed suit, and amidst much merriment, a universal holiday was proclaimed. Flags were hoisted, and children and officers partook of tea in the playground and on the balcony. Some of the little folks were curious to know if "Doctor would be President once a month," doubtless realizing that a holiday and tea in the open air, gooseberries and strawberries into the bargain, would be a most delightful monthly episode in their lives. An elder child asked, "What next would Doctor be?" and on being assured that the Presidential Chair was the highest rung of the Methodist ecclesiastical ladder, forthwith gave vent to her delight that "Our Doctor" had attained that elevated position.

'But greater still was the excitement and enthusiasm which prevailed when the President returned from Conference. The entrance to the Home was lined with boys and girls, Sisters and Officers, all ready to shout their welcome when the President and his daughter drove up. It was a veritable home-coming that could have been accorded, we dare venture to say, to no other man in Methodism. 'Doctor,' said one of the Sisters, 'money could not buy this welcome.' For little hands were thrust into his, baby fingers caught at Presidential coat-tails, the air was rent by shouts of welcome, and no wonder if for a few minutes the eyes of the greatest man in Methodism were dim with a suspicious moisture.

'Tea was laid for all in the schoolroom, and bright faces, best pinafores, and blue favours made a scene glowing with interest and life. Again the children cheered to the echo as the President and Sister Dora walked up the crowded room, and took their places. I noticed the President glance round for a peg on which to hang his hat before sitting down, but none being near, he placed it on the lowest form of a small gallery occupied by little girls. The child at whose feet it was placed looked at it with a wonderful reverence in her little face, and finally found vent for the feeling which evidently filled her little heart, by stooping and gently patting and stroking the brim of the hat of 'Our Doctor,' now invested with such a strange new dignity.

'In a graceful speech of congratulation and welcome, the Governor humorously impressed upon the children that no liberties must be taken with the

President such as were permitted when he was simply 'Our Doctor.' The children certainly must not cluster round him in the playground and cling to his arm, his hand, or even his coat-tails. The shouts of ironical laughter which greeted this statement, and the sight of the President in the playground with the children swarming round him in the prohibited manner during the rest of the evening, were quite sufficient to prove that the honour conferred upon the Founder of the Children's Home will not interfere one jot or tittle with the affectionate relationships which have ever existed between him and the children of the Home.'

At an early period in his presidential year, Dr. Stephenson was visiting Glasgow on behalf of the Children's Home, and was invited by the minister of Glasgow Cathedral to preach there, and allow the children to sing. In the sermon he preached on this occasion, entitled, 'A Plea for the Children of Sorrow,' he gives a very noble interpretation of the principles underlying the work of the Children's Home. We quote the following passage :

'Remember what our task is when a poor child comes to us from the deep places of London, Manchester, or Glasgow. He comes to us homeless, friendless, ignorant, or, perhaps, wise only in the things of which a child ought to know nothing. What is lacking in that child's life ? He is ignorant of God. He has lost the hand and voice of father or mother, or has never known any influence deserving those sacred names, and his life has been so unregulated and unsystematic, that the powers which are in it have not learned to spend themselves in any right or worthy direction. How then can you supply to the child the elements required for the right development of life? If you could throw that child into the bosom of some Christian family, and by some magic power instantly make him one of the family, what would happen? The child would find itself in an atmosphere of religious thought and feeling. Its life would be surrounded by all the sweet and gracious amenities and influences of a well-ordered family. It would receive adequate instruction, so that not one of its faculties should lie dormant, and in due time it would be introduced to some suitable and honourable occupation.

'Now in caring for children who have lost the influences of a well-ordered household, or who have never known them, it is needful to embody in your arrangements these cardinal provisions.

'There must be the highest and purest spirit of religion; no education can be complete without that. It is the very flower and crown of human life that men should fear God and become like Him. And a system which simply attaches certain religious observances to its routine as a necessary concession to public opinion, or which reduces the religious teaching and influences to the smallest possible point, is one which does not even seek to accomplish the highest and best results, and, because it misses these, necessarily misses the lesser and inferior ones. Now if you can gather the children into groups so small that each child in each group shall come directly under the influence of some superior heart and mind, and if especially you can secure that there shall live with that group of children, and play the true mother's or sister's part toward them, a Christian woman of education and refinement, you will have placed those children under conditions as nearly as possible approaching those of a well-ordered Christian family. Put the children by hundreds together into some barracks, and though you may make your building palatial in appearance, and though you may observe the newest demands of sanitary science, you necessarily deal with the children by police methods, you deal with them in the mass and not individually. Indeed, you cannot contrive any system applicable to a vast number of children together, which at the same time will allow play to the individuality of each child, and will permit that careful study of the peculiarities of temperament without which the best education of the heart and life are impossible. 'God' and 'home' are the two noblest words in the English language. These are the two thoughts to which this nation owes what it has been; and you must give to the child who has lost them, or never known them, the thought and the influence of God and home if you would have him become a good citizen.

'Scarcely less important in its sphere is the other principle which is embodied in our work, namely, that every young life should early be habituated to useful and honest work. This is necessary, not merely because without it the means of livelihood cannot be secured, but because worthy character cannot be formed either. Labour is almost everywhere the law of life. It is everywhere the law of that life which is worth having. It was no curse which was pronounced on man when he had fallen into sin that he was told that in the sweat of his brow he should till the ground. Rather in imposing upon him the necessity of duty and labour God was giving to him a strong shield against temptation, and a great power for keeping his life clean.'

Some question was raised at the Conference as to whether the President ought to leave the country during his year of office, and some brethren anticipated the possibility of serious Connexional difficulties arising if he did so. It was, however, universally felt that the presence of Dr. Stephenson at the second Œcumenical Conference, about to be held in Washington, could not be dispensed with. He accordingly took his place at the head of the British contingent. He won great favour by a speech at the Preliminary Reception in New York, from which we quote the following passage :—

'There are two strong bonds of sympathy between England and America, to which I may be pardoned for referring briefly.

'We both hate war. Our heads are not easily turned with "eppylets or feathers." Not that we cannot fight when need arises. The men who conquered at Crecy, and Naseby, and Blenheim have their descendants in the old land yet. And in that awful struggle in which you were engaged for the unity of the nation, you showed that the men who follow the plough, and wield the hammer, and ply the pen, can face sword and cannon when reason good is shown. Yes, we can fight when we need. "The British are a nation of shopkeepers," said Napoleon. After a while he attempted a mercantile transaction with us at Waterloo, and he did not get the best of the bargain. "America worships the dollar," said your enemies and critics; but your boys from many a farm, homestead, and city, soon proved to the world that what they cared for most was not the silver in the dollar, but the emblem that it bears.*

'Two great illustrations have been given of the fact that war is unwelcome to our race. The noblest army England ever had were those Ironsides who always prefaced their fighting with prayer, whose backs no foeman ever saw, and whose uplifted hand awed the tyrants and persecutors of Europe into quiet. But when the time had come for its being disbanded, that army sank once more into the mass of the population, each man resuming his trade of blacksmith or farmer, distinguished (as a brilliant historian has said) only by his greater sobriety.

'And when that herculean struggle of yours was over, the world saw with amazement your vast armies, blue and gray, sink into the substance of the people again, as the fallen snowflakes melt in the bosom of the ocean. Neither the Republicans of Old England, nor those of this Greater Britain, thought it necessary any longer to swagger about in cocked hat and feathers; they could be as true heroes at the forge and the plough as when rushing up the hill in charge upon the cannon on its crest.

'No, we do not love war for its own sake. God forbid that we ever should. I cannot recall without shuddering that one terrible moment in my life when war between my country and yours seemed

* 'In God we trust.'

almost inevitable. I have never ceased to thank God, and I thank Him once more to-night, that in that awful crisis there was in this land a great man, one whom God had raised from the soil, as He raised the first man from the soil, Abraham Lincoln, who used all the force of his personal character, and the powers of his great office, to hold in check the passionate feelings which might not unnaturally have arisen, and to give the nation time to think and let its better heart speak. And I thank God that in our land there was a woman, the best woman that ever sat upon a throne, who, when her ministers brought to her the dispatch which might have fired the first cannon, with her own hand scored out every word which a self-respecting nation should not write, and a self-respecting nation could not receive. Never were England and America greater than when that noble woman on the throne, and the equally noble man from the log cabin, said to the dogs of war, already showing their white teeth and growling, "Lie down, and disturb not the peace of two kindred peoples."

'But this is not all. I thank God that out of that great and terrible crisis came one of the most magnificent lessons ever taught to the world, and that this lesson was taught by England and America. For when your struggle was over, and you complained that we had not dealt fairly with you in your distress, there was in England a great Christian statesman who was not afraid of the sneers of the clubmen, or the curses of the worshippers of the great god Jingo, who stretched his hand across the sea to you and said, "Brothers, we are both of us strong enough to be calm and just. You say we have wronged you. If wrong there be, let not that wrong be made more wrong by hatred and bloodshed. Let us submit our case to arbitration, each agreeing to abide by the award, and to teach the world that there is a better way of settling international disputes than by letting loose the hell-hounds of war." Believe me, the time will come when men, looking back with amazement and disgust at the tiger-like thirst for blood which has so long impoverished and blighted the world, will date the beginning of a new era of peace and brotherhood from that great act of international dignity and justice.'

Dr. Stephenson's first task in the Œcumenical Conference was to deliver the sermon prepared by the Rev. William Arthur, which the latter, through the failure of his voice, was unable to preach himself. We are told that he did this with very great effectiveness, and afterwards, in the same meeting, responded as President on behalf of British Methodism to the welcome given by the American brethren.

The question of Methodist Union arose at an early period in the Conference, and Dr. Stephenson's action with regard to it has been the subject of a considerable amount of misunderstanding. The facts are as follows :

The topic for the third day was 'The Christian Church : its Essential Unity and Genuine Catholicity.' The Rev. T. G. Selby read a paper on 'Christian Unity,' in which he said, 'Let us promote this spirit by healing at the earliest possible opportunity, our own separations and estrangements as

Methodists. We can never become a providential force in the reunion of evangelical Christendom unless we first close up our own ranks and stand shoulder to shoulder. Let us go from this gathering with the steadfast faith in our hearts that we shall see a united Methodism.' These words awoke many echoes.

The Rev. Thomas Mitchell (Primitive Methodist), asked, 'Is the organic union of British Methodism desirable?' and answered his question in the affirmative. Then he asked, 'Is the organic union of British Methodism practicable, and if so, how?' He said, 'I speak for myself alone, and have no mandate from the Church to which I belong. . . . It may be that we shall not be the first to move, but Primitive Methodists are sensible people, and I may venture to prophesy that when the battalions of a united Methodism move as a leading force to the conquest of the world for Christ, the stalwarts of the Primitive Methodist contingent will not be found apart or behind.'

Another speaker, the Rev. W. B. Lark (Bible Christian), said, 'As regards the union of Methodism in the old country, there are many of us who believe that we are ripe for such a union, and if we are not, I do not see anything to object to in our hastening the ripening process.' Others spoke in similar tones, and the midday adjournment found men anticipating that the time had come for some decisive action.

At the Afternoon Session the Rev. William Redfern (United Methodist Free Church), made a direct appeal to Dr. Stephenson in the following terms: 'May I not, then, submit to Dr. Stephenson, the President of the Wesleyan Conference, and one of the most Catholic minds in Christendom, that if he will place himself in communication with the Presidents of the other Methodist bodies, and with the leaders of our Methodist world, and by their co-operation will initiate some step toward federation, he will make his presidential year the most memorable year since the time of John Wesley?'

Dr. Stephenson did not at once reply, and in the discussion which followed, the Rev. Price Hughes declared himself in favour of organic union as 'the only kind of effective co-operation between Methodists.' Dr. Stephenson, after first dealing with some statements made by Mr. Price Hughes, said, 'But, sir, I arose because a personal appeal was made to me. Although I have no authority whatever, or any mandate to speak for my Conference, and I therefore cannot pledge it to anything I may now utter, yet I am quite at liberty to say that it will be the greatest joy to me to meet my brother Presidents of the Eastern Section, and, if possible, devise some plan by which one step further in the direction of union can be taken, a step which I hope will be so wisely and carefully taken that we shall not have to draw back from it, a step which I trust may lead on to other steps, until, in God's own time, we may realize the fulfilment of all these hopes and prayers, and the Eastern Section of our great Methodism may be united together as it never has been before.'

Before the Conference adjourned, representatives of the United Methodist Free Church, the New Connexion, the Primitive Methodist Church, the Bible Christians, the Wesleyan Reform Union, and the Independent Methodist Church, all stated that they would be willing gladly to respond to the appeal which Dr. Stephenson had made. An impression was created that the Wesleyan Methodist Church had been pledged by this action beyond what it was prepared for, but certainly no word was spoken by Dr. Stephenson that did not carefully distinguish between his own private willingness to confer with the leaders of the other Methodist Churches on the subject, and official action as President of the Conference, which he was not at liberty to take. Even so, there was some protest and misunderstanding in the Conference itself; and it is possible that the cause of Methodist Union was hindered rather than helped by this episode.

We have the following picture of Dr. Stephenson preaching to a coloured audience at the Metropolitan Zion Church at Washington:

'The service before the sermon was conducted by the Bishop. It consisted to a great extent of chanting and musical responsive readings. Throughout the prayer the "Amens" and other ejaculations were continuous, and in no sense objectionable, but, on the contrary, intelligent and inspiring.

'The President in all his preaching has aimed distinctly at usefulness. He had a good time on Sunday night, preaching with great power and old-fashioned unction. For the after-meeting everybody remained. The President sang for the people and taught them to sing with him. During the prayers there were loud outcries, as there had been towards the close of the sermon. Several women were seized with peculiar convulsive shakings which they evidently strove to control. One sister, however, was hopelessly moved. She lifted up her voice, flung her arms around her neighbours, shook them, rose from her seat and seized a white woman, one of the few present, and greeted her with shaken expressions of joy. Finally she executed a flank movement along the aisle under the platform, halting in front of our astonished President, for whose special benefit she danced, leaping and shouting. The curious fact in this performance was that no one seemed to regard it as out-of-the-way. There are often much more exuberant manifestations. Sometimes the members will rise and march in procession, chanting their quaint negro melodies. But all this is a survival of a condition of things which is passing away. In the opinion of the wisest men who have inquired and taken personal observations, the coloured people are best left to work out their own destiny under the rule of their own Bishops and educated ministers—men of sense and piety, in many instances possessed of by no means contemptible scholarship.'

When Dr. Stephenson returned to England he threw himself into the great round of duties which the Wesleyan Church has come to expect from its President; and at the year's end he published a book entitled *The Words of a Year*, which contains some of the more important sermons and addresses he had given. Besides the Presidential Sermon and that preached in Glasgow Cathedral, to which we have already referred, this book contains others preached at the Œcumenical Conference, the re-opening of City Road Chapel, and at the

Portland Chapel in Bristol (after City Road, historically the most interesting chapel in the Methodist world, and the shrine and symbol of lay preaching). The principal subject of these sermons is the distinctive doctrines of Methodism. There are also discourses on Social Christianity, one preached in connexion with the London County Council Election, and another given at one of the Rev. H. Price Hughes' St. James's Hall Conferences. The book also contains the address at the reception in New York. These sermons show Dr. Stephenson at his best as a preacher, and bring out very distinctively the central character of his message. It was evidently the great essential doctrines of redemption which dominated his mind, and he expounds them with much lucidity and force.

During his Presidential year the Treasurers and Officers of the Children's Home, in order to relieve him of financial anxiety in connexion with his own special work, raised a 'Presidential Fund,' by means of which more than £9,000 was brought into the exchequer of the Children's Home; and he was thus set free to give his undivided attention to the public duties which were called for by his official relation to the whole of the Wesleyan Methodist Church.

CHAPTER XXI

Offer of Church in America—Grindelwald Conference—Baroness Langenau—Second Marriage—Chairman of First London District—Superintendent of Victoria Park Circuit.

IMMEDIATELY after the close of his Presidency, an offer was made to Dr. Stephenson of a very important position in connexion with the Methodist Church in the United States, namely the pastorate of the Metropolitan Church at Washington.

A letter exists which he wrote to a friend in connexion with this offer, and it is of the utmost value as affording an insight into the view he himself took of his own position and work. It is as follows :

'*October* 21, 1892.

'MY DEAR FRIEND,

'I have heard from Dr. Moulton, on the subject of my going to America. Like Dr. Rigg, he thinks that an enormous field of usefulness would lie before me there, and that I have been in a very unusual way prepared to enter upon it. On the other hand, he speaks appreciatively of the work I am now doing and of the public influence which he thinks I have gained, and much else to the same effect. Both of them feel the difficulty of my going to be great, and yet acknowledge the attractiveness and importance of the offer. So that, after getting the best advice, I have to judge for myself after all.

'And I confess I feel the difficulty of deciding to be great. If the proposal for my being connected with City Road had not been defeated, I should not have felt the same. But that is gone and cannot be re-opened. I do feel it a question whether I ought to do most of my preaching during the remainder of my life in a little chapel, to which we cannot even admit one hundred visitors. And, I think, this is *not* the expression of personal vanity. To remain in my position undoubtedly means that, so far as the wide public is concerned, I must be content with the pulpit and the audience which I had for many years before my Presidency—that, and no more.

'On the other hand—

'1. God has greatly blessed my work for the children: mine I may *here* call it, though I do not forget how much I owe to others.

'2. Many who have committed themselves to the work have done so in confidence that I should stand by it.

'3. New and important developments (Farnborough and Ireland) are before us. I don't think some of the money would be forthcoming if I were to go.

'All this makes the responsibility of my going very great.

'4. Then the Deaconess work is showing a wonderful spring and energy; and I think the mind and heart of the Connexion is turning towards me in confidence and expectation that this movement will be developed. I have a deep conviction that this Deaconess work, wisely and steadily developed, may be as important a work as the Children's

Home. But, on the other hand, I cannot help feeling that any decision I may now make must be for life. At fifty-two a man may begin a new career; but it is late enough. Let another five years pass, and any change will have become impossible. It is now or never.

'And if I remain here, some things are plain.

'1. My attention will have to be given more to the general direction of our affairs; with less attention to mere details.

'2. I cannot rush about the country as I have done. I must moderate my travelling.

'3. I cannot give solid fortnights to tours, with or without the choir, spending the days in waiting for the evening's engagement of an hour or half an hour.

'4. I must have a little more time for pen work; and I cannot refuse some attention to Connexional interests.

'5. I must have time to watch over and promote the development of the Deaconess work. I will never let this rob the Children's Home of its place —the first—in my heart and work; but I must feel that, consistently with my work for the Home, I am quite free to care for this other.

'6. I must move to another house, perhaps across the Park, where I can get a little more quiet than is possible to me when I am so near the Home, and its multitude of visitors. This might involve an additional £10 or £15 rent, but that is no very great matter.

'Moreover, I should wish to have with me ten or a dozen children, instead of five, as now. We should maintain them as we do the five, except that the clothing of the boys, not the girls, should come from the Home stores. This my daughter wishes, and I join with her. I don't imagine the Committee would object.

'7. I must have some help in Deputation work. I don't want an Assistant, at least not for some time to come. But I must be at liberty to ask occasional help from men like Mr. Curnock, who could give us a week's work, as men give a week or a fortnight to Missionary Deputations. I should run down to the principal meetings myself. This, with some little modification of arrangements which I do not need to specify particularly, would meet that part of the case.

'With such arrangements as these, I could be happy and useful—perhaps none the less happy because for the sake of the children I had parted finally with some not unworthy intellectual and public ambitions. But perhaps it is in this way that God calls me to a self-denial which, in other men, must assume other forms.

'I trouble you with this long letter because, to me at least, the matter is one of very great importance; and it is right, as well as agreeable to my own heart, that I should take you fully into my confidence. If you do not feel any serious objection to the general outline sketched above, that fact would help me to a decision of the case.

'Whether any guarded and brief personal statement should be made to the Committee, is a matter about which we might consult later on. But I should be glad to know your mind on the subject generally, because I cannot well keep the subject open in my own mind much longer.

'I may say that I have talked over the matter confidentially with Mr. Pendlebury, who sees no objection to such arrangements as are suggested above.

'Perhaps I ought also to say, in *perfect confidence*, to you, that I think it probable that I shall marry again after a while. But my daughter knows all my mind in this matter, is thoroughly happy in the prospect, and this, if it should take place, will not make any difference in our wishes and plans.

'With best regards, I am,

'My dear Friend,

'Yours affectionately,

'T. B. STEPHENSON.'

The year 1892 deserves to be remembered in the history of the Christian Churches of England as the time of the first Grindelwald Conference. Under the skilful and expert organization of Dr. Henry S. Lunn, who was supported by such men as the Bishop of Worcester, the Rev. Hugh Price Hughes, Dr. Berry, Dr. Clifford, and many other earnest religious leaders of the day, a large number of representative Christian people belonging to the Anglican Church, and also to the English Nonconformist Churches, gathered together amidst the Swiss Highlands to talk and pray over the problems of Christian unity. Their meetings, however much they may seem to have failed of their original purpose, which was nothing less than the restoration of unity to English Christianity, have, nevertheless, had a deep and permanent effect upon the religious situation in this country. The Free Church Federation of England owes its origin to these Conferences, though it was not the desired end of those who first promoted them. They sought a larger unity, and it was only when the sorrowful conviction deepened into certainty that the differences between the Established Church and the Free Churches could not at that time be composed, that any lesser organization was accepted at all.

Our interest in the Grindelwald Conference of 1892, however, is of a more personal nature. To it came Dr. Stephenson, with his daughter and with Sister Ella Macpherson. Of course he took his active part in conferences and consultations on a subject on which he felt so deeply. But we may turn away from such matters to affairs of a more intimate character. At Grindelwald Dr. Stephenson's party met the Baroness Langenau, a noble Austrian lady of very high rank. To Dr. Stephenson himself it was no new acquaintance.

She was a lady with a remarkable spiritual history. Immediately after a girlhood in which she received a severe Spartan education, she had been married to a husband who was very much older than herself, who also was of high rank, and served his country as the Austrian Ambassador, first at the Hague, and then at the Court of St. Petersburg. He died, leaving her one son, who was the idol of her heart, but who inherited his father's disease. She had done everything a mother could do to save his life, taking him at one time to a place among the mountains where they lived in a hut, and she slept on the floor. But all her efforts were unavailing, and he died before arriving at manhood. Her bereavement left her very miserable. She felt the hollowness and emptiness of Court life, and did not obtain from the Lutheran Church the true consolations of religion. She found a friend to whom she could tell her troubles and her spiritual needs in an English diplomatist, Sir Arthur Blackwood, who, though he was a member of the Anglican Church himself, introduced her to the little secret Methodist meeting in Vienna, as the place where she would be likely to find what she wanted. There she became soundly converted to God. Being now drawn toward the English Methodist Church, she came to England to inform herself with regard to it. Here she made the acquaintance of the Rev. Hugh Price Hughes, and of the Rev. F. W. Macdonald, who was then one of the Secretaries of the Wesleyan Methodist Missionary Society, and responsible for the work in Vienna. She also visited the Children's Home, was much impressed by the work and its methods, and formed a strong personal friendship with Dr. Stephenson.

On going back to Vienna she had started a Children's Home of her own. She tells the story herself :

'Since I have joined the Methodist Church I have pondered on the means of bringing some little children at least under the blessed influence of that Church without coming into open collision with the civil authorities ; for the State laws prohibit Wesleyan ministers from teaching Protestant school-children. At last I have resolved to start a Children's Home, and to sustain it myself, in order to prevent any one meddling with it. I had no difficulty in finding suitable premises, and in having them comfortably furnished ; seven poor little waifs from the street were chosen to be among the first inmates of the house, and on November 6, 1890, the Home was formally opened by a short and impressive service. There had been a great deal of rain of late, but on the sixth the sun rose in a cloudless sky, flooding our old Imperial town with its brightest rays.

'A little before four, my dining-room, which seats a hundred persons, was densely filled with an eager and sympathetic crowd. Mr. Roesch opened by stating that he had been invited by me to say a few words to those present, and explain the aims of the institution—to protect and train little girls, for Christ's sake. He earnestly besought God's blessing and guidance on the undertaking, and that it might not only rescue many from want, but from crime and ruin.'

Among the distinguished personages who were present at this opening ceremony were Princess Reuss, the wife of the German Ambassador, Countess Kielmansegg, wife of the Stadtholder of Lower Austria, and Chief Ecclesiastical Councillor Dr. Witz of the Reformed Church.

Baroness Langenau was not, however, content with these rented premises, but proceeded to build a new 'Wesley House,' which provided in Vienna a substantial memorial of the Centenary of Wesley's death.

She had great difficulty with the authorities, because Methodism was not a recognized form of religion in the city, and but for her own personal influence in high quarters, the services would probably have been stopped altogether.

She also formed a Deaconess Order of the women who gathered to help her in her work.

The Baroness Langenau was, as we have seen, one of the remarkable company who had been gathered together at Grindelwald ; and when she there made the acquaintance of Sister Ella Macpherson she desired her to come back with her to Vienna and assist her in establishing the Children's Home work which she had already begun. After some consideration, Dr. Stephenson took the Baroness into his confidence, and told her of the marriage which was then in contemplation between Sister Ella and himself, whereupon she very kindly arranged that the former should come back to Vienna with her to spend the time before the marriage took place.

Mrs. Stephenson describes the Baroness as a warm-hearted Methodist Christian, who could cry with joy when one of the girls of her Home decided for Christ. The Methodist services at this time were held in her 'gross zimmer,' with the police present to prevent the law being broken. On Saturdays a very different scene took place. From two to seven o'clock she used to hold a reception, which was frequented by the best society in Vienna. Here Sister Ella met many notable people. The Baroness was a great linguist, and everybody who came was received and spoken to in his own language. As soon as her guests were gone, she would turn to Sister Ella and say, 'Now let us be happy,' and the rest of the evening would be spent with the orphans at the Children's Home, where she would bathe the little ones, and put them to bed with her own hands. Her Christmas shopping for them was of a remarkable kind. The children were each of them to write out what they wanted, and every child had its wish without any hesitation as to price.

Early in the next year she gained her point with the authorities, and the Methodist Chapel in Vienna was legally authorized. Dr. Stephenson was the first to preach in it after this authorization, and soon after, on February 23, 1893, after a civil ceremony at the British Embassy, his marriage with Sister Ella Macpherson was solemnized within its walls, the service being conducted by a Scottish Presbyterian minister, assisted by the resident German Methodist minister, the Rev. G. F. Rösch.

After this Baroness Langenau kept in touch with Dr. Stephenson and his work. She attended the Deaconess Convocation at Birmingham in the year 1898. Five years afterwards, while on another visit to England, she died almost suddenly from the effects of imprudent bathing at Bognor. Her life had been, like that of Dorcas, 'full of good works.' Her interest in the work of Methodism in Germany was extended to the American organization as well as the British, and she heartily approved of the unification which was ultimately effected by the retirement of the Wesleyan Missionary Society from this field of labour, and the transfer of its work and workers to the Methodist Episcopal Church of the United States. She contributed generously to the funds of the Wesleyan Missionary Society, both before and after that transfer, and also in the final disposition of her property. The Rev. F. W. Macdonald, who had much to do with these arrangements, and in the course of them was often brought into association with the Baroness, says that he was greatly impressed both by her religious devotion and by a certain very attractive combination of simplicity and shrewdness in her character.

The movements of Dr. and Mrs. Stephenson after their marriage may be gathered from a paragraph which appears in *Highways and Hedges* for May, 1893, in which he says :

'During my recent visit to the Continent, I gained a large amount of interesting information on social, artistic, philanthropic, and especially religious questions. I gathered also nearly two hundred views of celebrated places, pictures, persons and things. Especially was I interested in the developments of Romish superstition, as illustrated by the fabric, the decorations and ceremonies of the Italian churches.'

He goes on to say that he hopes to give lectures on Vienna and Venice, Florence and Rome, and that he has obtained very fine photographs of Raphael's 'Transfiguration,' which he wishes to use as lantern slides in connexion with a sermon on the Transfiguration in various parts of the country.

Dr. and Mrs. Stephenson returned home on Thursday, March 16, and were warmly welcomed by a family gathering at Bonner Road. A re-arrangement had been made, by which the Wesley Deaconesses moved from 7 St. Agnes Terrace to 84 Bonner Road (at the same time transferring the name of 'Mewburn House' from their old to their new home), and Dr. and Mrs. Stephenson set up house-keeping at 7 St. Agnes Terrace. Though they had gone a little further in distance from the Children's Home, they made up for it by taking ten children into their house with them, of whom Mrs. Stephenson and Sister Dora took charge. Five of these children were maintained at Dr. Stephenson's own cost, as his subscription to the Children's Home. Writing about it, he says: 'This is not a new thing to me. Twenty years ago we received into our own house the first little girl befriended by the Home, and as I am continually asking Christian ladies to give themselves to this work, with whatever inconveniences and discomforts it may involve, we are glad to take our share of the burden, for we do not ask others to do what we are not willing to do ourselves.'

During this summer the question of the supply of the Approach Road Chapel was under consideration. It was finally arranged that the Conference should be asked to appoint Dr. Stephenson as Superintendent of the circuit, and that the Approach Road Chapel should be used for the Sunday worship of the Children's Home. Dr. Stephenson had been Superintendent of this circuit in 1871 and 1872. It was then known as the Bethnal Green Circuit, but the name was now changed to Victoria Park Circuit, and Dr. Stephenson and the Rev. T. Edward Ham were appointed the ministers. Dr. Stephenson's relation to the circuit was, as far as finances were concerned, purely honorary, and the Committee of the Children's Home took no responsibility in connexion with the Church, which was supported in the usual way. Still, the arrangement was regarded as mutually advantageous. Besides having Dr. Stephenson in the pulpit, the Church secured the valuable services of the Children's Home choir; the children and officers formed an interesting element in the congregations, and the work of the Church was helped by the presence of the Home community, and by the cordial co-operation of its officers in many branches of Christian enterprise. On the other hand, the Home was benefited by the new relationship. The officers and children came out of the secluded life of their own community, and took their place in a general congregation, joining in public worship, and learning something which is of great importance to children, namely, that they have their place in the Church of God. One of the greatest perils of such institutions is that it is extremely difficult to avoid giving children a limited view of life, so that when they go out into the world they are unable to fall into other ways than those to which they have been accustomed in the little world in which they have lived. The sharing in common worship is thus an important element in their education. The church stands at the end of the Terrace in Bonner Road, and actually joins the Home premises. It was thus most conveniently situated to be the ordinary place of worship for the community. The Wesley Deaconesses from Mewburn House also worshipped there, and the Probationers found in the many organizations connected with the Church scope for their energies, and an excellent sphere for training in evangelistic and philanthropic enterprise.

Dr. Stephenson was, however, somewhat overestimating his own strength when he took on this additional burden, especially as he had already been appointed to the office of Chairman of the First London District. He found himself compelled to resign this office at the beginning of 1894 (a time when he was seriously troubled with sleeplessness), and went out to the United States and Canada for a month's rest and change. After two years he gave up the Superintendency of the Victoria

Park Circuit ; but the arrangement which connected the Approach Road Chapel and the Children's Home was continued under the Rev. T. Edward Ham, who now became Superintendent, and again under his successor, the Rev. A. E. Gregory.

CHAPTER XXII

Different classes of Neglected Children—Society for Prevention of Cruelty to Children—Epileptic Children—Hope House opened—Crippled Children—Children in Workhouses—Twentieth Century Fund—'Family System.'

WHEN Dr. Stephenson began the work of the Children's Home, there was no very clear differentiation of the various kinds of children who needed such care as that which the Home provided. Much prominence was given to the waifs and strays; 'Poor little Scaramouch' was the kind of child mainly sought for, though it was recognized from the first that there were children who had fathers and mothers who were in just as great need of such assistance as those who were homeless and friendless. The effect of the work of such institutions as the Children's Home, Dr. Barnardo's Homes, the Church of England Waifs and Strays Society, and others of similar character, has been that practically the whole of this class of children is now dealt with. It would not be possible to-day to find in London, or in the country, the crowds of homeless uncared-for urchins, owned by nobody, whose sad plight first moved to pity the pioneers of this movement. Individual cases still exist, but the kind, strong hand of experienced Christian charity is at once held out to deal with them when they are discovered, and moreover, trained eyes are on the look-out for them. The Children's Homes and the Education Acts between them have made the England of to-day an entirely different country from that of 1870 in this respect.

The working of the Education Act soon brought into prominence another class of children, the unmanageable boys, and sometimes girls, who brought themselves within the reach of the law because of truancy, petty theft, and suchlike offences; and, responding to the new call, the Children's Home enlarged itself to take in an Industrial Branch.

One of the next special classes to claim the care of the Church was that of the orphans of godly people who through the misfortunes of life were unable to provide for them, and we have seen how the Princess Alice Orphanage was built specially to provide for them.

Meanwhile the work of the Society for the Prevention of Cruelty to Children was making the English people in general aware of the existence among them of an almost unsuspected evil, that of deliberate and malicious cruelty shown to children by some of those who had the care of them. The Rev. Benjamin Waugh, who founded this Society, maintained so vigorously that 'what is wanted is not the ever-open door of Institutions for the wretched children, but the ever-open doors of prisons for those who make them wretched,' that for a time he seemed to be attacking such men as Dr. Barnardo and Dr. Stephenson, rather than co-operating with them from another point of view. Mr. Waugh had first of all to get his own Society to agree with his estimate of the situation. More than three-fourths of his original Council fell away, and only then could his principles be considered as the adopted policy of the Society. Time and experience have proved the great value of this salutary demand for vindictive justice on the perpetrators of cruelty, but they have also shown that there are a good many cases where a shelter such as the Children's Home could give was absolutely necessary for the victims of cruelty; and especially from the year 1888 onwards the *Children's Advocate* and *Highways and Hedges* tell of case after case received into the Children's Home and protected and cared for there.

Another special class claiming the mercy and pity of the Christian Church was that of the epileptic children. In 1895 Dr. Stephenson wrote about them:—

'They are a very large class in the community; a much larger class than is generally supposed; and their lot is a most sad and pitiable one. The disease, as it runs its course, leaves them more and more helpless; shuts up against them one after another of the avenues of honest employment; draws over their minds a deeper and darker shadow; and brings them day by day nearer idiotcy. Two things are wanted for them: first, that they should receive such wise and appropriate treatment, medical and disciplinary, as will enable them to rise above and perhaps overcome the worst influences of the disease; secondly, that when the dreadful disease has struck its fangs into their system so deeply that they cannot be released, the life that is paralysed and darkened shall have its woes mitigated, its burdens lightened, and its gloom relieved by some gleams of sunshine, through the skilful and tender ministration of those who will see Christ and serve Him in the person of these sufferers. Some attempt is to be made for their relief by a public Committee. To that attempt we shall wish God-speed. Yet I confess that I believe the best way to deal with this work, so sorely needed, is by somebody quietly beginning to do a little of it.

'And the reason why I feel so strongly in reference to it, is because the necessity has been driven in upon our consciences by our own sad experience. We have frequently had epileptic children in the Home. We have some now. We have had to deal as best we could with these, by getting such help as was available here, there, and yonder; by obtaining for them temporary admittance to a hospital, or by some other difficult expedient. But in spite of all, we have watched more than one of our children slowly yielding to the fell disease; the eye becoming dull, the countenance swollen, the step heavy, the look more vacant; until at last we have been compelled by sheer helplessness to deal further with them, and against all our convictions of duty, and all our feelings of compassion, to hand them over to the workhouse authorities, to end their miserable existence there; and as I have done this I have felt ashamed of myself, and ashamed of English Christianity. Jean Bost, in France, could deal with them. Bodelschwingh, in Germany, can find money to meet their case, and devoted men and women to do the actual work. Cannot we do something, if it be only a little? I would be contented if we could but have only a little house, where a dozen such sufferers could be properly tended, and where we could nurse them for the life beyond. It would be a legitimate outgrowth of our work. It is a necessary adjunct to it, if we are not to abdicate our duty when some of our most hapless children need us most. It would cost little; for it would involve no extra charge for management and advertising. Would to God we could at least make the experiment! I believe it will be done some day: though perhaps I may not be permitted to see it. But surely He who said of an epileptic boy, 'Why could not ye cast out the devil? Bring the child to Me,' would smile upon an attempt to meet such pitiful and disabling sorrow as this!'

His appeal was not at once responded to, though it was never lost sight of, and in 1897 he writes:

'We waited some time before any such answer to our prayer was given which could indicate to us the Divine will in the matter. Then there came a kindly promise of £50 for furniture, and £50 for the first year's maintenance. This was followed by the welcome gift of £500 for the purchase of a cottage; and presently with the gift of £300 from another friend, together with some smaller though not less generous donations. The exact locality of our Bethesda is not yet determined; and these moneys, meantime, are held in hand; but we have under our care five young people who are suffering from this dreadful disease. In these cases we have already proved what can be done by dieting, suitable medicine, and constant loving care. One girl, who used to have a fit at least once weekly, has had only one in eighteen months. Another, who suffered from them frequently, has not had one for many weeks; and a boy, in whose case the results were scarcely less satisfactory, only relapsed when, owing to a mistake, the suitable treatment was for the time suspended. We have, of course, with so small an experience, no right to speak loudly, or prophesy confidently; but our belief is strengthened that if we had but the means to deal with this distressing form of human suffering, it could, in many cases, be alleviated; and in a large number life might be made tolerable, and even pleasurable, and in some cases, perhaps, the disease might be practically cured. To care for such sufferers is hard work. To do it rightly requires the very patience and tenderness and pity which the Master alone can give to His disciples; but I am proud to say that two of our Deaconesses have volunteered to devote themselves to the soothing of this bitter sorrow. I am hoping and praying that somebody will give us at a point within easy reach of Bonner Road, a house with a very large garden attached; or perhaps, better still, a house with a few acres of land adjoining, even if it were a little further out. We are content to wait for the finger of God to point the way in this as He has in all our history, but we are praying and watching for the movement of it.'

In May, 1898, he writes:

'Our enterprise for epileptic children, at present only a very modest experiment, must be put upon its feet, and got into thorough working order. We have only one house for this most pathetic and needy class of young sufferers. We ought to secure during the next year a second; because it is clear that boys and girls suffering from epilepsy cannot with propriety and comfort be treated in the same house. Our epileptic girls will inhabit Hope House, London;

the boys are temporarily lodged at Gravesend; but there will not be room for them at Farnborough. Will nobody give us a house, or pay the rent of one for us, say for three years, in the neighbourhood of our London Branch?'

'Our work for the epileptic children is still in a very experimental stage. The difficulties of such work are enormous. In many cases the dreadful disease has already made the little sufferer idiotic, and this puts it beyond our power to help the child (unless, indeed, we should, at some future time, be able to establish a department for idiots in accordance with the regulations very properly demanded by the Government). But even when there is the possibility of improving the condition of the sufferers, making life less burdensome to them, giving to them some work to do which is within their limited powers, and so putting into life a new interest for them, the difficulties attending such work are very great. It has not been possible for us as yet to get suitable premises, and it has not been possible for us systematically to receive boys at all. The one house which is devoted to this part of our work is occupied by girls. At present we can only wait upon God, and do with our best efforts the bit of work which He sends us, watching meantime for all providential indications of His will, and ready to follow where He leads. We may possibly not be able to develop this branch of work during the next few years. I, speaking for myself, however, cannot believe that it is the will of God that such work as this should be left to be done upon purely humanitarian principles. Such work ought to be saturated with the spirit of religion.'

The home for epileptic girls referred to above, 'Hope House,' under the charge of Sister Ray Forde, proved to be a very trying and difficult enterprise. It was, however, nobly maintained, and it is a comfort to know that Dr. Stephenson's ambitions with regard to this branch of the work have now been very largely attained in connexion with the Institution he founded.

The care of crippled children has since Dr. Stephenson's time become a very important branch of the work of the Children's Home. Although it was not given him to develop this work largely so far as numbers are concerned, he took the greatest interest in it on such a scale as was possible, and at the Children's Home Infirmary in Bonner Road some very extraordinary cases of success in dealing with crippled children were experienced. Dr. Tunstall, the Medical Officer of the Home, was deeply interested in this branch of his work, and had the co-operation of nurses who added Christian devotion to technical skill.

To turn to another side of the Infirmary work, the Home has its stories of romance connected with deserted babies. One of them, a little boy wrapped up in a brown-paper parcel, was adopted by a nurse, took her name, and has grown up to hold an honourable professional position. Another, who was brought to the Home a ten days' old baby girl by Dr. Hodge (later to be known by his heroic missionary work in China), was educated and adopted by a well-known worker in the Home, and she also has grown up to take a good position in the educational world.

Every stage of accomplishment in the good work of caring for neglected childhood seems to have been followed by a call for fresh effort in some other direction.

The case of the children of our Churches who were to be found in workhouses, under the care of the Poor Law Guardians, was prominently brought forward in the closing years of the nineteenth century, and a special opportunity for dealing with it offered itself. Under the leadership of the Rev. H. Price Hughes and Mr. Robert Perks a scheme was brought before the Wesleyan Conference for celebrating the commencement of the new century by another of those general collections, the earlier of which have already been described in these pages. The Twentieth Century Fund was to be the greatest of them all. A million Methodists were to give a million guineas. The names of the givers were to be inscribed on an 'Historic Roll,' which should hand down to posterity a list of the actual Methodist people who began the new era. This time none of the money was to be used to pay debts, but all of it to be devoted to the inauguration of new work. It was hoped that it would herald a great Forward Movement all along the line.

Out of the Fund it was resolved to give £50,000 to the Children's Home, with the understanding that provision should be made if possible to take *all* these children away from the taint of pauperism, and give them the larger advantage, and more definitely religious surroundings, of the Children's Home. This project appealed strongly to Dr. Stephenson's heart in the last years during which this work was under his care. In 1897 he writes about it as follows:—

'A large and important question awaits solution; and the attempt to solve it falls to the Children's Home. If we cannot solve it, who else can? The question is, Shall Nonconformist children, and especially Methodist children, be any longer brought up in Workhouse schools?'

From a careful calculation, he estimated that there were at that time about one thousand four hundred children in workhouses, or brought up by the Poor Law authorities, who belonged to the Methodist Churches.

'The question now is, ought they to be there? Are they likely to obtain there the religious, social, and educational advantages which they ought to have? Are they likely to receive that protection from unwholesome and degrading influences to which they are entitled? And if not, what is the duty towards them of the Churches to which their parents belonged?

'A further question is, how far can the Church, to which they have a right to look, utilize the provisions of the existing law, and supplement these by its own benevolence, so that these children shall have the social and religious advantages which we ought to secure for them?

'We ask, first, in what condition are they?

'Let it be granted that in some respects their circumstances are satisfactory. They live in substantial and spacious buildings. They have the necessary space in their bedrooms. Sanitary requirements are well met in most cases. They have a sufficiency of food. It is the very same, week after week, and it is served in a somewhat rough manner. But it is weighed out for them according to an approved scale, and the bairns need never to go hungry. Their schooling, though inferior to good Elementary Schools, is fairly good, though the subjects are restricted, and the attendance probably rather loose, as the children grow to be "handy." A chaplain of the Established Church is appointed to catechize, and hold religious services when necessary; and in a good many schools religious services are held by Nonconformist volunteers, at which, in some cases, the older children are allowed to be present. This does not prevail largely in the "Union Schools," in which the children of several federated parishes dwell together, apart from the workhouse proper with its adult inmates. With rare exceptions, the only religious services here are those conducted by the official—that is, the Anglican—chaplain.

'So far, so good. But several further facts must be considered, before the picture is accurate. Many of these schools are so large that individual treatment of the children is impossible. The whole system of discipline is necessarily mechanical and rigid. When you have sixteen hundred children in one great Barrack School, how can Johnny or Fanny be anything but items in a calculation—little human pawns moved indifferently here or there, by persons who know little of them? The officials may be attracted to a few children, and bestow upon them special attention and love; but they have to pay a heavy price for this in the jealousy and resentment of their less favoured comrades. The bulk of the children cannot have any such personal love and attention as every child ought to have; and they grow up to maturity with no sweet memories of home affection; with no adequate development of the finer elements of the nature; with no golden links of respect and regard for persons older and wiser, to act as checking and guiding forces in life. And this I say, without any reflection upon the humanity and integrity of the officials. The system is at fault.

'But further, these schools are not healthy. Though money is spent upon them without stint, and plans and arrangements have to be examined and approved by all sorts of authorities, some diseases, and notably ophthalmia, seem to be ineradicable. There seems little doubt that in spite of airy buildings and plentiful food, the vitality of the children is below the average. . . .

'The Church owes the duty of giving to them Christian home-life. They had it whilst their fathers and mothers were alive; they would have been enjoying it still had these been still alive, for their parents were Christian people in whose houses religion was a powerful factor. There the children were sheltered from the pollution of evil ways and evil practices; they joined in family prayers; they were sent to Sunday school; they were taken to the House of God; and the care which their parents exercised over them was the result, not of mere natural affection, but of deep religious conviction, and of the heart culture which grows with reverent worship of the Almighty Father. Surely, the Church's duty is to see that the children of its sainted dead, however poor, shall grow up amid influences as homelike, as tender and affectionate as those which they have lost.'

He proceeded to point out that the Local Government Board had the power to certify houses and institutions as suitable for the reception of children who would otherwise be in workhouse schools ; and that Boards of Guardians were authorized to contribute towards the cost of such children any sum not exceeding £30 per annum. He estimated that with what might be expected to come from this source, an additional income of £7,500 a year would be required to take care of them all. And beside this, that a considerable capital sum would be required for the erection of houses for the children.

This project was received with very much favour, and no doubt did much to win a welcome for the Twentieth Century Fund.

In 1898 he writes :

'It has been determined, with universal consent, that Fifty Thousand Pounds shall be devoted to the Children's Home, especially for providing the houses and other buildings required to realize fully our latest development, viz., the rescue of all Nonconformist children from the Workhouse Schools. Our calculations have always named £60,000 as the smallest sum required ; but we are thankful to have so substantial an amount as £50,000 placed to our credit, for it will keep us busy in extension work for several years.

'But, unless the matter is clearly understood by all our friends, it is likely to be a calamity instead of a blessing. . . . This huge Fund will require much time and immense energy in the getting. It cannot be expected that it will be gathered, so that its grants can be available, in less than about three years. During that time the needs of our work will exist day by day. The current income will require to be kept up. If the whole Fifty Thousand Pounds were paid over to us to-morrow, we could not do with one penny less of ordinary income, for this grant is not available for current expenditure.

'But again: These fifty thousand pounds, when they come to us, may enable us to build houses which will provide for about one thousand two hundred and fifty additional children. But this will involve the maintenance of these children. And, if they were all to come to us by arrangements with Boards of Guardians, at least £6,000 a year of additional subscriptions will be necessary if the houses are to be filled. To maintain fully the present subscription list, and to add to it a further amount of £6,000, is the preliminary condition of our being able to utilize this large promise.'

The Million Guineas of the Twentieth Century Fund was not got together without a large number of public meetings, held at every Wesleyan chapel of importance throughout the land. The speakers at these meetings naturally said much about the Children's Home because of the popularity of the proposal to give it substantial assistance. And the public attention thus called to the work and the prominence given to it meant the winning of many hearts. The ordinary funds of the Home gained additional support, and the actual grant of £50,000 was only one part of the good done to this work by this great collection.

It was not, however, given to Dr. Stephenson, but to his successor, the Rev. A. E. Gregory, to administer this money, and carry out, as far as was feasible, the project thus launched.

It was, however, never completely carried out, because a victory of another kind had been won, much more far-reaching in its results. The 'Family System,' which Dr. Stephenson had preached and practised for so many years, commended itself first to the Government, and then to the Boards of Guardians throughout the country; and the Industrial barracks schools, and the great Workhouse barracks schools, which he attacks with so unerring an aim, began to be changed for arrangements more after his own mind and heart. The great herd of children suffering from ophthalmia, and from lowered vitality, aimless and miserable through want of mothering, have been broken up into small groups under the kindly care of persons who can give them individual attention; and if there are still Nonconformist and Methodist children under the care of the Workhouse authorities, it is because in the main the great cause for complaint which Dr. Stephenson had against their condition has to-day disappeared. Perhaps, indeed, his witness for the 'Family System' was the greatest thing he did for the suffering childhood of Great Britain.

CHAPTER XXIII

Public Recognition and Honours—Sister Dora appointed Corresponding Secretary—Canadian Work—American Deaconesses—A Busy Year—Rev. A. E. Gregory Vice-Principal of the Home—Farnborough—Six Months' Rest—Rev. William Arthur—Dr. Creighton and the Home—'Young Leaguers' Union'—'Old Boys' and Girls'' Presentation—Resignation.

THE years following his Presidency brought to Dr. Stephenson many responsibilities and honours. He was now a well-known man, and came into contact with most of the great leaders, social, political, and religious, of his time. It is perhaps a matter of regret that he has left no record of his acquaintanceship with these people, but as he did not do so, it is not proposed to cumber these pages with a mere list of distinguished names. It must suffice to say that he had his full share of those appreciations and courtesies which English society shows to a man who had won distinction by honourable public work.

In 1893 he was a member of the Mansion House Committee on the Distress in London. This Committee considered the question whether in the economic crisis of the time it was wise that a Mansion House Fund for the relief of distress should be established. They unanimously reported against this, on the ground that it is scarcely possible to secure exact and discriminating administration of the Fund, and that it is certain that any Fund attracts to London a multitude of ne'er-do-wells, whose presence intensifies the difficulties of the suffering poor already there. No doubt the distress prevailing through certain parts of London at the moment was very grave, but England was at that time in a strait between two opposite theories as to the best methods of alleviation, and the question of the advisability of Relief work was hotly debated, and produced great division of opinion.

In 1895 the Anniversary of the Children's Home concluded with a service held at St. Margaret's Church, Westminster, on the invitation of Archdeacon Farrar. The Choir of the Children's Home, who rendered the musical service, wore the surplices, and conformed in every way to the usual ritual of the Church. Dr. Stephenson read the lessons, and Canon Fleming preached. Archdeacon Farrar was at that time about to leave London for the Deanery of Canterbury. His courtesy was so much apppreciated that no less than eighty Wesleyan ministers from the London Districts attended the service, and very warm expressions of approval of Dean Farrar's brotherliness were heard on all sides.

In 1897, the year of the Diamond Jubilee of Queen Victoria, the Prince of Wales invited subscriptions to the 'Prince of Wales' Hospital Fund,' and formed a Committee, on which he placed the name of Dr. Stephenson. On the accession of King Edward, it was known as the 'King Edward Hospital Fund,' and he served on this Committee, and took a great interest in its work for many years.

Next year, also on the nomination of the Prince of Wales, he was enrolled as an Honorary Associate of the Order of the Hospital of St. John of Jerusalem in England, a distinction reserved for those who have either done special service for the Order, or are 'persons eminently distinguished for philanthropy.'

The Order was founded in the eleventh century at Jerusalem, and migrated, first to Acre, then to Rhodes, and after years of wandering, to Malta. The English branch of it attained the status of an English Corporation in or about the reign of King Edward II, but was dissolved in the year 1540. About the year 1827 it was revived in England, and on May 14, 1888, in recognition of the excellent work performed by its members during the past half-century, and especially of the establishment of the St. John Ambulance Association, so well known for its examinations and certificates for 'First Aid to the Injured,' Her Majesty Queen Victoria granted a new Royal Charter of Incorporation, and was graciously pleased to become the Sovereign Head and patron of the Order, which had many Royal personages on the roll of its fraternity. Selection for enrolment as an Honorary Associate is made by the Chapter-General with the approval of the Grand Prior, but before any person selected can be admitted or enrolled, the name must be submitted to the Sovereign for approval and sanction. The Order has a very handsome Badge, in the shape of a Maltese Cross in silver, suspended from a black watered riband, which Honorary Associates are entitled to wear, by Royal permission.

In 1897 Mr. Francis Horner, who had been associated so intimately with the beginning of the work, but had been partially severed from it by business engagements and family cares, again became Honorary Secretary of the Institution.

At the same time Sister Dora Stephenson was appointed Corresponding Secretary. A little sketch of her qualifications for this office which she gave at the time, deserves preservation, because of its picture of the intimate relation between the life of Dr. Stephenson's family and the Home.

'I am always thankful that my life has been linked with that of the Home from the earliest days. I have no recollection apart from it. I have a hazy remembrance of a day when my old nurse, Jane, and a boy whose name I do not know, took a certain baby girl out in her perambulator. The baby was resplendent in a new white coat and hat. The nurse left baby and perambulator in charge of the lad while she made her purchase. When she reappeared, the boy, with a scared face, was picking the surprised baby out of the gutter, whither in his carelessness he had tipped her! I beg to state that the baby did *not* cry, even at the sight of the spoilt cape and hat.

'Another memory comes of a tiny three-year-old maiden, who felt considerably ill-used because a new baby was usurping so much of the attention of mother and nurse—the said baby being the *first* on the funds of the Children's Home, before, indeed we had a house for girls at all. Augusta ——— was the baby, and she "cried, and cried, and cried," much to the chagrin of the boy installed as under-nurse—William ———. I heard with keen interest of the coming of Captain Boss; of redoubtable Jack Baker, who so stubbornly resented the authority of Mr. Stephenson, but at last was conquered and won. I remember the distress there was at home when father came in, telling how poor little Francis ———, a new-comer, had been nearly killed by being bathed in a wrongly prepared medicated bath.

'I remember the event of Teddie ———, the first of our one-legged battalion; how Mr. Stephenson found it hard work to keep the artificial limb of equal length with the other, owing to the boy's growth, and how Edwin Pepper's fertile brain suggested the expedient of "getting a leg in a flowerpot that would grow along with him." I remember the summer outings to Farningham, the rolling down the hill, and the hearty welcome of our friends at the Mill. And Christmas in the old Schoolroom! Why, it took a week to cover up its imperfections, and the Principal had time to drive nails, and festoon chains, and build log cabins with his own hands! And the old drum and fife band, and the grand, never-to-be-forgotten advent of brass instruments, and befrogged uniforms, which Mr. Stephenson fitted on the boys, in the old schoolroom. I can see Willie ——— now as he emerged first in all his glory!

'Then came my first trip to Canada, about which I remember little clearly, though the home-coming is outlined definitely in my mind. A lighted schoolroom full of radiant faces, cheering children's voices, two little girl friends face to face hugging each other, and the basket that contained a ship's kitten, followed by whispered confidences as we walked up and down the yard. "Mother" McDougall says that for the next five years I was ring leader in mischief of all the girls in the Home. If so—and I fear the indictment is all too correct—the less said about those years the better. But some here will remember the escapades of those days, and officers of the present time may be thankful there is no sprite quite so mischievous to lead on the lasses to-day.

'The growing-up days were not quite so happy—times of transition can never be—but as soon as I was old enough I came into the Home, and as "Sister Dora" I have been happily at work for nine years.

'Why mention all this? some one is saying. Because I want you to realize that as child, girl, or woman, I have been in touch with nearly all the boys and girls who have belonged to the Children's Home. That is the reason why I have been made responsible for keeping in touch with all the boys and girls the world over. It is a very large order, and I have but begun to join up the old links of friendship; but it was thought that many would be interested in hearing something of their old comrades.

'The record of the year is, indeed, wonderful! It is impossible to give many details, but there are one or two broad facts that we all appreciate. We find that one or two lessons have been well learnt in the Home.

'First, we find that our boys and girls know that the best news they can give us is to tell us that they have come out definitely on the Lord's side.

'Second, old boys and girls are generally persuaded that to ensure a happy and healthy life, it is wise to eschew strong drink.

'Third, generally speaking, our boys and girls keep clear of "gold fever." They have learnt here that there is à nobler way of living than in the mere selfish heaping up of money. Some of our boys are "getting on in the world"; and for this we are thankful. But to "get rich" in money is not their first end in life.

'So at the present time I am glad to report that among our old boys are five ministers, three students for the ministry, three foreign missionaries. In connexion with our own work are—one Governor, six Sisters and Probationer Sisters, five heads of different departments, eleven assistants in positions of trust. We have trained at least eighteen public elementary school teachers. We know four old girls who are hospital nurses. You could find in Canada many young men farming their own land; many abroad and at home in positions of trust, and in this country scores of skilled artisans. Nearly thirty old boys are in H.M. Service, some as soldiers and some as sailors. Hundreds of girls are living usefully and happily in domestic service; while many more have entered another kind of domestic life where, as happy wives and mothers, they are indeed adding to the wealth of our nation.

'Our "grandchildren" are numerous, and of course they are charming. The dear bairnies here to-day have many little unknown cousins linked through mother or father, or both, with our Children's Homes. To-day, as our thoughts go out to them, and their parents the wide world over, we heartily pray, "God bless them every one."'

During this year the Canadian work demanded special attention. In some Canadian newspapers emigrant children were misrepresented as being the very residuum of English slums dumped upon Canadian territory, and there was some danger lest the Dominion Government should be induced to notice misrepresentations of the work, and take action which would render further emigration impossible. The objectionable statements were as far as was possible from being true, at any rate with regard to the work of Dr. Stephenson's Children's Home. His boys and girls were only sent after long-continued discipline and careful discrimination, and their record, as was proved by the investigations of Canadian Government agents, was exceptionally good; the demand for their services did not lessen, but year after year there was a long list of employers waiting for them before they sailed from Liverpool.

It should be remembered that the Children's Home at Hamilton was not so much a Training Home, as a centre for distribution and supervision of the children. The training could be better done before emigration, except so far as it was needful for the children to be familiarized with distinctively Canadian habits and practices, and this familiarity could best be gained in the actual experience of a Canadian household or a Canadian farm. Moreover, it was felt that the sooner young emigrants became absorbed among the population, and lost their distinctively English accent and appearance and habits the better. The Home at Hamilton was therefore first of all a Home for the reception of the new arrivals, and for their distribution among carefully selected Canadian employers. It was also the centre of an agency of supervision and protection, and the point from which regular visitations were made to all places where the children were living. Another purpose for which it was useful was the reception of boys or girls who, for any reason, were not suited in their first situation. The first distribution could not be expected to be entirely satisfactory in every case, and some children would have bad health and need special care; for these and similar purposes a local Home was wanted to which they could return in case of need. The results of the emigration enterprise were excellent, the failures were exceedingly rare. During the first twenty-five years, only two of those sent out were prosecuted and legally punished, a record which would surely compare favourably with any equal number of young people belonging either to English or Canadian families.

Dr. and Mrs. Stephenson went out to Canada at the beginning of August for consultation with Mr. Hills, the Governor of the Canadian Home, inquiries into the condition of the children, and visitation of such as could be reached in the time, as well as interviews with public men upon the new questions that were arising. He says, 'We conversed personally with nearly one hundred of our bairns. We saw some scores of the homes in which they are employed. We discussed, with the records before us, the history and character of all who had not reached twenty-one years, beside many older;

and we made careful estimates of their health, character, and prospects. The impression received was therefore no mere guess, but founded upon exact data. We know where our children are, and how they are doing. The result is on the whole very satisfactory. Some grievous disappointments there are. Over some we rejoice only with trembling. But the great majority are doing well ; a large proportion are doing excellently. Many are all that we could wish them to be. Our work is carefully and thoroughly done by our Hamilton representatives.'

'Recent legislation in the Parliament of Ontario and Manitoba, for the purpose of regulating the immigration of poor children from England, had caused us some anxiety. Not because we were afraid of any fair and reasonable inspection of our work, but because we could not be sure that in the hands of incompetent or unsympathetic administrators, it would not be a serious hindrance to us in the very cases which most need the new chance which emigration often affords. It is enough for the present to say that our fears were much relieved by the explanations and assurances given by the responsible officials of the Provincial Government. The Acts themselves can only be fully tested by the experience of two or three years. But at present we see no reason to suspend our careful and moderate work of emigration.'

Dr. Stephenson recounts an incident which occurred on this journey, which is significant with regard to Deaconess work :

'In August Mrs. Stephenson and I arrived at Buffalo Station, New York State, at six in the morning. We had travelled for twenty-one hours, and my wife had been seized with a severe though temporary illness. We had to change trains at this point, and we found ourselves unable to proceed. My wife could only lie down helpless and suffering on a settee in the women's waiting-room.

'What was to be done? My only friend in the city had removed elsewhere, a couple of years ago. To make matters worse, the station was thronged with a multitude of passengers. Every hotel in the city was crowded, for the "Annual Muster of the Veterans of the Civil War" was being held here, and 300,000 visitors were pouring in. Where were we to get medicine, or a doctor, or a quiet waiting-place? We had only been waiting a few moments, when up came a kindly, tactful, and sympathetic woman, accosted my wife, asked what was the matter, and set about soothing and helping her as only a woman can. We had never seen her before, but in my anxiety my heart went out to her as to an old friend, for she wore the costume of the American Methodist Deaconess. The neat black dress, with the black bonnet and white strings, commended her to our confidence in a moment. How kind she was—how she directed me to the chemist's for medicine, telephoned for a doctor from the hospital, brought out a pillow from her little store-room in the station, bathed the sufferer's head, brought her iced water, and in every possible way helped her, we shall never forget. She was gratified when she learned that, quite unconsciously, she had been helping those who are so closely identified with the Deaconess Order in England.

'But the incident is worth record here, because,

as we learned, this Sister's duty is daily at this crowded railway junction. From seven each morning till late in the evening, she is here to lead the blind, to help the lame, to advise the wandering, to comfort the sick, to protect girls and women, and to speak, as opportunity offers, a word for that Jesus for "whose sake" the Deaconess Order exists. Is it not beautiful ? It was delightful to see how everybody trusted and referred to this good Methodist Sister ; how the railway officials confided in her, and co-operated with her ; and how she had become a recognized and valued institution. In addition to all the other helpful ministries of her life, she has returned to their homes "eighty wandering girls" within the last two years. When will it be possible for us to appoint a Methodist Deaconess at even one of the great railway centres of England ?'

It was a very busy year. In Lancashire the Beckett Memorial House was opened, and other additions were made. At the Princess Alice Orphanage, two additional houses were built, for which the money was provided by two members of the Birmingham Committee, and other enlargements were required. At Farnborough a new branch to replace the Gravesend work was rising. At Alverstoke a new cottage and a new school were planned ; at Bonner Road the Hospital was enlarged, and additional office accommodation provided, and a new house for the Chief Resident Officer.

Next year (1898), the Rev. A. E. Gregory was appointed Vice-Principal of the Children's Home

THE CHILDREN'S HOME AT BONNER ROAD.

[face p. 364

More than twenty years previously he had spent two years as a voluntary worker in the Home. After this he had entered the ministry, and filled many important appointments with high credit. Dr. Stephenson's note about him, on his appointment, is as follows :

'His power of interesting and luminous speech, his literary skill, his sympathy with all true social advance, and his lofty conception of the child, as he may be, and ought to be, give him an uncommon fitness for his new office. His belief in woman's work, and his appreciation of the necessity of due training and equipment for such work as ours, promise much influence for good, in an enterprise which depends so largely on intelligent and consecrated women. His interesting and attractive preaching, and his facile and racy platform speech, will make him everywhere welcomed as a public representative of our work. To all our officers he is so well known that his appointment is most welcome. The Principal is thankful to have the assistance of such a Vice-Principal. We confidently bespeak for Mr. Gregory a hearty welcome in all parts of the country, and a frequent place in the prayers of all our well-wishers.'

The same year saw the General Committee of the Children's Home enlarged by the inclusion of representatives of the Methodist New Connexion, the Bible Christian, and the United Methodist Free Churches.

The lease of the Gravesend property expired in 1894, and a short extension was secured, but it was not judged wise either to purchase the property or renew the lease. A building at Farnborough, erected for an orphanage, had been presented to the Home; and though it was not, in its existing form, satisfactory, it lent itself to adaptation. The site was excellent, the position extremely healthy, and the existing building could be made to form an admirable centre block for the Institution. A large piece of adjacent land was purchased, making the entire site two acres and a half; schools, work-shops, drill-hall, laundry, bakery, stores, governor's house and drill-master's house were erected, and a fine playground big enough for football provided. The transfer from Gravesend to Farnborough took place in October, 1898.

The appointment of a Vice-Principal was made none too soon. At the beginning of November, 1898, Dr. Stephenson had a bad breakdown in health, and was ordered six months' absolute rest, during which he visited Italy and the Riviera.

At Cannes he saw the Rev. William Arthur. He writes:

'I had the great pleasure of spending a few days under his roof, during the winter of 1898. He was still active, but his energy was ebbing. He shrank from company, except that of a few old friends. He had practically given up literary work. But his interest in all that pertained to the Church of his life-long service was still keen, and his memory retained almost its full power. He recalled persons, places, and events, with a wonderful vividness. This was the more remarkable, because for several years he had paid no visits to England or to the British Conference. But he remembered his brethren of the ministry with a warm and touching pleasure and pride, and loved to talk about them.

By the citizens of Cannes he was greatly respected. Few persons of any eminence in the Evangelical world failed to pay their respects to him as they passed through the town.'

The friendship between these two men had been lifelong. There was one special service which Dr. Stephenson had been able to do for William Arthur again and again. A throat affection had taken away Mr. Arthur's voice. 'For many years he could never be sure of being able to fulfil public engagements. Sometimes his voice would have almost all its own clear resonance. Then within an hour or two he would be again reduced to whispering. . . . On some very important occasions, he was dependent on the voice of another. It fell to my lot to deliver for him a speech in 1870, on the admission of the laity to the Conference; his Fernley lecture in 1883; and his sermon before the Œcumenical Methodist Conference at Washington in 1891. He stood loyally beside me on all these occasions, with a look of most kindly appreciation on his face; but oh, how much the reader wished that his honoured friend had been able to do justice to these great utterances by his own voice and his own delivery.'

On Dr. Stephenson's return to his work just before Convocation, he was warmly welcomed at the Children's Home; but it soon became manifest that he had not recovered a sufficient reserve of strength to carry on the work that had now grown to such large dimensions.

At the Conference Meeting in support of the Children's Home, held in St. James' Hall, on July 29, 1899, the chair was taken by Dr. Creighton, Bishop of London, who had, a few days previously, paid the visit to the Children's Home to which we have already referred. In his public address the Bishop said :

'When Dr. Stephenson asked me to preside at this meeting, I knew of him by the hearing of the ear, and of his work from many of the clergy in the neighbourhood in which he works. It is one of the disadvantages—or shall I say advantages—of a Bishop, that he possesses an enormous amount of information. He is told all kinds of things—some pleasant and some unpleasant—and he knows a great deal more of what is going on in different parts of London than anybody else, except, perhaps, the Commissioner of Police.

'I had heard many times of the excellent work which Dr. Stephenson and his Institution were doing in the East End of London and other places ; but until this afternoon I had not the opportunity of judging the work by personal contact. When Dr. Stephenson expressed the hope that I would visit the Home, I assure you I did so with very great pleasure and delight. The excellencies of the Institution are obvious to the eyes of anybody who knows its temper and arrangements. Children are perfectly straightforward. It is quite imposssible to get them to be deceitful in their early days. I am afraid that is left for us to do when we grow older. They are, thank God, by nature the most straightforward and direct of human beings, and it is easy in walking among them to see what is their interest in life, and what are their relations with those with whom they stand. I have not seen in many places the children run from their play and put their hands in the hands of the officers, as I saw them do this afternoon. I would bear my testimony that this Institution in all that I saw was all that could be desired. It is in seeing things like that, that one feels the great advantage of the system by which at present we do our philanthropic work.

'The children I see around me, and the children I saw this afternoon, filled my heart with joy, as they would fill the heart of any one of you here. We trust that there are many of them who, when they have grown up as honourable citizens, will look back with delight to the help and kindness they received from all concerned with the Children's Home; that when they have gone out into the world, they will turn back and say, "Thank God, that in the days of my youth, I knew what was the example of a Christ-like life, that I was taken out of the evil of the world, into the hearts of those who served Christ; and I was taught the lessons of that life by the message which was brought home to me by the loving eye and the smiling face of one who, for no other reason but the love of Christ, held out her hands to me, and took me to her bosom.'

The year 1899 saw the beginning of a development of the Children's Home work that has since grown to so great an importance that it ought to be chronicled here, although in truth Dr. Stephenson himself was in such bad health that he was able to have very little to do with it. The 'Young Leaguers' Union' was a very successful endeavour to organize the interest of the happy children of Christian families in this great work. Its beginnings so nearly synchronize with the time when

Dr. Stephenson laid the work down that it would be quite fair for the Young Leaguers to regard themselves as successors, in part at least, to the great enterprise which he founded.

At the end of 1899, at the urgent advice of his doctors, Dr. Stephenson removed to 109 Mount View Road, Stroud Green, London, N., which was some considerable distance from the Home in Bonner Road. This was, of course, done in order to secure for him rest and relief, of which he was feeling in great need.

The Christmas Festival of the Home for this year fell upon Dr. Stephenson's sixtieth birthday. A presentation was made to him from the Old Boys and Girls, and Dr. Waller, who was his lifelong friend, and had been nominated for the ministry by his father, undertook to make the presentation on their behalf. A letter had been drawn up from the Old Girls and Boys, and a writing-desk, with a picture of the Interior of the Chapel at Bonner Road, were the mementoes selected. Dr. Waller said:

'I have been asked to perform a unique and to me a very agreeable duty. By a happy coincidence this day of Annual Festival is your birthday, and your friends desire to mark the event. On the ground of old friendship I have been asked on this interesting occasion to present to you the congratulations of this meeting, of the friends of the Children's Home in both hemispheres, and I think I may add, of your brethren in the ministry.

'Perhaps you may have a little misgiving as to whether it is a matter altogether for your congratulation to enter upon your Sixth Decade. For the sake of your work, we could have wished that it had been your fiftieth instead of your sixtieth birthday! Few lives have been crowded with more useful work, and we do most sincerely pray that you may long be spared, and that God may crown your life with every needful blessing.

'Our friendship is of long standing, for it began in the prime of our youth—before either of us had entered the ministry. Your father was the Superintendent of the Whitby Circuit, in which I resided, and it was he who nominated me for the ministry. I well remember our first acquaintance when you came home from Wesley College for your holiday. I can see you now in my mind's eye, as a slim youth with certain traits of character which you have never lost; for in your case, "the child was father of the man." It is a long track of time we have to look across to a certain bright Sabbath day when we walked across the stretch of yellow sand to the fishing village on the N.E. coast of Yorkshire, where you made one of your first attempts to preach. The text I well remember—"When they saw the star they rejoiced with exceeding great joy." From that day forward I have watched with sympathetic interest your progress and your ever-increasing influence, both as a minister and as a Christian philanthropist.

'Your rise in the ministry was rapid. Soon I had to admire you "shining from afar." From the first you were appointed to very important charges—to Norwich, Manchester, Bolton, and London. I regard it as providential that six of those early years were spent in the County Palatine. Lancashire thenceforward became the base of your constantly widening and cumulative influence, and of the special work to which you were afterwards called.

'Your appointment to Lambeth marked a crisis and formed an epoch in your ministerial career. Whilst fulfilling your circuit duties, the last thing you dreamt of was to be satisfied with merely "taking your appointments." It was then that your heart yearned over the homeless and friendless waifs and strays of our great city; and it was then that you began to bring the whole forces of your ardent nature to bear on the work of evangelization in one of the vilest quarters in London, south of the Thames. That was the time when you were providentially led to the work with which your name will always be associated, namely, that of saving the children. Little did you think, little did others think, whereto this work would grow!

'I have seen a good deal of your work both in this country and across the Atlantic. There is not only the London colony, but that yonder at Edgworth, where the wild moorland has been turned into a fruitful field—typical of the moral transformation wrought in many of the inmates of those Homes. It must be peculiarly gratifying to you that those who were first associated with you, more than thirty years ago, when the first little cottage was opened as a Refuge and a Home, are with you in the work to-day.

'It was inevitable that you should be wholly set apart to this work. I well remember the deep interest your honoured mother took in your work in Lambeth, and afterwards in Bethnal Green; and I also remember how solicitous she was when you were allowed to withdraw from Circuit work, and devote your whole time to the Home. "I am anxious," she said, to me, "lest Bowman should be drawn off in any way from the work of preaching to which God has called him." That has never happened, and your mother's wish has been fulfilled. If you had given up your great vocation you would never have risen, as you have done, to the highest position in the Wesleyan Methodist Church; and what is more, you would never have been able to do the great work for Christ in connexion with the Children's Home.

'At a very early period in your ministerial life, your voice was heard in Conference debates. In those days, it was deemed rather an audacious thing for a young man to speak in the Conference. Grey locks—or, at least, a bald head—were deemed almost essential to any one who took part in that august assembly. But you, sir, had then neither of these qualifications; and yet you were listened to by the grave fathers, and some of your important and far-reaching proposals have been embodied in subsequent legislation.

'Dear sir, you have risen to the highest position in Methodism. Your brethren have honoured you with the Presidency. But the work by which you are most widely known, and by which your name will be handed on to other generations, is the Institution of the Children's Home. To few men God has given the honour of accomplishing a work so great and so abiding!

'I have to congratulate you on the attainment of your sixtieth birthday, which I do most heartily. For your work's sake we could wish you were a stronger and younger man. But after all, you are not so very old. How can you be old when I am your senior? From fifty to sixty is said to be the youth of age; and from sixty to seventy the manhood of age. We trust that after another decade there may then be before you a long eventide full of light. We wish you health, happiness, and prosperity; length of days, and life for evermore! We pray especially that God may pour abundantly upon you His richest spiritual blessings.

'My dear Dr. Stephenson, as an old friend, who knew your father and mother, your brothers and sisters, allow me to use the words of St. John: "Beloved, I wish above all things, that thou mayest prosper and be in health, even as thy soul prospereth."'

When the Annual Meeting of the Children's Home Committee was held on May 9, 1900, it was more largely attended than any other previous gathering. The Ex-President, the Rev. Hugh Price Hughes, was in the chair; and the President and the Secretary of the Conference were also present during part of the Meeting. For it was assembled to receive the resignation of Dr. Stephenson. His decision was conveyed in the following letter:

'My dear Friend,

'I shall be obliged if you will convey to our General Committee my wish to retire from the office of Principal of the Children's Home at the coming Conference. I do this under medical advice. You are aware that my health has been uncertain for some time past. My medical advisers declare that I have no organic ailment, and that I am physically equal to any ordinary charge. But they say that the strain involved in carrying the chief responsibility of our great enterprise, with its multitude of cares and anxieties, is more than I ought to bear longer. I had hoped that the arrangements so kindly made to ease the pressure upon me would have enabled me to continue in the position which I have occupied from the beginning of the work. But in this I am disappointed, and with the great increase of our work, and the prospect of more rapid increase within the next few years, I am convinced that you ought to have as colleague a man in the full vigour of life. I feel it, therefore, my sorrowful duty to retire.

'It may avoid misconception if I say that I have no engagement or prospect for future work. But, if it please God to give me some years more of life, I doubt not He will also give me some work to do for His Church. And to the end of my life it will be a joy to me if I can, at any time, or in any way, help the Children's Home, which I might have served better, but could hardly have loved more.

'I am, my dear friend,

'Yours affectionately

'T. BOWMAN STEPHENSON.

'To the Rev. A. E. Gregory.'

The Rev. A. E. Gregory writes the notes on this meeting for *Highways and Hedges* :

'And now a few words as to the future. The Conference may appoint a successor to Dr. Stephenson as Principal of the Children's Home, but no man can ever be to this work what Dr. Stephenson is and has been. It is not simply that a man of his genius, versatility, ingenuity, courage, devotion, cannot be found to succeed him, but even if Methodism were rich enough to provide such a successor, and he were available for the post, there is only one man who is, or can be, the father and founder of the Children's Home. Yet the work must go on. Dr. Stephenson has, by God's blessing, by the generous aid of God's people, and by the wise and loyal co-operation of his fellow workers, built so firmly and so well, that it may not only be sustained, but greatly extended.

'My own intimate knowledge of and interest in the Children's Home goes back for some twenty-eight years, and much as I admire the material development of the Home, this is not, in my judgement, the most striking feature. There are plenty of men who can build houses and chapels, but there are not many who could have impressed upon an Institution the spirit which animates the officers, and to a very large extent even the children of the Children's Home. In this respect, Dr. Stephenson has accomplished a work vastly more important and much more difficult than what is generally understood by "founding an Institution."

'And this fact makes the task which awaits the new Principal very much lighter than it would have been if a different class of workers, animated by a less admirable spirit, had been engaged in the work. The man who takes up this duty and responsibility will come into "a goodly heritage," not only in the beautiful and flourishing branches which are scattered throughout the country, but in the staff with whom he must co-operate, and in the children to whom he must minister.

'What as to finance? I do not think that God's

people will allow "these little ones" to suffer through any change in the administration. The one thousand one hundred children of the Home have a safe and a warm place in the hearts of tens of thousands, who will take care that their "bread" shall still be "given" and that every year the door shall open more and more widely to admit the children of want and sorrow. The Lord hath been mindful of us. He will bless us.

'And now, will our friends pray for us? God has blessed His servants and their work: let us ask for still larger blessing. Let us pray that the great Father of all may grant to Dr. Stephenson many more years of faithful, happy, fruitful service in whatever place He may see fit, that the divine wisdom may guide His Church in the choice of those who shall carry on this Christ-like ministry to those who need us most, and that grace, strength, courage, and tenderness may be given to all who labour in the Children's Home.'

When the Conference met it passed the following Resolution:

The Conference hears with profound regret of the resignation of Dr. Stephenson. The Conference expresses in the most emphatic terms its sense of the inestimable service Dr. Stephenson has for so many years rendered, and of the great loss which his retirement must be to the work of the Children's Home. The Conference could not bring itself to entertain the idea of Dr. Stephenson's retirement, were it not for the strongly expressed judgement of his medical advisers that this step is inevitable, and that his release from the cares and anxieties of the Home may, by the blessing of God, secure to him restored health, and power to render further service to the Church. The Conference remembers with devout thankfulness how this work was founded by Dr. Stephenson, and has grown from the very smallest beginnings under his fostering care. His courage, perseverance, and enthusiasm secured for the Home the support and affection of the Methodist Churches at home and abroad, and not of the Methodist Churches alone, but of many others to whom this beautiful and blessed enterprise has commended itself as one of the most admirable of the philanthropies of the time. Dr. Stephenson's breadth of view and varied genius have given to the Children's Home a character altogether different from, and incalculably superior to, that of the ordinary charitable institution. By the adoption of the 'Family System' and by instituting an order of consecrated Christian women for the service of the orphan and the destitute, he has taught British philanthropists the best and most effective way of dealing with the children of sorrow. It is impossible to express in the compass of any resolution the value of such service as Dr. Stephenson has rendered to the Church and to the country. But the Conference is confident that the Institution he has so successfully established will, for many generations, do its beneficent work on the lines laid down by its founder. The Conference trusts that in the providence of God Dr. Stephenson may yet be spared for many years of fruitful service in the Church on earth. It trusts that he will still preserve a close and happy association with the Home, and assures him that his counsel will always be valued by the Committees, and that his presence will ever be welcome in the gatherings of the children and officers. The Conference prays that the remainder of his life may be full of joy and blessing, and that the memory of the thousands of young lives saved from sorrow, shame, and sin by his instrumentality may be to him a constant source of comfort and inspiration.

Many kind expressions of affection and sorrow were received by Dr. Stephenson at his resignation. We content ourselves with printing one which is peculiarly touching:

'MY DEAR DOCTOR,

'Your letter brings me a message that causes me the keenest and most sincere grief. I am wondering what can be the occasion of your taking this sad step. I am wondering whether the condition of your health, or unhappiness caused to you in any way and by any means by any of us, is the cause. Perhaps I may yet be favoured with a little more information that will throw light upon it.

'I cannot tell you what an unnatural thing it seems to me that you should in any sense, even nominally, resign your place in your own work. I do trust that effect will not be given to this, and that some intervention will occur.

'I tell you, you are so treasured in all our hearts that our future life in the Home will be overcast with cloud if you are not with us. I speak of all your old workers. You can depute a Principal, but a Principal will never take your place—we want you, the Father and the Founder. Part of my strength will go from me and from my work if you go, and my chief happiness in life will leave me if you leave the work. I have never failed in my heart's love for you and yours. You are the one man to whom I cling with an affection, which, however unworthy, is still sincere and deep, and more than twenty-five years old. No other man can ever become a friend to me in any real sense. I am not writing evanescent sentiment, but truth which abideth.

'My love and sympathy to Mrs. Stephenson. I earnestly hope that you may be able to change your decision in this momentous matter.

'I am,
'My dear Doctor,
'Yours always affectionately,
'J. PENDLEBURY.'

The Rev. J. Watts-Ditchfield, Vicar of Bethnal Green, writes:

'From my boyhood, the name of Dr. Bowman Stephenson has been familiar to me, but I little imagined that, in the order of God's providence, the first independent charge to be committed to me in my ministerial life would include the Children's Homes which will be for ever associated with his life and work. It was a great joy to me to find myself welcomed in a most real and heartfelt way by Dr. Stephenson. I was welcomed to the Homes not only as a visitor, but also as a friend, and I hope it will not shock the Methodist supporters of the Homes to learn that the children, following their Principal's lead, soon began to call me "Vicar." It was my privilege frequently to meet Dr. Stephenson, and the more I saw of him the more I realized the bigness of his heart, the wisdom of his statesmanship, and the real underlying devotion to his Lord which made his whole life one of service to the Great Father by striving to help the little ones whom He loved. During his long connexion with Bethnal Green, Dr. Stephenson made his influence felt in various directions, and into all that concerned the morality and the purity of the people, especially on the Temperance side, he threw himself with all his heart, and time after time co-operated with Dr. Winnington Ingram, the then head of Oxford House. Great as was this work, however, his real life was with the children. They loved him because he loved them. Dr. Creighton, the then Bishop of London, visited the Children's Homes, much to the delight of the children who looked upon the gaiters and episcopal hat with wonder and with awe. Dr. Creighton was immensely pleased with all he saw, but accustomed as he was to paying official visits, he realized that even Methodists might have been pardoned if they had made just a little preparation for the visit of the Bishop of London to their Homes; but in crossing the courtyard even the presence of the Bishop did not prevent the children from crowding round Dr. Stephenson, seizing hold of his hands and coat-tails, and running with joy by his side as he talked with the Bishop. The Bishop was quick to notice this, and turning round, said, "This cannot be done to order. This is not part of the arranged programme, but it shows that this place is what it professes to be—a real Home." May I be permitted to add one word as to the real grief it was to the good Doctor to retire from the work. As I talked with him, I realized that he felt it was the best thing he could do for the sake of the Homes, and therefore he had no option, for to him the Homes came first, and Dr. Stephenson last.

'I may be pardoned if I add one word more. Few Methodists realize the heroic figure of his successor, Dr. Gregory. I use the term heroic advisedly, because his physical weakness, his pain and sickness were such as to cause ninety-nine men out of a hundred to abandon so great a task, but he, with the heroism begotten of the Spirit of Christ, stuck to his work even to the last. These two men, so different in character, so varied in gifts, formed a unique combination. They were united in their common love to the Homes, and in death they were not divided, and we believe that for both there will be a "Well done" from the Master whom they sought to serve.'

CHAPTER XXIV

Development of Deaconess Work—First Public Consecration Service—Use of Surname—Sanction of Conference—Council of Management formed—First Missionary Deaconess—Work in South Africa—Miss Willard's Visit—Ceylon Work started—Sister Rita Hawkins.

In the years following his Presidency, Dr. Stephenson gave much time and thought to the development of the Deaconess work. We must go back for some years to pick up this new thread. In 1893 he writes about it :

'Twenty-five years ago, two thoughts were given to me which crystallized ere long into purposes. One was to teach our Church practically to care for the bereaved and the wronged children of the land. I was soon enabled to make a beginning in that work : a beginning which has grown into the Children's Home, as it is to-day. The other idea, was to develop in connexion with the Church the systematic, skilful, and sanctified work of devoted women. To some extent, this also has been accomplished in and by the Children's Home, the Sisters of the Children being themselves the witnesses thereof. But in its other and more public aspects, this latter enterprise has had to wait. At length, within the last two years, a healthy beginning has been made ; already seventeen Deaconesses are at work in various parts of the country, and twelve others are in training. If it should please God to spare my life for fifteen or twenty years, I hope to see a development of this work as remarkable and interesting as that of the Children's Home. Nevertheless, in this as in all else, I would say, "The Lord's will be done."

'Here it may be well for me to repeat that the funds of the Deaconess Institute are entirely distinct from those of the Children's Home. The two enterprises are very closely associated in sympathy by the fact that the Principal of the one is the Warden of the other, and that notices of both appear in the same monthly magazine. But it must be clearly understood that the Committee of the Home, as such, undertakes no responsibility for the Deaconess Institute, though several of the best friends of the Home are also generous supporters of the Deaconess work. Up to the present time, in fact, I have personally taken the entire responsibility for the conduct of this enterprise; backed, however, by the valuable and liberal co-operation of Mr. Perks, who is Treasurer, and of several ministers and lay gentlemen, who act as a council of advice. It is the more important that the mutual independence of the Home and the Institute should be clearly understood, because our friends will then realize that the Deaconess Work has no well-established fund on which to draw, and that it can only be continued and developed if funds are forthcoming.'

The first public Consecration Service at which Wesley Deaconesses were 'set apart' took place during Dr. Stephenson's Presidential year, on September 17, in the Chapel of the Children's Home, when three Sisters from Mewburn House were formally received as Deaconesses.

An analysis made by Dr. Stephenson of the number of women workers in the Wesleyan Methodist Church in the year 1892 shows how far the Deaconess idea was already taking hold of the Methodist Church, especially in those places where the need for progress was most keenly realized. It was as follows :

Sisters of the Children, including Probationers	47
Sisters of the People (West Central Mission)	30
Lady Workers (East London Mission)	20
Wesley Deaconesses	15
Mr. Clegg's Evangelists, Halifax	Number Unknown
Yarmouth Sisterhood	Number Unknown
Central London Mission	3
South London Mission (Bermondsey Settlement)	6

He estimates that about one hundred and forty women were in this way devoted to the work of God in connexion with Methodism. 'They vary greatly in the work they do, in their educational and other qualifications, in the training they received, and in the compactness of the organization to which they belong, as well as in other matters. It is probably well that several varying experiments should be tried before any system can be formally approved by the Church and accepted as the best. Meantime, specially in connexion with the Wesley Deaconesses, widespread interest is being aroused in many parts of the country, in which it is hoped to be able to reap the advantage of being able to secure for local enterprises the services of duly trained and authorized Sisters.'

At the Conference this year, a Committee of Inquiry respecting the Deaconess movement was asked for by some who were 'doubtful of this thing, whereunto it would grow'; but the Conference declined to enter upon such an inquiry, and did so in such a fashion as to show that it looked upon the movement with no unfriendly eye.

It was very soon discovered that the title 'Sister,' with the Christian name only, was not sufficiently distinctive when the number of deaconesses began to increase, and at the beginning of 1894 it was agreed that Wesley Deaconesses were to follow the Kaiserswerth usage, and employ the surname also for purposes of distinction.

In September of this year a Deaconess Home was opened at Gravel Lane, Salford, in which two or three Sisters resided.

At the Conference this year a Committee was appointed, on the motion of the Rev. Dr. Stephenson, 'to consider whether the Wesley Deaconess Institute may be brought under the sanction or direction of the Conference, and if so, in what manner this may best be done.'

When this Committee met at the end of the year 1894, there were forty-three Deaconesses and Probationers in the Order. The statement which Dr. Stephenson made before this Committee is a most interesting one:

'Thirty years ago I became aware of the extraordinary spread and influence of the Deaconess movement on the Continent, and read carefully on the subject. In the year 1870 I had the opportunity of visiting Kaiserswerth, and seeing something of the work of the Deaconesses in connexion with the Franco-German War. From that time I have never wavered in the opinion that here is an arm of service of the highest value to the Church, and particularly in times like our own, when the work of the Church must touch social conditions at so many points. When the London Lay Mission was established, I endeavoured to introduce and embody the Deaconess idea, but the times were nor favourable. But the idea has been embodied with increasing thoroughness in connexion with the Children's Home, all the work of which is done by women who have given themselves to it from religious motives, and who have passed through a two years' period of testing and training, and are, in fact, Deaconesses devoted to the care of the children.

'About five years ago I had the opportunity of making an experiment of Deaconess work on a wider field, through the kindness of Mr. Mewburn. When I received his offer of £500 for this purpose, I asked the attendance of a number of leading ministers and laymen at an informal meeting. To that meeting I explained, as fully as circumstances would allow, my wishes and hopes. I did not ask that they should accept definite responsibility, or that they should form a committee of management, but that they should give me an assurance of their sympathy and help in making an experiment. Such assurance was given, and several ministers and other gentlemen allowed me to use their names as a Council of Advice, which might be called together if necessary.

'The undertaking was then commenced; a house was taken and furnished. Mr. Perks consented to accept the treasurership, and from that time the work has progressed with a rapidity and success beyond all that I had hoped. During the period of its existence I have been called to the special labours of the Presidency and Ex-Presidency, and it has been impossible for me to give to this work all the time and attention that I should otherwise have bestowed upon it. One result has been that, modest as has been its expenditure, I could not have carried it on to this time but for the help of a few friends, and of one friend especially, whose generosity and confidence in me and this work have been very great. From the first, however, it has avowedly been an experiment, and I have felt for some months past that the time has arrived when the question of its coming under some form of Connexional supervision and control should be considered.

'Some reasons for this opinion are the following:

'1. Though the expenditure involved is not likely to be large, it is more than any man, who has upon him such responsibilities as the Principal of the Children's Home, should be expected to bear without some Connexional sanction. Hitherto I have had to seek the necessary money amongst my friends, and to appeal to them on grounds which are more or less of a personal character.

'2. I am convinced that the employment of women in such work as that which the Deaconesses do, ought to come under some better control. Women are being extensively employed in our churches. All of them, however engaged and directed, stand before the public as officers of the

Church. Many have had little testing, and no training; and if for any reason they cease to be wanted at any particular place, they have no certain prospect of another appointment. In some cases also, those who have proved unsatisfactory in one place are accepted and employed elsewhere, without any inquiry from those who had to dismiss them. In a word, the employment of women amongst us has reached a stage in which discrimination and control ought to be exercised; though it should be introduced gently, tenderly, and with great care. It is, however, no wish of mine that the Committee should express any judgement upon any other case than that of the Wesley Deaconess Institute. If that Institute should receive Connexional sanction in some safe form, I am quite sure that it would make its way into the confidence of our people, and take its proper place in our economy. It would attract to itself the best of those who desire to be employed in such work, and its existence under such conditions would go far to prevent mischiefs which, without a recognized Institution, would be likely to arise.

'What then is the Wesley Deaconess Institute?

'It may be said to embrace three parts: First, three Training Homes, in which women, who believe that they are called of God to this work, and are recommended by the ministers and other friends of the circuit in which they have resided, are trained for the work of Christian Deaconesses.

'Secondly, one Deaconess Home, at New Gravel Lane, Salford, in which a group of three Sisters live together. Though at present there is only one such home, this is probably the best way in which the services of Deaconesses can be employed in towns, or large sections of towns.

'Thirdly, an Order of trained Deaconesses, who are at work in connexion with Circuits or Missions in England, and, in one case, on the Foreign Mission Field. There are at present twenty-three Deaconesses, thirteen Probationers of the second year, and seven Student-Probationers. For the most part Deaconesses are appointed by the Warden, at the request of the Superintendent minister who employs them, and if they are unable to remain in a particular neighbourhood, they are appointed to some other sphere, so that as long as their conduct is satisfactory, every Deaconess may expect an appointment.

'The probation of a Deaconess extends over two years, of which the first is spent in one of the Training Homes, the second in work upon a Circuit or Mission. During the twelve months' residence the Probationer receives instruction in medical nursing, which fits her for all the emergencies which are likely to arise amongst sick people in the course of her visitation. She is encouraged to visit Institutions and Missions from which she may hope to gather hints which will be useful to her in her after-work, in which some hours of every day are spent. If her year of training proves satisfactory she is then appointed to a station or circuit for her second twelve months; and if during that period her work and character prove satisfactory, she is then 'recognized' as an accredited Deaconess, in connexion with the Annual Gathering, in a simple, solemn service.

'Here comes in naturally the question of the relation of a Deaconess to the Circuit in which she works. In the Circuit she is wholly under the direction of the Superintendent minister. If he choose to confide the direction of her work to a Committee, or to one of his colleagues, that is his business, with which we do not interfere. We appoint no Deaconess, except at the request of the Superintendent minister. and we know no other responsible person than him. The Superintendent can dismiss a Deaconess at three months' notice. The Institute may withdraw a Deaconess at three months' notice given to the Circuit, but with the Circuit she is wholly and only responsible to the Superintendent minister.

'The Circuit employing a Deaconess pays an agreed sum for her services, which varies, according to the cost of living in localities, from £50 to £60 a year. In a permanent system these sums might probably need revision. No direct payment passes between any person in the Circuit and the Deaconess. She receives her payment from the Institute. There are many reasons for this, which will occur to the mind of the Committee, which it is scarcely necessary to mention.

'It will be seen from the above that as soon as her year of residence in the Training House is completed, the Deaconess ceases to be chargeable to the Institute, except for some small and incidental expenses. Her maintenance is provided by the Circuit or Mission employing her. The charges upon the Central Committee will therefore be: The maintenance of the Training Houses; the cost of correspondence and oversight, and the cost of the Annual Gathering. I merely mention here another question of considerable importance, but which can better be considered separately, the question whether some small provision should be made for the retirement of those who shall have spent many years in the service of the Church.

'Taking the three items above mentioned, let me say, first, that, in my judgement, it is not necessary to contemplate the employment of a minister separated to this work. I cannot foresee that that would become necessary within any period which it is worth our while to consider. What may be necessary many years from now none of us can say. So far as we can see, for many years to come no such appointment is likely to be required.

'If you calculate £150 a year for what one may call 'central expenses,' including the cost of the Annual Gathering, that in my judgement will be ample. Then probably two of the three Training Houses at present in existence would be enough to supply the demand that is likely to occur for many years to come for trained Deaconesses. It is not desirable that these agents should be multiplied too rapidly. It is very desirable that those who are employed should reach a very high standard in character and efficiency. If we could send out of the Training Houses *ten* yearly, this would, I think, supply the wear and tear, and meet the demand for additional places. After careful examination of the cost of the houses during the past four years, I am of opinion that the sum of £650 would be sufficient, especially if, by the purchase of a house, rent could be saved. This would make the total expenditure required £800. But if to be secure we calculate the possible requirements of the Institute at £1,000 a year, it would be allowing an abundant estimate.

'One Wesley Deaconess is already employed in the Mission Field. She is working at Durban, in South Africa. I have received from ministers at work in India, China, and other parts of the world, inquiries as to when we may be able to assist them by sending Deaconesses to their fields of labour. Undoubtedly such agencies are urgently needed, and would be highly valued. The work of the Christian Deaconess embraces the care of the children, the sick, the poor, and the lapsed, and there is in the Foreign Mission Field an almost unlimited opportunity for the employment of such women, in Orphanage and other schools ; in Zenana work, and the visitation of the people from house to house; in the instruction of the people ; and in all sorts of domestic arts, as well as the assistance which such women could render in religious meetings of all kinds. The bearing of this enterprise, therefore, upon the Foreign Mission Work ought not to be overlooked ; and I may say in passing, that several of our Deaconesses have expressed a strong wish to be employed in the Foreign Field, and that whilst two of them have already passed the examinations required by the London Obstetrical Society, one of these has done it in order that she may be ready for that work when the call shall come.'

The Committee reported to the Conference as follows :—

The Committee is of opinion that the work of Deaconesses and other women workers is of great value to the Church, and deserves to be encouraged. That whilst not prepared, at present, to recommend that the Wesley Deaconess Institute should be brought under the direction of the Conference, the Committee learns with satisfaction that a responsible Committee of Management is being formed, consisting of members of our Church, and suggests that the Conference should cordially recommend the work to the confidence and sympathy of the Connexion.

The Conference adopted the Report, and recommended the work to the confidence and sympathy of the Connexion, as the Committee had requested; and a responsible Council for the management of the Institute was formed.

This Council of Management met on June 19, 1895, and a Draft of the Constitution for the Deaconess Institute was prepared, to be considered at a further meeting of the Council in September.

At this September Meeting a Code of General Regulations was adopted, which forms the basis of the existing Rules of the Order.

Meanwhile a very interesting development of the Deaconess work had been taking place in South Africa. The first Wesley Deaconess to leave the country for work abroad was Sister Evelyn Oats, who sailed for Durban on March 17, 1894, after having been set apart at a special Consecration Service at the Children's Home. On her arrival at Durban we find her realizing that a new country may have its scenes of wretchedness as well as an old. She writes:

'I went to visit a woman who was ill one day, and oh! what a wretched abode it was. I had to sweep the floor clear from the heaps of ashes and refuse, empty slops, and fetch water from outside. There was no fire, and the only basin in the whole place was an enormous tin one full of dirty clothes, plates and dishes, in slimy water. I wanted the basin, so I emptied the contents, and proceeded to cleanse it with cold water, and certainly got off several layers of dirt. Then the doctor came in and told me to use a syringe for the patient, but added, "I wouldn't use that dirty basin if I were you." I felt like annihilating him, you may imagine, after all my pains. In future I carried my own basins and towels.'

Before very long, however, we find her in Johannesburg, where she had been asked to take the place of another woman who had been serving as a Deaconess, who met with an untimely end, being found alone in her little rooms at Stephenson Cottage three days after her death. Sister Evelyn did not hesitate to take up the work thus laid down, and to continue living at the cottage. She writes:

'It is satisfying to find you thought I had acted wisely in coming here. I can but believe that God chose me and arranged my path with His own wonderful knowledge of need and supply. Mr. Hudson sends his kind regards, and I am to say that they are *very* glad to have me. The work is very heavy; the distances to be covered enormous, and lying at extremes. One lives all the time at high pressure, in the rush and racket of a very London. Here are the same thronging crowds, the vehicular traffic, the busy mart and 'change, the slum life, the blighting effects of drink, misery, and sin visible daily; but Wesley says, "Go not only to those who need you, but to those who need you most," and having done so, I am in my element.'

A second Deaconess was soon required at Johannesburg, and Sister Miriam Scriven went out in

May, 1896. The work there was of a most sensational character. The startling contrasts of wealth and destitution, the abject misery and pain, the defiant vices of this amazing community come out again and again in the correspondence of the Deaconesses.

The remarkable nature of this work, and the superb courage with which it was done, did much to create an ideal in the minds of the members of the Order. One extract from a letter may help to enable our readers to realize something of the situation :

'I have had some strange experiences lately. Another burglary in Stephenson Cottage, between 8 and 8.30 p.m. on Saturday, during the open-air service on Market Square. I had my money with me, but had left my watch and chain off in the morning, having to work in a dirty house which necessitated an old gown, watchpocketless. I thought the watch safer at home !—gold watch and chain ! Also, the thief took down a beautiful little loaded revolver which had been given to me after the last burglary, and kept it. That was all. Really, I felt nonplussed, and inclined to ask, "Why is it permitted ?" for I was on duty bent again. The working men brought me £10 and a big old bull-dog revolver, which is too heavy for me to fire, but may serve to intimidate. Moral, "Lay not up for yourselves treasure upon earth." However, I have been preserved from danger in a very remarkable way lately. Last Saturday week, about 8.30 p.m., a young man came to tell of a house where lay two women and a child in one room with smallpox, and no one would go near them. I asked, "Could they afford to pay a nurse?" and he replied, "Oh, yes, they *must* afford it; if help didn't go soon they would die." "Then why don't you help?" said I. "Oh," he replied, "that is just why I came to you; nobody will go." "It will mean being carried away to the lazaretto when the inspector comes to-morrow, and most likely it will mean death, and it is now too late to get to explain to any one, and my folks at home, they may never hear the rights of the story, nor know that duty called." All this flew through my mind, and I confess I hesitated. Then I remembered that "He" went even to certain death for me; should I fear danger for Him? Did Christianity mean nothing that it should fail me at the test? What was I better than the neighbours who had fled? Of course I went, and after crossing the threshold knew no more fear. How glad I was I went! and I had reason to be gladder later on. The disorder was terrible, but that was soon changed, and the patients fed and sponged. Then seeing how very seriously ill the elder woman was, I spoke to her of her soul's welfare, and prayed. Almost deaf and with blackened mouth, I was forced to bend over her, and she clasped my hands with her feverish ones as she said, "You'll think it strange, Sister; but I'd rather die if the Lord will take me; life is so hard." And her daughter explained that a brutal husband made life a burden; a recent kick in the stomach having caused rupture. This younger woman's husband lay ill of a supposed fever, which afterwards proved smallpox. At 11.30 Sunday morning the inspector (long delayed) came, pronounced it smallpox of a virulent type, and ordered the whole household to the lazaretto. I gave him the names one by one, even of the suspects, and he wrote on, promising to send the ambulance as soon as possible. He went off, and lo! my name was spared! Oh! what a lesson to trust in God and do the right. I do not understand the escape even yet, but "though thou walkest through the fire thou shalt not be burned." Verily He had given His angels charge to keep me! At 3 p.m. I saw the procession off, climbing the wagon to give a last drink to quench their burning thirst. Then the yellow flag was hoisted, and I walked home, down the middle of the road, let myself into Stephenson Cottage, and subjected myself to severe disinfection, after which I went off to get vaccinated, but found the doctor out. (I arranged for this to be done a couple of months ago, but the appointment failed.) Six hours later the elder woman died, every "suspect" has had it, besides two men who were in the house to a meal a week before. Of course, I may yet fall a victim, but "all is well."'

In January, 1897, Sister Evelyn Oats opened a Convalescent Home. It was a daring private venture, but proved an immense success. During the first year more than a hundred passed through it. She writes:

'They enter by certificate, in all stages of convalescence, and receive the tender care, the individual thought, that is one of the chief charms of a home (spelt with a little h). There are *rules*, framed chiefly for the patients' own welfare, but these are never obtruded, and have rarely indeed been broken. The diet is simple, but plentiful, and of the best quality, cooked by a North countrywoman whose home-made bread and delicious puddings are long remembered by old patients. The *charge* is two guineas per week; but a large number of the patients have contributed nothing, being both friendless and penniless.'

At the Convocation of 1896 the Deaconesses had a visit from the well-known American philanthropist and leader of women's social work, Miss Frances Willard. She was in very frail health, and quite unable to stand while she spoke. None who were present will ever forget that address. Much of it was too sacred to be reported. She spoke as a sister to sisters, sometimes using the familiar address, 'my dears,' as though it were a gathering round the fire-place of the old home. Her references to discipline through which God's providence had put her in early life, to her first public work, and the trials and sacrifices it involved, and to the peace and strength which through and in all she had derived from communication with the All-sufficient Father, were accompanied with a wonderful spiritual power. Her words about her own health, and the necessity of the Deaconesses caring for theirs, were full of wisdom and sisterly affection. And as she dwelt upon the fact that life's opportunities were fast passing away, and the eternal realities growing nearer and plainer, the listeners felt that 'all heaven was open.' It meant much to all the members of Convocation, at the close of the session, to have a hand-shake and a sisterly word from this gifted and affectionate woman.

She was indeed not far from the end of her life. In little more than a year she had passed away;

and her memory was kept green at the Children's Home by the name given to the Training House for Workers—Willard House.

This Convocation was also notable for a visit from Mrs. Trimmer, the wife of a well-known Wesleyan missionary in Ceylon. Mrs. Trimmer pleaded for the work in Ceylon, and the question was raised whether the Deaconesses could manage to support one or two of their own number as missionaries to the women of Ceylon. The Rev. G. J. and Mrs. Trimmer were deeply interested in a call that had come to them from Puttur.

Puttur is a village, and the centre of a group of villages inhabited by Tamil people, many of whom are of high caste. It is in the densely populated peninsula of the north of Ceylon, a district where the main industry is the cultivation of rice, curry stuffs, and tobacco. The nearest large town is Jaffna, which is ten miles distant to the south-east. 'Jaffna (Puttur)' stands as a separate circuit on our *Minutes*, under the North Ceylon District, a Tamil minister being appointed there, under the care of the Superintendent of the Jaffna station, the Rev. George J. Trimmer, who is also the Chairman of the District.

When Mr. Trimmer returned to England on furlough in 1895, he brought an earnest request from the people of Puttur: 'Remember our need; bring help back with you.'

Truly the need was urgent—the supplying of the need was apparently impossible. When the Women's Auxiliary regretfully had to refuse assistance, Mr. and Mrs. Trimmer felt that they must give up hope. But away in Ceylon and at home in England God's people were praying, and God answers prayer in His own time and way. When Dr. Stephenson wrote and asked Mrs. Trimmer to speak at the Convocation of 1896, she did not know that his letter was God's answer, but it was so. The pressing need of the women of Ceylon was laid before that company of Christian women, Wesley Deaconesses and Sisters of the Children, assembled in the chapel at Bonner Road, and the Spirit of God breathed upon them. When an appeal was made for one worker from that assembly the response was ready, and before the day closed it had been decided that not one, but two Deaconesses should go out to Puttur, and that the responsibility of supporting them there should be undertaken by the members of Convocation.

'When we left the Convocation,' says Mr. Trimmer, 'feeling that the appointment of two deaconesses might be considered certain, the uppermost feeling in our hearts was, "Now to Him that is able to do for us far more abundantly than we can either ask or think, to Him be the glory."'

Sister Gertrude Nettleship was selected for the work, and sent out to Puttur in July, 1897. A second worker was not found until the next year, when Sister Faith Hunter joined Sister Gertrude in October, 1898.

Sister Evelyn Oats returned to England in 1899, and was present at the Convocation, where she gave a most vivid account of her work; but as to what effect her work had had upon public opinion in the Gold Reef City she naturally did not speak. That was left to the Rev. W. Hudson, who for many years has had charge of the Central Johannesburg Circuit, and who was on furlough in this country. 'I don't know another lady in all Johannesburg,' said he, 'who has there the place that Sister Evelyn has. The work of the Deaconesses has secured them a sort of immunity, and their persons are sacred in the streets by day or by night.' When the Diamond Jubilee celebrations were over, there was a balance of £4,000 unspent, and suggestions were invited as to what would be the best means of expending this sum. A public meeting was called in the Exchange, and lawyers, politicians, and men of wealth expounded their schemes; but at length Sister Evelyn got up and stated her case in favour of a Victoria Convalescent Home, and to-day, on a plot of ground which was given to the Sister, who is also a trustee of the Home, Johannesburg has its Convalescent Home. The Sister beat the lawyers, and carried the meeting with her.

The first Sister-in-Charge at Mewburn House, Sister Rita Hawkins, passed away on April 3, 1900. She had given her services without salary to the work, and her gracious, dignified, yet unassuming manner made her a singularly suitable person to influence the probationers committed to her care. She was much more than the head of Mewburn House. Among the poor women of Bethnal Green her name was as ointment poured forth. For their sakes she underwent training as a nurse, and became a most efficient helper in time of trouble to patients of all kinds. To the Church work at Victoria Park she gave her leisure time. Her class for women was always crowded, and her men's Bible-class was very successful. In 1899 she resigned her position to marry the Rev. W. C. Williams, of Loughborough.

She at once entered upon circuit life with only too much zeal, but in the midst of her work came the unexpected call to rest. Her death was felt as a great loss by all the members of the Order.

CHAPTER XXV

Superintendent of Ilkley Circuit—Deaconess Institute—*Flying Leaves*—Lady Associates—Œcumenical Conference—Deaconess College acquired—Ceylon Fund—Badge of the Order—Opening of the College—Death of Sister Dorothy Coy.

WHEN at the Conference of 1900 the resignation of Dr. Stephenson of his position as Principal of the Children's Home was accepted, he did not go into retirement. Although he felt himself unable to bear the very great strain of the work of the Children's Home, he believed himself to be still capable of service as a circuit minister, and declared himself ready to take an appointment from the Conference in the ordinary course. After some negotiations with other places, it was decided that he should be appointed as Superintendent to the Ilkley Circuit, and he came there in September, 1900.

At first the relief from the old burdens gave him new spring and energy, and he threw himself into the work of the circuit with great zeal, re-organizing and renewing everything. Soon a project for a new Sunday-school building was started ; a Holiness Convention was arranged to be held in Easter week ; Dr. Stephenson's Service-Book and Supplemental Hymnary were introduced into the Chapel ; and a 'Circle of Young Disciples' was formed to help the

"Doctor" and one of his Bairns.

Photo, Russell and Sons.

Dr. and Mrs. Stephenson and Sister Dora in 1900.

[*face p. 105.*

children to find the way into the Church and to join in its spiritual life.

Meanwhile he had not resigned his connexion with the Wesley Deaconess Institute; but it was at first understood that Dr. Gregory, whom the Conference had appointed Principal of the Children's Home, should continue to assist him with the Deaconess work also. Mewburn House was still head quarters, and Calvert House, Leicester, was also training some Probationers, under the Sub-Wardenship of the Rev. Joseph Posnett, who had succeeded the Rev. William Bradfield in this office; Sister Dorothy Coy being Sister-in-Charge.

There were at the time seventy-four Deaconesses and Probationers belonging to the Wesley Deaconess Institute, as distinct from the Sisters of the Children belonging to the Children's Home. The financial year had been closed with a debt of about £500. An endeavour was made at this time to start a Superannuation Fund, both for the Sisters of the Children and for the Deaconesses. The two funds, however, were to be kept entirely distinct.

There was good news from Ceylon: 'Leading officials in the Civil Service say that they never could have believed it possible for any mission enterprise to have laid hold upon the native population as the medical work of our Sisters at Puttur has done. Sometimes as many as one hundred and fifty persons are waiting to be dealt with in the verandah of the little Mission House. Prejudice is disappearing with wonderful rapidity, and the ministry of healing is preparing the way for the gospel. Our Sisters, Gertrude Nettleship and Faith Hunter, have mastered the difficulties of the language, and are able to converse freely with the people. We hear that they hope to be able shortly to conduct services without the aid of an interpreter. The educational work also is very prosperous. When it is remembered that Puttur has been for many years a kind of forlorn hope, and that we were warned by experienced missionaries that in sending our Sisters there we were condemning them to a hopeless enterprise, our friends will the more readily understand the importance of assisting so good a work.'

Next summer the Convocation was held in London, and the Consecration Service was conducted by Dr. Stephenson in Wesley's Chapel, City Road, when twenty-two Sisters were set apart for the work, ten as Sisters of the Children, and twelve as Wesley Deaconesses. In the evening the Annual Meeting was held at City Road, with the Rev. Dr. H. J. Pope in the chair. Dr. Stephenson made a special statement in view of the fact that the next Conference was to be asked to take the Institute under the official care of the Church. He gave some reasons why the Institute should be fully acknowledged by the Conference. In the first place it had fitted itself to become so by the fact that it had been made a strong arm in the service of the Church. Then the character of the work, of which much ignorance existed in many parts of the country, needed to be made public ; also Connexional confidence must be won for the movement ; and further it was obvious that such an Institution must have important connexion with other departments of our Church work. Finally, it might be expected that larger numbers of suitable candidates would be ready to offer themselves if they knew they were becoming connected with a recognized branch of the Wesleyan Methodist Church.

The Conference agreed to the request that was made to it, and took the responsibility of itself appointing a General Committee for the management of the Institute. It also gave its provisional approval to the Regulations, directing the Committee to consider them during the year, and report specially upon them to the next Conference. It appointed the Rev. Dr. Stephenson as Warden; the Revs. Simpson Johnson and Dr. Arthur E. Gregory, Secretaries; Mr. Robert W. Perks, M.P., Mr. Francis Horner, and Mr. Albert W. Bain, Treasurers.

From this time the office of the Institute was definitely removed to Ilkley, and Dr. Stephenson took into his own hands that part of the work which had been done for him during the year by Dr. Gregory.

The Wesley Deaconess Institute had up to this time, by permission of the Committee of the Children's Home, used the *Highways and Hedges* as its organ; two or three pages of that magazine being usually given to Deaconess matters. But now a separate periodical was felt to be necessary, and *Flying Leaves*, taking its name from the *Fliegende Blätter*, of Kaiserswerth, made its appearance on September 1, 1901, and has from that time been the official organ of the work.

The second number of *Flying Leaves*, published on November 15, 1901, is distinguished by the commencement of the 'Lady Associates' of the Wesley Deaconess Order. The idea was partly suggested by the 'Third Order' of St. Francis of Assisi. Lady Associates are women who have the Deaconess spirit, and acknowledge the call to this service, but their duties in life are such as prevent them from actually becoming deaconesses themselves. They undertake to pray for the work, to give countenance and sympathy to all who are engaged in it, and to assist it financially by giving or collecting a guinea a year for its funds. They receive the badge of the Order, made in special colours, as an Associate's Badge, and are welcomed to the meetings of the Sisterhood.

At the same time that the Order was strengthened by the accession of the Lady Associates, it was limited by the fact that the Sisters of the Children were no longer counted as members of it. There remained, however, a memory of much kindly fellowship in the past, and a warm feeling of mutual interest between the workers belonging to the two associations.

The first list of Lady Associates was published on December 15, and contains fifty-three names.

In the autumn of the year 1901 the third Œcumenical Conference was held, this time at City Road, London. The reports of the previous Conferences in 1881 and 1891 had each been prefaced by an Introduction written by William Arthur, and Dr. Stephenson felt it to be an honour to be asked to perform the same task on this occasion. The paragraph about the chapel in which they met shows his love for City Road.

'The third Œcumenical Conference met, as did the first, in Wesley's Chapel. It found the venerable building renewed, beautified, and more commodious, while every characteristic and historical feature of the edifice had been preserved with a most reverent care. It was gratifying to the Wesleyan Methodists, who are especially the guardians of the venerable church, that their brethren from all parts of the world should find Wesley's Chapel, in its structure and adornments, not unworthy of its great history. Their pleasure, too, was enhanced by the fact that so many of the Churches of the Methodist stock had gladly taken a part in the work of restoration. For centuries to come, if the world should last so long, ever-increasing throngs of the loyal children of Methodism will journey from the ends of the earth to meditate and pray on the spot where Wesley most frequently preached, and where his "bonnie dust" reposes.'

He still adhered to his strong convictions on the topic of Methodist Union.

'Nevertheless, the needless existence of separate Churches is to be regretted, and separation is needless, except when sufficiently grave variations of creed, method, or polity compel it. It can scarcely be denied that in some of the now divided Churches of Methodism there are no sufficient causes for their separation. In such cases economy of men and means might well be promoted, and a larger result of a higher kind expected from labours which would be no longer in any degree expended upon rivalry or self-protection. True everywhere, this is especially true in new and sparsely-populated countries. Hence it was a cause of deep thankfulness that, whilst the second Œcumenical Conference was heralded by Methodist Union in Canada, the third could rejoice over a like Union in Australasia, all but completed.

'It would have added to the joy of the Conference if any decisive step could have been reported towards Union between at least some of the several Methodist Churches in Great Britain and in the United States. But it was tacitly recognized that in the countries where Methodism has been longest planted, is most widely and strongly entrenched, and has the memory of past struggles still surviving, the difficulties in the way of Union are the greatest. The Conference, however, greatly rejoiced in the fact that controversy between Methodist Churches is a thing of the past, and the relations between those Churches are cordially harmonious, and show promise of an increasing intimacy of relation and feeling as the years pass on.'

He regretted that 'woman's work in the Church was only represented by an extemporized public meeting added to the programme.'

At the first Œcumenical Conference a Memorial Service had been held for President Garfield. Now for a second time a President of the United States was struck down by a murderer. The grief of the Conference was the more acute because President McKinley was a loyal and consistent Methodist.

The topic allotted to Dr. Stephenson in the Conference itself was 'Interdenominational Fellowship among Methodists.' He began by saying, 'I do not like my subject, and I have tried to get out of it, because if I speak honestly about it I know I shall not please everybody, and I doubt very much if I shall please anybody. . . . It does not touch many of the most serious evils with which we have to deal. It does not touch, for instance, the undue and wasteful competition that is going on here and there, the overlapping which we cannot help regretting at so many points of our work. It does not affect the needless extra management expenses of three or four separate Missionary Societies; it does not touch the fact that we have small Theological Colleges which cannot be so effective as larger and better equipped Colleges would be, and yet which cost relatively more. It does not touch the miserable scandal of two or three little chapels standing side by side in villages at needless expense of money and men, and more than that, to the destruction of all wholesome Church discipline. . . . I do not think fraternal fellowship, good, sweet, pleasant, and helpful as it is, can go very much farther. There are sentimental young men and women who sometimes desire to assume to each other the platonic relation of brother and sister. It ends in nothing, or it ends in something warmer. We were told yesterday about a courtship that had been going on in Australia, and one cannot help asking in reference to some courtships, how long they are to go on. Courtship too long continued is apt to become tedious and fretful, and even quarrelsome. It may possibly end in action for breach of promise. Marriage, if there is to be one, should really not be put off too long. A friend of mine was crossing the Atlantic. There was a bright little boy on board, and he asked him how old he was. "Six." "Would you like to be seven?" "Yes." "Would you rather be seven or eight?" "Eight." "Why?" "Because I want to hurry up and be married.'' Speaking only for myself, it appears to me that we have got just about as far with interdenominational fellowship as we are likely to get. We may continue as we are, and we may even somewhat improve our relationship to each other, but I believe we have reached the point at which any serious further advance spells Union, and nothing less. . . . I am not going to discuss Union; I am not at liberty to do it, it is not my subject, and I know there are plenty of difficulties in the way; but in my judgement, if any serious further advance in this direction is desired, it is only possible by way of Union, and we may well ask, " Shall we have grace and sense and wisdom to do the right thing under these circumstances ? " I pray God we may.'

No action, however, was taken by the Conference on the subject.

One more Œcumenical Conference fell within the actual life-time of Dr. Stephenson, that which was held in Toronto in 1911, but he was far too ill to be able to attend. Methodist Union had made some further progress; the Methodist New Connexion, the United Methodist Free Church, and the Bible Christians having joined together to form the United Methodist Church in England. Discussions were going on between the Methodist Episcopal Church and the Methodist Episcopal Church, South, though no formal action had been taken; and a union was being contemplated in Canada between the Methodist and the Presbyterian Churches. The whole process, however, seems exceedingly slow. There appears to be more spiritual vitality about the actual organizations in which men are grouped than most people imagine, and such organizations tend to preserve their individuality, though the amount of reason that can be given for their separateness is exceedingly small. But slow as the process of union is, the tendency is all one way at present, and if the Methodists become convinced that devotion to Christ and His work, and brotherly love, demand organic union, the obstacles that are presented by this curiously persistent individuality of existing organizations will surely be finally overcome.

To turn back to the Deaconess work, it will be seen that it had now come to a critical moment in its history. Institutions in London and Leicester could not be efficiently managed by a minister who was subject to the ordinary Methodist three years' system, and might be appointed now at one end of the country and now at another; and the Wesley Deaconess Institute, if it were to develop, needed a home of a different character from either of the houses referred to. At this juncture the way was opened for advance in a surprising and unexpected manner. To Dr. Stephenson himself, the events about to be narrated came with a spiritual content that can only be appreciated when we remember the bitterness and pain it had been to him to give up his work in connexion with the Children's Home. The new prospect came as an assurance to his soul that God was still using him for great purposes, and the consolation and strength it brought enabled him to carry through to a successful issue a new development which gave the Wesley Deaconess Institute an assured prospect of unfettered development in close relation with the Wesleyan Methodist Church.

He tells the story himself :—

'During the past few weeks our gracious God has been giving to me wonderful proofs of His favour and goodwill. I cannot doubt this. If I did, I should have to give up my faith in a special Providence. For seldom, if ever, has a chain of remarkable circumstances been made by The Hand of Power and Skill more plainly than in the circumstances I am going to relate.

'To understand it all, I must go back a little. For thirty-one years I was the principal officer, as I had been permitted to be the founder, of the Children's Home. When twenty-one of these years had elapsed it was given to me to commence another movement, which I should have preferred to be a development of the work of the Children's Home, the whole thus becoming a great Institute of philanthropic Christianity. But that was not to be. The Wesley Deaconess Institute, therefore, was separately organized, and grew up side by side with its elder sister—the Children's Home. Ten years passed, during which this work of the Deaconess commended itself to the wisest and most responsible men in our Church. At the end of the thirty-first year I was compelled to withdraw from the Principalship of the Children's Home, but I could not also withdraw from the Wardenship of the Wesley Deaconess Institute. No one else was quite ready to take it up, and so, when I left London, we had to pack up our books and documents and transfer the business of the Institute to my study in the country.

'Another twelve months elapsed, and the Conference of the Methodist Church adopted the Wesley Deaconess Institute as its own, and resolved to appoint annually a Committee for the government of it. So, though the youngest Institution of the Church, and possessing no strength beyond the buoyancy of youth, the Institute took its place alongside of the Missionary Society, the Home Missions, the Theological and Normal Colleges, and the other recognized departments of our organized activity.

'But in the year which had elapsed it had become evident that no arrangement could be more inconvenient than for the Warden to be living two hundred miles away from the principal training house of the Order. During the year of resident Studentship, the Probationers ought to become well known to him, and his influence ought to be exerted upon them, especially as for many years afterwards he must be in correspondence with them when scattered in their stations throughout the world. Besides this, he must mainly determine their spheres of labour, and act on their behalf, as well as on the behalf of the Church, in many ways, possible only to one who knows the Deaconesses personally and well. It seemed, therefore, as though the Warden must give up his connexion with the work, or go back to London, or else the head quarters of the work must move northwards.

'It will be understood that these alternatives caused much anxious and prayerful thought. To myself the matter was one of great moment. I had accepted a warm and hearty invitation for my next circuit, to one which was very attractive to me, by its position in a great city, by its inspiring congregations worshipping in large churches, and by the opportunity it would give me to promote aggressive movements in a large population. I had accepted this invitation with every confidence that, if life were spared, I should be able, when I left Ilkley, to go to this new and attractive sphere. But as the months went on, and I found that Connexional claims in all parts of the country were becoming more rather than less, and that the work of the Wesley Deaconesses was commending itself more and more, and promising to develop largely, I felt that I must reconsider the position. I shrank from undertaking the charge of an important and enterprising circuit, unless I could give to it my best and fullest energy and attention. It appeared possible that I could, in the years of life left in me, serve the Church of my fathers and my choice in various ways, both by voice and pen ; and it seemed also plain that by God's blessing I might be able to do for the consolidation and establishment of the Deaconess work of our Church, what, perhaps, no man could do who had not had my experience. It was not easy to give up prospects of work which were very attractive, but after full consideration I felt that I ought to release the circuit in question from its obligation to me, leaving the future to be shaped for me by that kind and wise Hand which had never failed me in the past. I acted accordingly, without, at that time, having any anticipation of the events which were shortly to occur.

'But events ripened rapidly. Opinions, which I was bound to respect, urged that I should retain my responsibility for the Deaconess enterprise which

I had commenced, and that, therefore, it would be better that the Training House and Offices of the Institute should be moved northwards. But the personal element in the case was not the only determining one. Our Church is powerful in the great cities of the Midlands and the North; and in the great populations of those parts of the country, social and religious problems cry for solution not less loudly than in London. A large number of our Wesley Deaconesses are at work in the great belt of population which stretches from Hull to Liverpool, and from Leicester to Newcastle, and somewhere within that region it seemed desirable that the centre of the movement should be fixed. But I am a circuit minister, subject like my brethren to the itinerancy; and the uncertainty involved in this fact added gravely to the difficulty of the problem. The funds of the Institute were in no condition to accept a considerable charge for the maintenance of its chief officer, nor had Conference been asked for a minister to be devoted to this work. What was to be done? The chief Home of the Institute might be brought northwards, but it could not be moved from place to place every three years; or the perplexities would recur ere long. What could be done, except to commit the whole matter into the Hand that is too strong to fail, and the Wisdom that makes no mistake? Prayer was offered, much and often, for power to do this, and one day, as I was speeding along in the train to fulfil a preaching engagement, there came to me a rich and wonderful manifestation of the power of God. To His glory I humbly record it. My heart burned within me, as did the hearts of those travellers who, long since, were going to Emmaus. I felt the Hand of God was on my head, as a father's might be on his child's, in blessing. It was difficult, even in the railway carriage, to refrain from shouting aloud to the praise of His glory. I could but cover my face with my hand, that I might thus be alone with God, even in the presence of my fellow-passengers, and so wonder and adore. Then came the thought, Why is this? Is this a signal that my work is done, or is it a sign that there is some specific work yet for me to do? And to this question I could but say, "Be it according to Thy will."

'Not long before this, a large vacant building had been suggested as suitable and amply sufficient for the purposes we had before us, but, though it could probably be bought up favourably, the lowest cost seemed far beyond any means at our disposal. A small portion of the Century Fund was to come to the Wesley Deaconess Institute out of the amount allocated to Home Missions, but at the most liberal expectation it would be quite insufficient for making such a purchase. Now, however, the idea of this building returned powerfully to my mind, and, after much thought and prayer, it seemed to me that we might reverently put God's will to the test. The time was most inopportune for launching any wide general financial scheme, but if a very few friends of the work should be made willing to bear the cost, that would not only make the purchase possible, but might be taken as an indication of the mind of God concerning it. Eventually I wrote to a friend of many years' standing, saying that I would like to put before him a piece of work that I thought needed doing; that having heard the particulars of it, he might, if he were led to think it proper, in some way aid it. Through his kindness, a long evening was spent in his hospitable home, talking frankly of the work, its needs, and the possibility of giving to it permanent status and ampler development, through the purchase of this building At the end of the conversation, my kind friend said, " You shall hear from me in a fortnight"; but next morning at the breakfast table, he said, " We think we had better strike while the iron is hot, and I shall be glad, if you can carry out this scheme, to give you £2,000 towards it."

' It now seemed possible that if the building were purchased favourably, and a substantial amount could be relied upon from the Century Fund grant, the acquisition of the property might be achieved, but still some alterations would be necessary in the building, the whole would have to be thoroughly cleansed and put in order, additional furniture would be wanted, and some margin must be allowed for contingencies which it was impossible to foresee. Prayer and meditation led me to ask another friend of many good works to let me tell him about what was going on. He proved himself as kind and hospitable as the former. It is good to find shrewd and successful men of business deeply interested in all details of the work of God, and considering proposals for the extension of that work with as much care and thoroughness as they examine the details of their own business, or the enterprises of municipal government. After many inquiries, freely made and frankly answered, my friend promised to give £1,000. Again my heart leaped in wonder and gratitude! £500 will still be needed, but amongst our generous friends, especially in the neighbourhood in which the Institution will be placed, we cannot think there will be any difficulty in realizing this amount.

'Two further steps were necessary. The General Committee of the Wesley Deaconess Institute must consider the policy involved, and the practical steps proposed. A large and representative meeting in due time assembled. The whole matter was thoroughly discussed. The entire Committee expressed by vote its judgement that the head quarters of the Institute should henceforth be located north of the Trent, and, with only three neutrals and none voting in the negative, the meeting authorized the purchase of the property in question, subject to certain prudent conditions. Seldom has any Committee meeting been held in which was felt a deeper sense of the overshadowing presence of God. The frankest discussion of the subject, from every point of view, did not for a moment interfere with that deep emotion, and the decisive vote was given with the conviction in every mind that "this thing was of the Lord."

'The Home Mission Committee had still to be consulted. It assembled a few days later. The case was put before it, and was thoroughly discussed, some of our most trusted and beloved Missioners taking keen interest and active part in the consideration. Again there rested on the meeting a gracious sense of the presence of God. It was felt that the Church was being led to take a step full of promise for all our enterprises on behalf of the religious and social benefit of the people. By a unanimous vote, the Committee expressed its gratification with the proposal, and its willingness to devote the expected grant to this purpose. So, by the consent of many minds, some privately consulted, others comparing their views in large and important Committees, this project has been cordially welcomed and heartily blessed.

'Connected with it is a personal question, to which I must refer in order to avoid misunderstanding. Such a building being secured, there will be more need for the careful oversight and administration of one who is familiar with the work, who may be able to give it a right shape during its early and formative years. There is, however, no intention of asking the Conference to set apart a salaried minister to this work. If God should spare my life, it will be my joy to serve this enterprise for a few years, without drawing upon the funds of the Institute; and if those years be not permitted to me, the God who has led us up to the present point will take care of His own work in His own way. So to Him be all the glory! "Brethren, pray for us."'

The building referred to is of course the College now known as the Wesley Deaconess College at Ilkley. It had been erected as a boarding-school for boys, but had not proved a financial success, and was therefore offered on very favourable terms.

It was purchased in February, 1902. It is very interesting to note what was the programme for its use, as it first appeared to Dr. Stephenson's mind.

'To return to our new possession. For what will it be used? First, it will provide the offices necessary for the correspondence and general business of the Institute. This has already become voluminous. There are eighty-six Deaconesses, Probationers, and Students in the Wesley Deaconess Order. They are residing in all parts of England, in Scotland, Ireland, South Africa, New Zealand, and Ceylon. Their appointments have to be arranged yearly, and in some cases changes have to be made during the year. Correspondence must pass between the Warden and Superintendent Ministers, Local Treasurers, and others, as well as between him and the Deaconesses, whose relation to the Warden entitles them to receive consideration and advice from him frequently. Whilst their work in the Circuits or Missions is wholly under the superintendence of their ministers, many occasions arise which require that the Warden should be informed, and that the Deaconesses should be advised and directed by him.

'The preparation and publication of this little magazine, necessary in order that our friends and subscribers may be kept well informed, and that new friends may be secured, also demands time, thought, and room. Correspondence with applicants for admission to the Order, with Circuits or Missions desiring to employ our Deaconesses, and with people of all sorts "who want to know," and the proper keeping of the records of what is already a considerable federation, demand suitable offices. These the new building will provide.

'It is thought that provision should be made for the training of twenty student-probationers. The wear and tear of the work, and its gradual extension cannot be met with fewer annually in training. Usually the Wesley Deaconesses have had—

certainly they ought to have had—a fairly good education before they come as candidates. But there are cases of women whose intellectual power, force of character, and deep piety make them eligible candidates in spite of defective early education. It may perhaps prove necessary that some such should receive a longer period of training. It is certain, therefore, that accommodation for not less than twenty students should be provided.

'But we wish to be able to meet the needs of ladies, who, not feeling called to become Deaconesses. and desiring still to live "amongst their own people," yet wish to receive some instruction and training which would qualify them to do better service in their own circuits and neighbourhoods. Six months' or, better, twelve months' residence in a College for Christian workers would be of immense value to such young ladies. Guidance in Bible study, in Christian sociology, in the practical methods of Home Missionary enterprise, in medical nursing and medical cookery, would enable such women to return home trebly equipped for the gentle and powerful ministry which, unpaid, and living in their own localities, they might fulfil amongst the people around them. At no cost, and without the name of Deaconess, they might do true and invaluable Deaconess work.

'This idea has been practically tested in American Methodism. At Chicago, Mr. N. W. Harris has built at great cost a Training School for Home and Foreign Missions, which accommodates two hundred students. Of these, a good proportion become Deaconesses, but many do not. Nor is the intention to become a Deaconess a necessary qualification for entrance. After their term of training is over, many move out upon various lines of Christian service, and many return home to bless with their enlarged powers their own families, their own local Churches, and their own towns. In comparison with the imposing work of our friends at Chicago, our experiment must be a very modest one ; but we are sure it is worth trying. We may be able to accommodate ten such students, who, of course, would meet their own expenses, which need not be large.

'Our new building will also provide residence for our Deaconess Evangelists, and for those Deaconesses who, needing rest and reinvigoration, can come "home" for a while. Occasional visitors from the various Missions in Australia, Canada, the States, and elsewhere must be welcomed, and put into possession of what we can teach them, if the comity of world-wide Methodism, and of the Christian Churches, is to be preserved. For all these purposes our new "Mother-house" will be none too large.

'But there is yet another element of great importance in the case. The primary aims of the Deaconess Order are spiritual. It is a "soul-converting" agency. It must employ to the full all social influences and expedients, but in all, its object must be "soul-winning." It is therefore of first importance that during their student year our sisters should be familiar with the constitutional arrangements and methods of the Methodist Church, and should learn to prize them, to be at home with them, and to "work up to them" when they go into appointments. At the same time the existence of an Institute of Christian work forms a natural rallying-point for earnest spirits in all the region round about. It would be greatly to the advantage of our Church's work throughout the West Riding, and indeed through the North of England, if meetings were sometimes held of Class-leaders, Local Preachers, Sunday-school Teachers, Guild workers, and others who are active in their own neighbourhoods. And no better or more inviting centre for such meetings could be found than Ilkley. The College Hall, which is part of our purchase, and which will hold nearly three hundred persons, will lend itself admirably to such meetings. They will bless alike the visitors who come to the conventions, and the residents who will gladly promote and serve these meetings, and who will themselves gather knowledge and catch enthusiasm from them.

'Meantime it may be well to explain two words which frequently occur in speaking of our work. One is the word Institute. The Conference has sanctioned the "Wesley Deaconess Institute." By many people the word Institute is supposed to apply to a building, and the chief training house of the Wesley Deaconess Order is taken to be the Wesley Deaconess Institute. An Institute is indeed something instituted or established ; but it may be much greater than any building, or, indeed, it may be entirely without a building. You may have, for instance, an Institute of Architecture, which is a voluntary association of architects for certain purposes. They may not, and probably in the early days did not, have any building of their own, but met, say, in a room in an hotel. They are an Institute nevertheless.

'Usually, however, the word means both property and persons; persons forming the association, and the property being the building in which they have their headquarters, and where their business is done. In like manner the Wesley Deaconess Institute means the Warden, Officers, and Members of the Wesley Deaconess Order, and their training houses, or other buildings which they may possess, as their centres of operation. As the years go on other houses would, no doubt, be occupied, which might be even in distant parts of the world, but the whole of the enterprise, under the guidance of the chief committee of the Order, together with all persons and properties involved, would form the Institute. It is in this wide sense of the word that it is used amongst us.

'What, then, is meant by an Order? This is an ecclesiastical term, often used very loosely, and sometimes having attached to it a meaning which it does not rightly convey. An Order in the Church is a body of workers recognized by the Church, having their own distinctive work and place. So the Ministry is an Order of men who have committed to them preaching and pastoral functions, and who are set apart to such a work from all ordinary cares. So local preachers are an Order, a body of men recognized and authorized by the Church fo the work of preaching. So the Deaconesses, recognized by the Church and authorized by it, are an Order of women set apart for such work as is particularly suitable to their sex. It is *an* Order; we do not claim that it alone can do the work needed. But it is a part of the Church's organization: it bears her authority and is subject to her direction, and so the Order of Deaconesses has its proper place in our system.

'And not in our Methodist system only. This order is recognized in the Church of England. Deaconesses of that Church act not under "superiors" who are largely independent of the Bishops, but directly under the authority of the Bishops. In the Church of Scotland Deaconesses exist under the sanction of the General Assembly, and under its direction given through a Committee. In the Methodist Episcopal Church of America, Deaconesses work under the direction of the Board of Bishops, and under the supervision of the several annual Conferences which hold jurisdiction over the vast territories of the United States. The same is true in the Lutheran Church, and now happily amongst ourselves. It will be seen, therefore, that the word Order applies mainly to the persons who are at work, and to their status and responsibility to the Church which authorizes them. The word Institute is a larger word, and includes the buildings and machinery which are necessary to the proper direction and management of the Order, to its cohesion, and to the proper training and instruction of those who from time to time shall become members of it.'

Convocation this year was held at Oxford Place, Leeds. The roll of the Order showed fifty-eight Deaconesses, of whom forty still remain in the work at the Convocation of 1913; and twenty-five Probationers, fifteen of whom are now fully accredited Deaconesses.

At this Convocation the question of the continued

co-operation of the Sisters of the Children with the Wesley Deaconesses in supporting the Ceylon work was considered, and it was agreed to continue it a little while longer.

The financial responsibility was, however, left with the Wesley Deaconess Committee. The difficulty was the greater because the first Deaconess sent out had concluded five years' service, and needed to come home on furlough. Her colleague's furlough would also be due in another twelve months. A third Deaconess must, therefore, at once be sent out to fill the first vacancy, and to remain while the second Deaconess took her furlough. Some friends kindly came to the rescue, the financial difficulty was surmounted, and the work maintained. The 'Ceylon Fund' needed some help from the General Funds of the Institute for a few years, but sufficient money is now raised every year for this special purpose, and it is possible that other developments may come.

The Conference, which was held that year at Manchester, acknowledged the liberality which had enabled the property at Ilkley to be purchased and fitted up; and also approved the Regulations of the Order, giving them the authority of its sanction.

A badge was adopted for the Order, a blood-red square cross, with a wide ring round it. On the circle are the words, 'To seek and to save that which is lost.' These words form the motto of the Children's Home, and were now appropriately inscribed on the badge of the Deaconess Order, which was established in such close relation with the Children's Home. On the transverse are the words, 'For Jesus' Sake,' the motto of the Deaconesses of the Methodist Episcopal Church, U.S.A. On the upright is a figure of a dove, the emblem of Kaiserswerth, and below, an open book. The badge for the Lady Associates is precisely similar, except that the circle has a blue instead of a white ground.

The College was informally opened on September 30, when seventeen students commenced their studies, with Miss A. M. Gregory, L.L.A., as Resident Tutor. Next day the Rev. Frederic Platt, B.D., who undertook to teach Theology, gave his introductory lecture. The formal opening took place a month later, on October 30, under the auspices of the President of the Conference, the Rev. J. S. Banks, D.D.

Some months previously Dr. Stephenson, who was still the Superintendent of the Ilkley Circuit, removed from the Minister's house, and took up his residence in the College.

The opening ceremony was overshadowed by the death of Sister Dorothy Coy, which took place on October 22. For nearly twelve years Sister Dorothy had been a striking feature of the public life of Leicester. She had been Sister-in-Charge of Calvert House from the commencement of the Deaconess work in that town. In 1896 she greatly added to her usefulness by becoming a member of the Board of Guardians, where she did admirable work in connexion with the women and girls in the Workhouse and in the Cottage Homes. She won for herself a public position of much honour in the town, and with it the warm affection of the people. She was a great sufferer from a nervous and bodily weakness of such a grave character that most people would have held that it absolved them from anything like a strenuous life. It was said, and was possibly true, that she had shortened her career by the labours with which she filled it ; but surely, the ' one crowded hour of glorious life ' that she lived was better far than a long-drawn-out invalid existence of misery to herself and burden to others. Her heroic will triumphed over her bodily frailties. Her brave constancy never shirked a duty because it was disagreeable, and her modest firmness, without ever courting publicity, never shrank from accepting responsibility which was brought to her by duty. Her real kindliness and compassion for the weak and suffering reigned royally over a naturally somewhat austere temperament ; and she left a name in the town of Leicester, and among the Deaconesses who had lived with her at Calvert House, that cannot be forgotten.

CHAPTER XXVI

Warden of the Wesley Deaconess Institute—Chairman of the District—Visit to Kaiserswerth—Hull Convocation—Visit of Sister Julie Borges—Visit of Mrs. Lucy Rider Meyer—Commencement of work in West Africa—Retirement to Finchley—Resolution of Conference—Last illness—Death and Funeral.

WHEN Dr. Stephenson gave up the minister's house at Ilkley and took up his residence in the College, it became clear that his main duty would be in connexion with the Deaconess Institute, and he gave up all thought of accepting an invitation to another circuit. During his third year at Ilkley the Conference granted him the services of the Rev. Harold B. Mallinson, B.A., as an assistant. At the end of the year the Rev. Dr. Maggs was appointed Superintendent of the Ilkley Circuit; and Dr. Stephenson's name stands on the Minutes as Warden of the Wesley Deaconess Institute. Although this appointment was really the 'setting apart' of a minister to a new department, it was not technically so regarded, because Dr. Stephenson did not receive any remuneration for his services from the Deaconess Institute. Nevertheless, the appointment was not that of a Supernumerary minister, but preserved for him his position as a minister in full work, and made it possible that he should be elected Chairman of the District in

1905, when the Rev. Silvester Whitehead, who previously held that office, was removed by the Conference to the Governorship of the Theological Institution at Handsworth, at the close of his Presidential year.

In the autumn of 1903 Dr. and Mrs. Stephenson were able to take a holiday in Germany, and he revisited Kaiserswerth, which he had not seen since 1871. He found the Deaconess House greatly enlarged and beautified, the system confirmed in all its essential features, and the number of its deaconesses much increased. There were nearly twelve hundred belonging to the Kaiserswerth Order, and fully fifteen thousand Deaconesses and Probationers belonging to other 'Mother-Houses,' which looked to Kaiserswerth as the source of their inspiration.

Soon afterwards Sister Julie Borges was welcomed as a representative of Kaiserswerth at the Convocation held at Hull in the year 1904. One pathetic incident which Sister Julie related in connexion with her visit, referred to the daughter of Pastor Theodore Fliedner, the Founder of the work. Sister Mina Fliedner had since her mother's death been at the head of the Kaiserswerth Institution, until, six years previously, the failure of her health had compelled her to transfer her duties to other hands. Since that time she had been living in the 'Feierabend-Haus' (Evening Rest-house), the venerated adviser and friend of all connected with the Order. When Sister Julie Borges was about to come to England to attend the Wesley Deaconess Convocation, she went to Sister Mina and asked her for a message to the English Deaconesses. She replied, 'No, I think I can send them no message, as I do not know them well enough ; but you may tell them that I love them all in the Lord Jesus, and that while their Convocation is meeting, I shall be praying for them night and day.' Sister Julie left with these words in her memory and her heart. Two days afterwards Sister Mina was found in her room dead on her knees. She had passed away in the very act of prayer.

Sister Julie Borges, who spoke English with great precision and accuracy, gave the Convocation a most interesting address. After presenting greetings from the Pastor and Deaconesses of Kaiserswerth, she began with an apology. 'I have never spoken to so large an assembly, and never in my life before gentlemen, therefore I must ask you to bear with me, and to take my ardent wish to serve for the deed. I propose to say a few words about the Deaconess work in Germany, its beginning, its subsequent progress, and its present state.' She gave a most interesting and graphic account of the origin and progress of the great Institution from which she came, and a sketch of its present position.

After leaving the Hull Convocation, Sister Julie Borges visited Florence Nightingale, who had received training as a nurse at Kaiserswerth, and who was at this time in a state of extreme weakness. Sister Julie's account of the interview is as follows :—

'I arrived at King's Cross Station, and found Sister "Kathleen Mavourneen." She was quite ready to go with me, and proved a very amiable companion.

'At last we rang the bell at Miss Nightingale's house. A servant opened, and when I wanted to send up my card, she said, "It is not necessary ;

you are expected." Then we were shown into a pretty room, and Miss Nightingale's lady-secretary received me kindly. Sister Kathleen asked whether she, too, might be admitted, but was told Miss Nightingale received only one visitor at a time. She might come a few days later. Then we got some tea, and Miss Cochrane cut me some flowers from "Miss Nightingale's London Garden," to take them to her friends at Kaiserswerth. Then the girl came to conduct me to her. In a large, light room her bed was standing, and Miss Nightingale stretched out both her hands in welcome. She was looking very sweet, with a bright, very clear complexion, and her hair was beautifully white. I was going to kiss her hand, Continental fashion, in the emotion of my heart, when she drew me to her, and kissed me and called me "My dear, dear Sister."

'I gave my message from Kaiserswerth, and told her that she was still remembered there. "Dear Kaiserswerth," she said, "how well I remember it!" Then she asked me, "How long have you been a Sister?" and when I said more than thirty years, she said, "Have you always been happy?" Now I did not know what to say. Always is a long word, and I could neither answer yes nor no, so I said, "Dear Miss Nightingale, if I had to live my life over again, and if it were ten times, I should always wish to serve the Lord as a Kaiserswerth Deaconess."

'Then she said, "Thank God! Oh, thank God! It is a blessed life when we can live it for others."

'Then I told her about our Convocation in Hull, and I said, "All the Sisters send their respectful greetings." Then she folded her dear hands, and said over and over again, "Thank you!"

'When I asked, " Could I deliver any message ? " she said, " My blessing," or some such words, which I did not quite catch. After a while I said pleasantly, "Miss Nightingale, they call you the Queen of Nurses. You now must be good to yourself, and send me away if I tire you." Then she said, " No, I am not tired, stay a little longer," and then, " Have they given you some tea downstairs ? " " Where are you going to sleep ? " So I told her I would cross that very night. " I shall think of you," she said, and repeated, " Where do you stay for the night ? " Then I knew she was getting tired, and I got up to take my leave. Then she folded her hands again, and said, " Pray ! " So I knelt down to thank the Lord for everything He had done for us poor women, who desired to glorify His name only. She kept saying, " Amen," and " Praise the Lord," so that I came to the conclusion that she must be a devout Wesleyan. So with my heart full of prayer and praise I came away.'

At the next Convocation, held at Birmingham in 1905, there were visitors representing the American Deaconess work ; Mrs. Lucy Rider Meyer, M.A., M.D., Principal of the Chicago Training School ; Miss Addie Grace Wardle, M.A., B.D., then Vice-Principal of the Chicago Training School (now President of the Cincinnati Missionary Training School) ; and Miss Helen Ingram, an English woman born in India, who had been brought up in connexion with an American Methodist Mission, and had ultimately devoted herself to the work in India as a Deaconess of that Church ; so that the Wesley Deaconesses had the opportunity of acquainting themselves with some of the leaders of Deaconess work in the United States, and in their Indian missions.

Unfortunately their addresses are not reported, but a note tells us that Mrs. Meyer 'added to hers a distinct element of interest by singing to music of her own composing the pathetic little song, 'Dat little brack sheep.' A report of another meeting says, 'Mrs. Meyer made a speech, during which the auditors felt that laughter and tears were near to each other as they listened, and the meeting broke up at a quarter past ten o'clock, not a dozen of the audience having stirred from their seats.'

During the time with which we have been dealing another development of Wesley Deaconess work had been in the air. This time it was from the West Coast of Africa that the call came, or rather, two calls in succession. To the first it was not possible to respond, but the second meant the beginning of an important and growing work. The first arose from the need of English trained nurses in West Africa. Miss Mary Kingsley, the well-known West African traveller, was deeply interested in the subject. She held that no women ought to go there 'unless they were people who thought their work not only worth living for, but dying for'; and declared that nursing in West Africa was only fit for religious women. An experiment was being tried by the Colonial Office, then under the direction of Mr. Joseph Chamberlain, with Lord Ampthill as Under-Secretary. Some arrangements had been made which did not work well, and Lady Ampthill, meeting Miss Mary Kingsley, consulted her on the situation. Miss

Kingsley, with a vigorous statement that the Government could not manage women, advised that the Wesleyans should be applied to, as they had effective Mission organizations on the Coast. This suggestion being favourably considered, Miss Kingsley gave the name of the Rev. Dennis Kemp as a Wesleyan missionary in West Africa who was personally known to her ; and he, on being applied to, referred the matter to Dr. Stephenson. Unfortunately, the Deaconess Institute was not in a position in which it could undertake the regular supply of a series of nurses for such service ; but the application had called the attention of the Order to West Africa, and volunteers had declared themselves ready to go there. So that when not long afterwards the Wesleyan Missionary Society appealed to the Deaconess Institute for workers in this part of the Mission field, they met with a prompt and ready response.

At the Hull Convocation (already referred to in connexion with the visit of Sister Julie Borges), another visitor was the Rev. William Findlay, M.A., one of the Secretaries of the Wesleyan Missionary Society. He brought an invitation from the Society, which had already been presented to the Committee of the Wesley Deaconess Institute, and now, with their sanction, was laid before the Deaconesses. He said, 'The situation in West Africa which has led us to seek for help is this. We have been working in that region for from eighty to one hundred years, and have only men missionaries, either young unmarried men, or men who have left their wives in England. Christian womanhood, as it exists in Europe, is practically unknown in West Africa, and the case is getting urgent. There is a growing cry that West Africa should throw off European customs and manners, and go back to primitive West African ways. This is not professedly a movement to throw off Christianity. Its advocates are leading our members to hold the idea that they can keep their Christianity, their Bible (with the polygamy which they say it teaches), and throw off our culture and pure family life.

'If this teaching can be averted, it must be by the girls and women being taught what true Christian womanhood means. This Order can provide what West Africa needs. It needs continuity of service, and you can supply a succession of agents. Mr. Bartrop writes hoping that two deaconesses may go back with him after Conference to the Cape Coast School. That is the first place for which we want workers. Mrs. Ellis, the widow of the Chairman of the District, after leaving West Africa on her husband's death, returned to start a boarding-school where the daughters of our Christian men on the Gold Coast were gathered, and she taught them cleanly ways, and purity, and kindness. She had wonderful success, and the leading natives gladly sent their children. She worked alone for more than twelve months, a piece of heroism seldom matched even on the Mission field, but her health gave way, and she came home, and could not return. For the last two years they have been holding on with native teachers, hoping some one would go from England. I leave these words in your hearts, I know you will help.' In answer to a question as to what technical qualifications would be needed,

Mr. Findlay said the Deaconesses should be able to prepare pupils for the College of Preceptors Examination; but the training of scholars in Christian household ways would be one of their most important duties. One Deaconess should be a good housekeeper. It was proposed that there should be three Deaconesses for the school, two on the field, and one at home on furlough. Several volunteers offered themselves at the meeting, and the first two Deaconesses, Sister Annie McVicker and Sister Ethel Worthington, sailed for the Coast on September 17, 1904.

The second school, at Freetown, Sierra Leone, was staffed in the same way twelve months afterwards, a third at Accra in January, 1908, and a fourth at Lagos in April, 1912. The work wins the warm approval of the Wesleyan Missionary Society and of their missionaries in that field; and promises to be a most effective instrument for the establishment of the ideal of a true Christian home life among the West African peoples.

Writing at the beginning of the New Year, 1905, Dr. Stephenson says:

'We are thankful that at this moment our Deaconesses are a body of intelligent and earnest women, who find their happiness in a life of constant effort and devotion. The Methodist Church is displaying an increasing confidence in this Institute, as is shown by the most practical proof, that of an increasing demand for Wesley Deaconesses. This, indeed, is a happy embarrassment, for we are unable to meet all the requests which reach us; and during the past year several circuits, having applied in vain to us, have had to find help elsewhere.

This difficulty will, however, become smaller as the Order becomes larger.

'It is satisfactory also to note the fine spirit of mutual regard which increasingly binds the members of the Order to each other. This is unquestionably a source of great strength. It is impossible that some of our workers should avoid an occasional sense of loneliness and depression. With no other Sister within, perhaps, a hundred miles of her, a Deaconess cannot help feeling lonely, however kind the people may be amongst whom she may be working. But the arrival of a sympathetic letter from the Mother-House, the coming of the new number of our Magazine, the reception of a loving message from some former comrade, lightens the darkness. And even more helpful and gracious in its influence is the knowledge that every day each Sister is prayed for by all. How calming, strengthening, and sustaining this sense of a real though invisible fellowship amongst us is, cannot be estimated.

'And the widening of our circle of personal interest constantly goes on. The number of Wesley Deaconesses at work beyond the four seas is still small; not quite a dozen; but these are surely pioneers. The blue veil with the white stripe is known, at least by some, in Europe, in Asia, Africa, and Australasia. And only financial bondage can prevent such appointments becoming much more numerous. Calls are reaching our ears from other parts of the world, to which it would be a privilege to make a favourable response. There is a great future before the organized work of trained and tested women in the Wesleyan Methodist Church.'

This year and the next (1906) were times of development and growth, in which there is little to record. The work won favour with the Methodist people, the organization was established and perfected, and Dr. Stephenson preached the ideal of the Deaconess wherever he could get attention to it. He also worked hard at the finances of the Institute. In this he was nobly seconded by Mr. Pliny Hepworth, who had accepted the Treasurership of the Institution in 1903, and by the Rev. John Elsworth, who was appointed Secretary to the Institute in the same year. Aided by the great liberality of the Senior Treasurer, Mr. T. R. Ferens, M.P., of Hull, they succeeded in obtaining a Guarantee Fund of £500 a year for five years, which was of the greatest value in putting the finances on a permanently sounder basis. Mr. Elsworth also gave very valuable help in connexion with the records of the Order.

In the winter of 1906–7 it became evident that the Warden's strength was failing. A particularly welcome donation of £300 to the Deaconess Superannuation Fund, given by Miss Hamptonne, of Jersey, came at a time when it brought much encouragement to a weary man.

Convocation was held in Southport in 1907 and Dr. Stephenson's weakness was scarcely noticeable to those present, but in the month of June he writes a personal note to his Deaconesses for the next issue of *Flying Leaves :*

'It is never pleasant to talk about one's self ; such talk may be easily misunderstood. Hence the apology with which I begin a brief personal statement to all friends of the Wesley Deaconess Institute.

'It is widely known that I am about to withdraw from the post of Warden, which I have held since the beginning of the enterprise. The work owes so much to the faith and courage and generosity with which we have been supported, that our friends have a right to know the facts. There has been no whisper of discord, no note of discouragement, no lack of success in this work. The responsible Committee has not suggested my retirement, but on the contrary has expressed most kindly its regret that such a retirement has become necessary. The whole matter is simple.

'My medical advisers have unitedly insisted upon my laying down some of the burdens which I have been carrying for so long, and amongst them they insist that I must sever myself from the responsibilities of the Wardenship, and that this must be done forthwith.

'I confess that I cannot understand it; but I know well the faithfulness, the skill and kindness of those who are advising me, and I dare not take the responsibility of incurring perils to life and health which may perhaps be avoided or postponed by obedience to medical orders.

'It is of course a terrible wrench for an active and enthusiastic man to retire from all responsibility for a great Christian enterprise which he has been permitted to establish. It must strike a solemn note through all his thought. It is, it must be, "the beginning of the end," though there may yet be some years of quiet work. But I have no murmur on my lips or in my heart. It is close on fifty years since I left my father's house to begin the work of regular preaching; and it would be unreasonable and unworthy to murmur when the Providential command comes: "Cease, for your day's work is done."

'I am very thankful that the work is well established, and I believe has before it a bright future. The Methodist Church will give some man to the care of this work who is worthy and capable. The Church of God never depends on any one man. And so long as it pleases God to spare me I shall take a deep interest in the Order.

'The Deaconesses have invariably treated me with respect and kindness which could hardly be surpassed. Loyal friends have gathered round, and have helped me by their contributions, their advice, and their co-operation.

'Whatever I may have done, the most important and valuable work has been done by my dear wife and my dear daughter, who have in many ways rendered loving and valuable service to it.

'Others, I doubt not, will be raised up to do all they have done, and our Treasurers and Secretaries and those who are most experienced on the Committee will continue their care, oversight, and assistance.

'I shall hope at some future time to bear my testimony to the valuable work of these honorary workers. For the moment this acknowledgement must suffice; but it is offered by a full and grateful heart.

'May God bless the Wesley Deaconess Order, and make it a hundredfold more useful than hitherto; and may God bless with His abundant grace all those who by prayer or gift or in any other way have helped it.'

The Conference received his resignation, and passed the following Resolution :

The Conference receives with great regret the resignation of Dr. Stephenson as Warden of the Deaconess Institution, and in acceding to his request to become a Supernumerary desires to express its high appreciation of his distinguished ability, and of the great service which he has rendered to our Church. Rising early to distinction, he has for many years taken a leading part in the development of our Church Constitution and in the administration of Connexional affairs. Called early to the Presidency of the Conference, he fulfilled the functions of this high office so as to command the approval of all. As the Founder and Principal of the Children's Home and Orphanage in the first place, and as the Founder and Warden of the Wesley Deaconess Order and Institute in the second place, he has accomplished a work which is unique in the history of Methodism, which will bring blessing to multitudes, and cause his name to be remembered for many generations. Dr. Stephenson's reputation extends not only through British Methodism, but also through our Colonies and the United States of America. While he has been recognized as one of the philanthropists of the age, he has not limited himself to the promotion of the objects of general benevolence. His supreme aim has been to serve the highest spiritual purposes contemplated by the Christian Church. He has combined humanitarian sympathy with loyalty to evangelical doctrine and spiritual experience, and he has united devotion to popular evangelism with a true appreciation of Church principles, and with earnest efforts to develop, not only the higher life of the individual, but also the corporate life of the Church. The Conference hopes that, when Dr. Stephenson is relieved from the strain of work, he will improve in health, that he may be able for years to come to use his ability and experience in the service of the Church, and that the evening of his life will be bright with the promise of life eternal.

The Conference appointed a special Committee during its sessions to investigate the somewhat irregular position of the Deaconess Institute as one of the 'Departments' of Methodist Church life. On the report of this Committee, it was at once decided to regularize the position, and appoint a Warden who should be 'set apart' to the work in accordance with the usual custom of our Church. The Rev. William Bradfield was honoured by being selected for this post.

Dr. and Mrs. Stephenson retired to Clare Bank, Dollis Park, Church End, Finchley; but on September 24 he was back attending a Deaconess Committee in Leeds, and came to the College to spend a night, being determined, as he himself put it, 'to get over as soon as possible the strangeness of feeling that the College was no longer his own residence.' The consideration Dr. Stephenson gave to his successor was of a character never to be forgotten; the gracious courtesy of it, the willingness to let the new man see from a new point of view, the watchfulness for opportunities of showing approval, went straight to that successor's heart. Dr. Stephenson made it quite plain that while, on the one hand, he did not want to lose touch with the work, yet, on the other, he did not intend to interfere with the new management, but to help it by all means in his power; and surely never man was better helped than the present Warden by a predecessor who kept up so long as he could the closest interest in the work, and yet never tried for a moment to resume the reins he had laid down.

For a time he was able to interest himself in Connexional work, and attended Conference, where, on the death of Dr. Rigg and the Rev. C. H. Kelly, the coveted seat of the Senior Ex-President fell to his lot. The disease from which he was suffering, however, re-asserted its power and laid him low time after time, although at first he had very considerable intervals of better health.

An incident occurred in Conference involving his name, in which he took no personal part, of which the significance has been altogether unduly exaggerated. The Committee of the Children's Home, whose work had grown very largely, and appealed to a very much wider public since the days of his retirement, had somewhat altered the name of the Institution, and called it 'The National Children's Home and Orphanage,' and in many of their announcements the name of Dr. Stephenson had entirely disappeared. A good deal of objection to this was taken in Conference, and finally the Conference directed that the words, 'Founded by Dr. Stephenson,' should be added to the title. He was not at the time strong enough to bear the strain of feeling that his own name was thus becoming the centre of a somewhat stormy discussion. It was generally supposed that the personal relations between himself and Dr. Gregory, his successor in the Principalship of the Children's Home, were very seriously strained by this incident; but the writer can testify that not very long after this, in grave personal troubles, his heart turned to Dr. Gregory at once as a trusted friend of whose sympathy and help he was sure, and that he met with a response from the latter which was as full and frank and tender as Dr. Stephenson had evidently felt sure it would be. The last occasion on which the writer ever met Dr. Gregory, not very long before his own last illness, was in order to take consultation with him with regard to the condition of Dr. Stephenson. We little thought then that the younger man would go first, but he passed away on June 21, 1912, and Dr. Stephenson lingered nearly a month longer.

Throughout his last long illness, which was sometimes of an extremely painful character, the skilled, loving care of his wife never failed him, though it is wonderful how she was enabled to endure for so long a time the heavy and heart-breaking burden that rested upon her. Another loyal and efficient helper was 'Florence.' She came into Dr. Stephenson's house as a little child. Hers was a sad story, as indeed every case whether of the waif or orphan class is. Her attachment to him from the first, when she was but seven years old, was very beautiful, and it proved to be the abiding and ever-growing inspiration of her life. During the Doctor's residence in Ilkley, Florence was provided with an excellent situation, but her love never failed, and when the Doctor retired from active work it was Florence who offered to leave her good situation and come and serve him.

She came, and very soon, in days of family sickness, developed more than ordinary gifts for sick nursing. As 'Doctor' had always put his children's best interests first, it was decided that valuable as she might be in the home, her sphere was nursing, and she must go into training accordingly. She was entered at one of the London hospitals, where she received full training, and won all needful certificates.

But all through her absence she visited her friend and watched with anxiety his increasing weakness, only desirous that if ever he needed her she might be free. Her term of probation expired and her equipment as a sick-nurse was completed at the time of the commencement of the last stage of the Doctor's illness; and when she heard that her life-long friend needed a nurse, she went to him, and cared for him affectionately through months of suffering and untold weakness, until at last, with his hand in hers, he fell on sleep, and she closed his eyes in death.

It is a remarkable coincidence that both Dr. Stephenson and Dr. Gregory were gently led through the valley of the shadow of death by nurses trained from childhood in the Children's Home.

The Methodist Conference was just about to meet at the time of his death. Mrs. Wiseman, the great leader of the Women's Auxiliary of the Foreign Missionary Society, had passed away on Sunday evening, July 14, 1912. On Tuesday morning, July 16, another great Methodist leader, the Rev. H. J. Pope, D.D., was called home; and a few hours later on the same day Dr. Stephenson also passed to his rest. When the Conference met on the following day it was under the shadow of a threefold bereavement such as had never previously taken place.

The funeral service was held at City Road on Saturday, July 20, and was attended by large numbers of representatives of the Children's Home, and its old boys and girls, and by many members of the Wesley Deaconess Order. He was laid to rest in the City of London Cemetery at Ilford, in the plot of ground set apart for those who had died at the Children's Home. In his chapter on 'Dr. Stephenson as a Musician,' Mr. Sharpley has already spoken of the scene; and truly one cannot forget the long procession in the summer sunshine, the strangely beautiful singing, and the deep emotion of a company, so many members of which were mourning the loss of a friend who under God had redeemed their lives from destruction.

'Blessed are the merciful, for they shall obtain mercy.'

APPENDIX

WE are very glad to give the following statement in order to show the signs of permanent vitality in both the Institutions which Dr. Stephenson founded.

A. THE CHILDREN'S HOME.

Figures from the Report for 1911, giving some idea of the growth of the Children's Home.

Year.	*No. of Children.*	*Ordinary Income.*
1869	29	£307
1879	456	£9,335
1889	729	£14,054
1899	1,076	£28,330
1909	2,008	£49,859
1911	2,201	£54,715

The estates presented to the National Children's Home and Orphanage, and money expended upon the purchase of property, and for the erection of schools, houses, workshops, &c., considerably exceed £200,000. There is not one penny of debt resting upon these establishments. All contributions are spent upon the actual support and development of the work.

Total number passed through the Home ..	6,780
Total number resident	2,201
Total number received to Mar. 31, 1911 ..	8,981

Disposals.

In the United Kingdom—		
To situations, friends, &c. ..	3,995	
Died	230	
Adopted	172	
		4,397
By Emigration—		
To Canada	2,333	
To Australia and New Zealand ..	50	
		2,383
		6,780

Children Received.

The children received this year have been of the usual classes.

1. The (so-called) waif and stray. There are not anything like so many children literally without any home or shelter as there were thirty or forty years ago. The ' waif ' of to-day comes, as a rule, from the common lodging-house, from the workhouse ward, from the home of the deserted mother, or the widow left in hopeless poverty by the death of her husband.

2. As ever, we have had a considerable number of children whose father and mother, not infrequently both, have been drunkards. Ever and again we find the cause of death of the parent said to be ' drink.' Usually, of course, the drunkard's death is attributed to some special disease, but we have many children whose parents have actually died simply from excessive drinking.

3. This year again, we have received a number of the children of criminals. The murderer, the forger, the coiner, the thief, the perpetrator of unnameable crimes, are amongst the parents of ' these little ones.'

4. The Industrial Schools Act and the Children Act have again contributed to increase our family. These are children who surely need us most. I am thankful that, in our Farnborough Branch especially, we are able

to deal with these cases. Our great difficulty is that when the time expires for which they have been committed by the magistrates we have no further legal control, and cannot prevent a boy from going back to the evil surroundings from which he came. We are glad to get as many of these boys as we can to Canada and have them safely settled there before their 'time' expires.

5. But many of our children belong to none of these classes. They are the children of respectable parents, often of parents who have been valued and earnest members in some branch of the Church of Christ. In caring for these we are but repaying in part a debt due to faithful workers. Our Birmingham Branch is specially devoted to the care of orphan children of Christian parents.

6. We must not forget our cripples. What would the Home be without them? We should miss some of our merriest, brightest, and most successful children. The work at Chipping Norton is as difficult as in any of our branches. Many of our cripples can, sooner or later, take their place in an ordinary branch and give a good account of themselves, but Chipping Norton must care for the most helpless, having long patience, and even then may reap what seems but a poor return for so much toil and care. We have many disappointments in this department, but are very thankful for the opportunity of ministering to these sadly afflicted children and for the wonderful success which has crowned our work in not a few instances.

7. The number of children who have lost one or both parents by tuberculosis is much the same as before, about one-fourth of the admissions. By no means all of these children are themselves afflicted, but many are, and we are able now to deal much more promptly and effectively with those who need special treatment than we could before the establishment of the Harpenden Sanatorium.

B. The Wesley Deaconess Institute.

At the retirement of Dr. Stephenson the figures reported to the Conference of 1907 were—

No. of fully accredited Deaconesses ..	..	98
No. of Probationer-Deaconesses ..	..	56
		154

Ordinary Income—

	£	s.	d.
Payments from Circuits and Missions	5,738	8	8
Subscriptions, Public Meetings, &c. ..	894	1	4
Special Subscriptions (for five years) ..	529	0	0
	£7,161	10	0

Superannuation Fund, Accumulated Capital	£2,090	13	5

At the Conference of 1913 the figures were—

No. of fully accredited Deaconesses ..	..	170
No. of Probationer-Deaconesses ..	..	59
		229

Ordinary Income—

	£	s.	d.
Payments from Circuits and Missions	10,975	1	4
Subscriptions, Public Meetings, &c. ..	1,441	0	11
	12,416	2	3

Superannuation Fund, Accumulated Capital	£5,210	10	11

INDEX

JARROLD & SONS, LTD.,
THE EMPIRE PRESS, NORWICH.

Lightning Source UK Ltd.
Milton Keynes UK
UKOW03f2000190813

215623UK00016B/1042/P

9 781290 503884